# JEWISH HEROES & HEROINES

# JEWISH HEROES & HEROINES

## Their Unique Achievements

Darryl Lyman

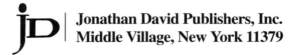

Jonathan David Publishers, Inc.
Middle Village, New York 11379

# JEWISH HEROES & HEROINES:
## Their Unique Achievements

Jonathan David Publishers, Inc.
68-22 Eliot Avenue
Middle Village, New York 11379

2 4 6 8 7 5 3 1

**Library of Congress Cataloging-in-Publication Data**
Lyman, Darryl, 1944–
    Jewish heroes and heroines : their unique achievements / Darryl Lyman.
        p.      cm.
    Includes index.
    ISBN 0-8246-0388-5 (hardcover)
    1. Jews—Biography.          I. Title
    IN PROCESS
    909'.04924—dc20
    [B]                                                              96-728
                                                                       CIP

*Book design by Marcy Stamper*

**Printed in the United States of America**

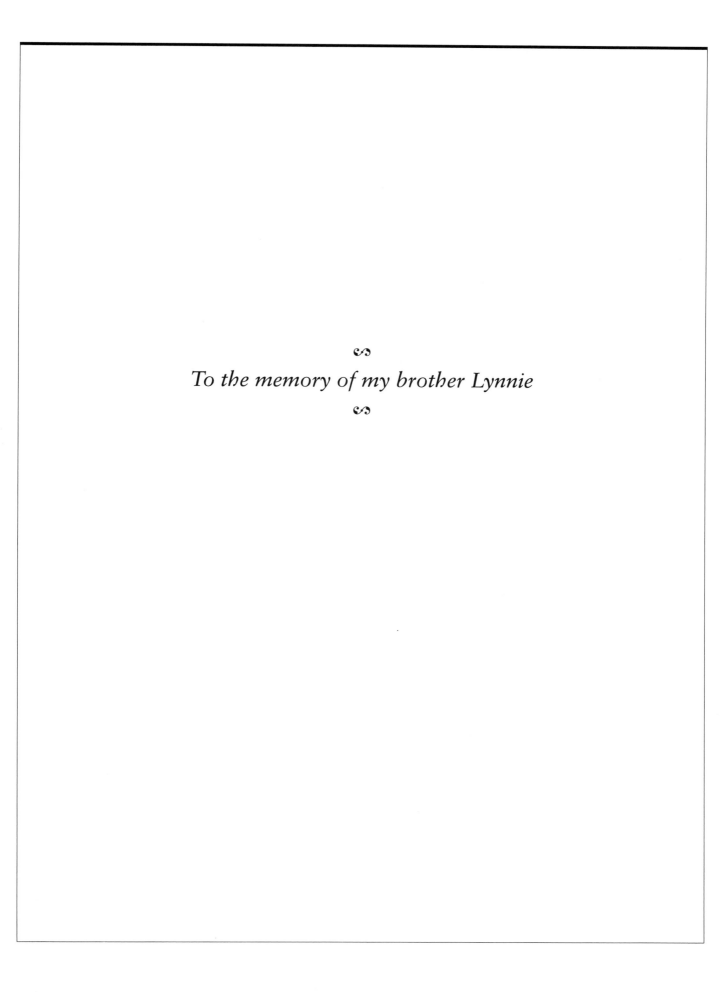

*To the memory of my brother Lynnie*

# CONTENTS

e

# INTRODUCTION

❧

*Jewish Heroes and Heroines: Their Unique Achievements* is a compendium of hundreds of stories of outstanding accomplishments by Jews. The book is organized into fields of endeavor ("Government and Military Service," "Physical Sciences," "Music," "Sports"), principally from the modern world. Biblical personalities, who could easily fill an entire volume by themselves, are excluded.

Who is a Jew? This book follows the most widely accepted definition: a Jew is anyone who was born of a Jewish mother or who converted to Judaism. People fitting this definition are included even if they did not practice Judaism or if they converted to another religion. Excluded by this definition are people born of a Jewish father and non-Jewish mother, such as the author J.D. Salinger, the feminist Gloria Steinem, and the scientist Otto Warburg; the impresario Oscar Hammerstein and his grandson the lyricist Oscar Hammerstein II both had non-Jewish mothers. The rare exception to the above rules is noted and explained in the text.

What is a hero or heroine? In this book, a hero or heroine is a person widely admired for his or her achievements that have substantially benefited humankind. Those benefits include such diverse positive results as providing entertainment, creating businesses (and therefore jobs, products, and services), and discovering lifesaving medical treatments.

The word *unique* is used here in its original two meanings: "being the only one" ("sole") and "being without a like" ("unequaled"). Not intended by the word are its extended senses of "unusual" and "distinctively characteristic" ("peculiar").

*Jewish Heroes and Heroines: Their Unique Achievements* commemorates special contributions of Jews to the world community in a wide range of fields. Specifically, it records unique (one-of-a-kind) achievements by Jews (those born of Jewish mothers or converted to Judaism) whose bestowal of benefits on humankind raised the achievers to the status of heroes and heroines.

# 1
# GOVERNMENT AND MILITARY SERVICE

❧

AMONG THE MANY JEWS WITH UNIQUE ACHIEVEMENTS *in government and military service were four Nobel Peace Prize winners—Menachem Begin, Henry Kissinger, Shimon Peres, and Yitzhak Rabin. Begin, prime minister of Israel, won the 1978 award for his efforts to achieve peace with Egypt. Kissinger, head of the United States National Security Council, won in 1973 for his negotiations to end the war in Vietnam. Peres and Rabin, Israeli foreign minister and prime minister respectively, both won in 1994 for their efforts to reduce tension in the Middle East by negotiating an agreement for limited Palestinian self-rule in Israeli-held territory.*

*David Ben-Gurion and Chaim Weizmann played crucial roles in the founding of modern Israel. Ben-Gurion was the nation's first prime minister, while Weizmann served as the first president.*

*Pathbreaking Jewish women in politics included Bella Abzug, Barbara Boxer, Dianne Feinstein, and Golda Meir. Abzug was the first Jewish woman to serve in the United States Congress. Boxer and Feinstein were the first pair of women to represent a state in the United States Senate. Meir served as the first woman premier of Israel.*

*Jews have headed countries and founded political parties. The most notable example was Benjamin Disraeli, who founded England's modern Conservative party and became Great Britain's first prime minister of Jewish origin.*

*Jews have also excelled in the armed forces. One of the most significant twentieth-century advances in military hardware was the nuclear submarine, pioneered by Hyman Rickover.*

# A Jewish Woman Wins a Seat in the United States Congress

## Bella Abzug

❧

*Bella Abzug was born in New York City on July 24, 1920. Her original name was Bella Savitzky. As a child, she was profoundly influenced toward feminism when, with other females at her synagogue, she had to sit behind one side of a curtain while the men prayed on the other side. In the mid-1940s she married Martin Abzug, a stockbroker and novelist, and earned a law degree at Columbia University. She practiced law in New York City, specializing in civil rights cases. In fact, she helped write the legislation that became the Civil Rights Act of 1964 and the Voting Rights Act of 1965. From 1971 to 1977 she was a member of the United States Congress. Later she worked as a lawyer and writer.*

Courtesy of Bella Abzug

Bella Abzug made history when, in 1970, she became the first Jewish woman elected to the United States Congress. She sought and used that position to further her outspoken advocacy of civil and women's rights. "Jews believe," she said, "you can't have justice for yourself unless other people have justice as well. That has motivated much of what I've done."

Her New York City district was largely Jewish, but it had diverse elements as well, including Chinatown, Little Italy, Greenwich Village, and much of the Upper West Side. During her 1970 campaigns, she became known for her trademark wide-brimmed hats and her way of emphasizing points by jabbing with her fist. Because of her dynamic speeches, reporters dubbed her Battling Bella and Hurricane Bella. Abzug won the Democratic primary by defeating Leonard Farbstein, a seven-term congressman. In November she defeated the Republican-Liberal Barry Farber to become the first Jewish woman to serve on Capitol Hill.

"I was lonely and an oddity," she later said of her time in Congress, "a woman, a Jew, a New York lawyer, a feminist, a Nixon opponent from way back, a peace activist who passionately opposed American involvement in Indochina, and just as strongly favored aid to democratic Israel." Abzug held her seat till January 1977. She then returned to New York City as a lawyer and writer, continuing to fight for the causes that had motivated her pathbreaking congressional victory.

### Also Noteworthy

▲ Alexander, Moses (born November 13, 1853, in Obrigheim, Bavaria; died January 4, 1932, in Boise, Idaho). The first known Jewish governor of an American state (Idaho, 1915–19). (David Emanuel, governor of Georgia in 1801, may or may not have been Jewish.)

# SIGNING THE 1978 PEACE ACCORDS
## Menachem Begin

ɐↄ

MENACHEM BEGIN, PRIME MINISTER OF ISRAEL, shared the 1978 Nobel Peace Prize with President Anwar Sadat of Egypt for their joint efforts to achieve peace between two nations that had long been enemies.

In November 1977 Sadat made an unexpected peace initiative. Begin, a long-time hard-liner against the Arabs, reasoned that if Sadat were willing to expose himself to extremely harsh criticism from his fellow Arabs to make the peace gesture, then the Egyptian president must be sincere. He accepted the overture, but the initial talks faltered. President Jimmy Carter of the United States intervened and invited Begin and Sadat to America. During a thirteen-day conference in the United States, Begin and Sadat established a basis for the signing of "A Framework for Peace in the Middle East" and "A Framework for the Conclusion of a Peace Treaty between Egypt and Israel." In return for a full peace, Israel agreed to give back most of the Sinai region captured from Egypt during the Six Day War of 1967.

> *Menachem Wolfovitch Begin was born in Brest Litovsk, Russian-ruled Poland, on August 16, 1913. He earned a law degree at the University of Warsaw (1935), was an active Zionist during the 1930s, commanded the militant Irgun Zvai Leumi (National Fighting Organization, 1943–48), entered Israeli politics, and served as prime minister of Israel (1977–83). He died in Tel Aviv, Israel, on March 9, 1992.*

The peace treaty itself was formally signed on March 26, 1979. It was the first Israeli-Arab agreement that genuinely tried to establish a lasting peace. For their efforts, both Begin and Sadat were

State of Israel Government Press Office

◄ Menachem Begin (*left*) and Jimmy Carter meet at peace talks.

strongly condemned by many of their own people. Sadat, in fact, was assassinated in 1981.

### ALSO NOTEWORTHY

▲ ALLON, YIGAL (born October 10, 1918, in Kefar Tavor, Galilee, Palestine; died February 29, 1980, in Afula, Israel). Leader of the Palmach, the Israeli army's main striking force, in the nation's most decisive victories during the War of Independence.

▲ BARUCH, BERNARD MANNES (born August 19, 1870, in Camden, South Carolina; died June 20, 1965, in New York City). Financier and public official known as "the advisor to the presidents." Son of the physician Simon Baruch.

▲ BEAME, ABRAHAM DAVID (born March 20, 1906, in London, England). The first Jew to serve as mayor of New York City (1974–77).

# EARNING THE TITLE OF FATHER OF ISRAEL
## David Ben-Gurion

❧

*David Ben-Gurion was born in Płońsk, Russian-ruled Poland, on October 16, 1886. His original name was David Gruen ("Green"). His father, a Zionist, greatly influenced him at an early age. "One day I will be the leader of Israel," the boy once boasted. Later David was an active Zionist and, in fact, did become the leader of modern Israel. He died in Tel Aviv, Israel, on December 1, 1973.*

ON MAY 14, 1948, DAVID BEN-GURION delivered Israel's declaration of independence, and soon thereafter he became Israel's first prime minister. Both were fitting honors for a man who had done as much as, or more than, anyone else to bring about the Jewish state.

In 1906 he moved to Palestine to be a farm laborer. There he helped found the first modern Jewish defense organization, Hashomer ("The Watchmen"). In 1910 he began to write articles under the name Ben-Gurion ("Young Lion") "because," he said, "it sounded like a name out of the Bible." After World War I he helped found Haganah, the Jewish underground army in Palestine, as well as Histadrut, a confederation of Jewish workers. In 1935 he became the chairman of the Jewish Agency for Palestine, and throughout the 1940s he was one of the leaders in the fight to create a Jewish state.

After delivering Israel's declaration of independence, Ben-Gurion headed the new state's provisional government and successfully led the

Photo: Werner Wolff

defense, known as the War of Independence, against the armed attacks by Arab countries. In March 1949 he was officially elected Israel's first prime minister, and he also continued in his role, since 1948, as defense minister. He held both positions till 1953, and again from 1955 to 1963. In 1956 he ordered the successful Sinai campaign when Egypt nationalized the Suez Canal.

From 1963 to 1970 he served in the Knesset (Israeli legislative body). When Ben-Gurion retired in 1970 after his lifetime of service to the Jewish state, he was revered by the masses as the Father of the Nation.

# Two Women Represent a State in the United States Senate

## Barbara Boxer

ço

WHEN BARBARA BOXER AND DIANNE FEINSTEIN *(see page 17)* won California's two United States Senate seats in 1992, they made history: the election marked the first time that any state had chosen to be represented in the Senate by two women. Boxer, like Feinstein a Democrat, defeated the Republican Bruce Herschensohn.

In the 1992 race for the Senate, she drew a sharp distinction between herself and her conservative opponent. Boxer favored women's rights, gay rights, health care, AIDS research, environmental protection, and military reform. Though she and Feinstein had previously had some political disagreements, they pulled together during this campaign and often appeared jointly. Their victories in the November election were attributed to their stand in favor of abortion rights and environmental protection, to the scarcity of women in the Senate (only two before this election), and to the general need for change in Washington. Boxer kept her campaign promises by sponsoring much legislation in the Senate after her history-making election.

Courtesy of Barbara Boxer

*Barbara Boxer was born in Brooklyn, New York, on November 11, 1940. Her original name was Barbara Levy. In 1962 she married Stewart Boxer, graduated from Brooklyn College, and passed her exams to be a stockbroker. When she had difficulty getting a job, she was convinced that employers were rejecting her simply because she was a woman. That experience generated her interest in women's rights and in politics as a way of gaining those rights. After moving to the San Francisco area, she worked as a journalist (1972–74), a congressional aide (1974–76), a member of the Marin County Board of Supervisors (1976–82), and a member of the United States House of Representatives (1983–93) and Senate (since 1993).*

## ALSO NOTEWORTHY

▲ BENJAMIN, JUDAH PHILIP (born August 16, 1811, in Christiansted, Saint Croix, Danish West Indies; died May 6, 1884, in Paris, France). The most prominent nineteenth-century American Jew. He was the first professing Jew elected to the United States Senate (1852); during the Civil War, he served as the Confederate attorney general (1861), secretary of war (1861–62), and secretary of state (1862–65).

▲ BLUM, LÉON (born April 9, 1872, in Paris, France; died March 30, 1950, in Jouy-en-Josas, near Paris). The first Socialist, and first Jewish, premier of France (1936–37).

▲ BRISCOE, ROBERT (born September 25, 1894, in Dublin, Ireland; died May 30, 1969, in Dublin). The first Jewish lord mayor of Dublin (1956–57, 1961–62).

# CREATION OF ENGLAND'S CONSERVATIVE PARTY
## Benjamin Disraeli

જ્જ

*Benjamin Disraeli was born in London, England, on December 21, 1804. His surname was originally spelled D'Israeli. In 1817 Benjamin's father, after quarreling with his synagogue, had his family baptized as Christians. Young Disraeli, following in his literary father's footsteps, began publishing novels in 1826. To gather color for his stories, he toured the Mediterranean and Near East areas during 1830–31. The conditions he found there influenced his later politics, encouraging him to support Britain's imperialism. Disraeli was elected to Parliament in 1837 and served as the British prime minister during 1868 and 1874–80. He died in London on April 19, 1881.*

BENJAMIN DISRAELI WAS GREAT BRITAIN'S FIRST PRIME MINISTER of Jewish origin. He was also the founder of Britain's modern Conservative party.

In 1837 he won election to parliament and began his rise to power. At that time the Conservative party was new, an outgrowth of the old Tory party, which had stood primarily for law and order as well as the interests of trade, industry, and the landed gentry. Under Disraeli's leadership the party formed a new alliance between the old aristocracy, the country gentry, and the impoverished masses.

With that broad backing, he rose to the position of prime minister for a brief period in 1868 and then held the office again from 1874 to 1880. To hold his political alliance together, Disraeli developed a two-pronged domestic policy: (1) he defended the monarchy, the House of Lords, and the church; (2) he instituted social reforms, such as slum clearance, public health programs, laws to prevent the exploitation of labor, and laws to clarify the position of labor unions. His foreign policy was based on consolidating the British Empire. In 1875 he acquired shares in the Suez Canal for England, and in 1876 his efforts in India were so successful that Queen Victoria declared herself the empress of India. She was so fond of Disraeli that she ennobled him as the first earl of Beaconsfield.

The alliance and policies that Disraeli used to mold the Conservative party still affect not only that party but British politics in general.

### ALSO NOTEWORTHY

▲ BUSH, SOLOMON (born 1753 in Philadelphia, Pennsylvania; died 1795 in Philadelphia). The highest ranking Jewish officer in the American revolutionary forces (lieutenant colonel, 1779).

▲ DREYFUS, ALFRED (born October 19, 1859, in Mulhouse, France; died July 12, 1935, in Paris, France). French army officer at the center of the Dreyfus Affair, from 1894, when a military court, with false evidence, convicted him of treason, to 1906, when a civilian court cleared him.

▲ FRIEDMAN, WILLIAM FREDERICK (born September 24, 1891, in Kishinev, Russia; died November 2, 1969, in Washington, D.C.). Cryptologist who, as head of the Signal Intelligence Service of the Army Signal Corps, led teams that broke various secret Japanese codes in the 1930s and 1940s, notably the "Purple" machine cipher (1940).

# TWO WOMEN REPRESENT A STATE
# IN THE UNITED STATES SENATE

## Dianne Feinstein

෨

WHEN DIANNE FEINSTEIN AND BARBARA BOXER *(see page 15)* won California's two United States Senate seats in 1992, they made history: the election marked the first time that any state had chosen to be represented in the Senate by two women. Feinstein, like Boxer a Democrat, defeated the Republican John Seymour.

As a child, she had an uncle who took her to meetings of the Board of Supervisors in San Francisco and encouraged her to get an education so that she could make the city better. She kept that progressive spirit throughout her rise in San Francisco politics, and eventually it led her to seek a high office beyond the city limits.

Courtesy of Dianne Feinstein

In 1992 Feinstein ran for the United States Senate. One of her principal motivations was her desire to ensure individual rights. Judaism, she said, "increased my sensitivity with respect to isues of discrimination and human rights in general." Though she and Boxer had previously had some political disagreements, they pulled together during this campaign and often appeared jointly. Their victories in the November election were attributed to their stand in favor of abortion rights and environmental protection, to the scarcity of women in the Senate (only two before this election), and to the general need for change in Washington.

Feinstein filled a seat vacated by Pete Wilson, who was elected in 1988 but left early to become governor of California. In 1994 she was reelected to the Senate and thereafter continued to fight for the principles that propelled her to her history-making 1992 election.

*Dianne Feinstein was born of a Jewish father and non-Jewish mother in San Francisco, California, on June 22, 1933. Her original name was Dianne Goldman. At the age of thirteen she was confirmed in the Jewish faith, and as an adult she chose to live as a Jew. She majored in history and political science at Stanford University (B.S., 1955), married the neurosurgeon Bertram Feinstein in 1962, served on the California Women's Board of Terms and Parole in the 1960s, and was a member of the San Francisco Board of Supervisors in the 1970s. In 1978, after Mayor George R. Moscone was assassinated, Feinstein became acting mayor of San Francisco. The following year she was officially elected to the office, and she served in that capacity, the first woman to hold the position, from 1979 to 1988. In 1992 she became a United States senator.*

# NEGOTIATING THE VIETNAM PEACE
## Henry Kissinger

❧

Ron Hall

*Henry Alfred Kissinger was born in Fürth, Germany, on May 27, 1923. His original first name was Heinz. He immigrated to the United States in 1938, earned a Ph.D. in political science from Harvard University (1954), taught there (1954–69), became President Nixon's assistant for national security affairs (1968), headed the National Security Council (1969–75), and served as America's first foreign-born secretary of state (1973–77). After he left public life, he was a writer, lecturer, and international consultant.*

HENRY KISSINGER, AMERICAN STATESMAN, shared the 1973 Nobel Peace Prize with North Vietnam's Le Duc Tho for their negotiations that led to the ending of the war between their countries.

When he joined President Nixon's team, Kissinger was a hard-liner on Vietnam. While he was advising the president on their "Vietnamization" policy of progressively disengaging American troops and replacing them with South Vietnamese, Kissinger also advocated the increased bombing of North Vietnam and Cambodia. But during 1970–71, he made a dozen trips to Paris for secret meetings with North Vietnamese representatives. Further negotiations resulted in a January 23, 1973, cease-fire agreement between the United States and North Vietnam. The agreement was that America would withdraw its troops and North Vietnam would release American prisoners of war.

Kissinger's efforts helped end the most divisive foreign war in the history of the United States.

---

### ALSO NOTEWORTHY

▲ **HOLTZMAN, ELIZABETH** (born August 11, 1941, in Brooklyn, New York). The youngest woman, at thirty-one, ever elected to Congress (1972), and the first female district attorney in New York City (1981).

▲ **JAVITS, JACOB KOPPEL** (born May 18, 1904, in New York City; died March 7, 1986, in Palm Beach, Florida). Four-term United States senator who introduced the War Powers Act of 1973, which aims to limit a president's ability to wage war without congressional approval.

Courtesy of *The Jewish Week,* New York

**ELIZABETH HOLTZMAN**

# A Woman Becomes Israel's Premier
## Golda Meir

୧୨

GOLDA MEIR WAS THE FIRST WOMAN to hold the office of prime minister of Israel. As a leader in peace and war, she had a sincerity, simplicity, and grandmotherly image that endeared her to millions, but also a courage and strength that opponents learned to respect.

From her earliest days in Palestine, she devoted herself to Jewish causes. She was motivated by her own childhood fear of pogroms. "If there is any logical explanation...for the direction which my life has taken," she later explained, "it is the desire and determination to save Jewish children...from a similar experience." From the 1920s to the 1940s, she held various posts in the Jewish community in Palestine. On May 14, 1948, she was a signatory of Israel's declaration of independence, and soon thereafter she became the only woman member of the Provisional Council of State, Israel's first legislature. She then served as the first minister of labor (1949–56), hebraized her name from Goldie Myerson to Golda Meir (1956), and held the post of foreign minister (1956–66).

*Golda Meir was born in Kiev, Ukraine, on May 3, 1898. Her original name was Goldie Mabovitch. She came to the United States with her family (1906); married Morris Myerson, a sign painter (1917); and moved to Palestine with her husband (1921). There she was politically active and served as Israel's prime minister (1969–74). She retired in 1974 and died in Jerusalem on December 8, 1978.*

From 1969 to 1974 Meir reigned as Israel's prime minister. During the Yom Kippur War of October 1973, she led the successful counterattack against the Arabs. "When peace comes," she said after the war, "we will perhaps in time be able to forgive the Arabs for killing our sons. But it will be harder for us to forgive them for having forced us to kill their sons."

After her death, it was learned that she had kept secret the fact that during her last twelve years of life she suffered from leukemia. It was another example of the courage that characterized Israel's first woman chief of state.

### ALSO NOTEWORTHY

▲ KREISKY, BRUNO (born January 22, 1911, in Vienna, Austria; died July 29, 1990, in Vienna). Chancellor of Austria from 1970 to 1983, a record tenure.

# Negotiating Palestinian Self-Rule
## Shimon Peres

cs

*Shimon Peres was born in Wołozyn, Poland, on August 16, 1923. His original name was Shimon Perski (or Persky). In 1934 he moved to Palestine. When modern Israel was born in 1948, he entered the defense ministry, and eventually he served as minister of defense (1974–77) and prime minister of Israel (1984–86). In 1992 he became foreign minister under Prime Minister Yitzhak Rabin. On November 4, 1995, Rabin was assassinated and Peres once again took the reins as prime minister.*

FOREIGN MINISTER SHIMON PERES OF ISRAEL, along with Israeli Prime Minister Yitzhak Rabin and Palestine Liberation Organization (PLO) Chairman Yasser Arafat, won the Nobel Peace Prize in 1994. They were so honored because "in a situation marked by war and hatred, they had to take the risk of showing their opposite numbers at least a minimum of trust" and of "confidence that if they offered an outstretched hand, there would be someone there to take it."

In 1993 Peres publicly stated that Israel must make peace with the Palestinians or face a revolutionary situation similar to that in the former Yugoslavia, endangering the very existence of the Jewish state. While Peres and Rabin were engaged in talks with the Palestinians, the Jewish leaders came under verbal assualt by Israeli hard-liners. Nevertheless, Peres negotiated an agreement with the PLO on limited Palestinian self-rule. On May 4, 1994, Rabin and Arafat signed an agreement for Palestinian self-rule in the Gaza Strip and the West Bank enclave of Jericho. "We had a dream before we had a map," Peres said that day. "Now we have a dream and a map together."

► Shimon Peres chats with actress Lauren Bacall.

IPPA, Tel Aviv

In October 1994 the three principals—Peres, Rabin, and Arafat—were awarded the Nobel Peace Prize for making "substantial contributions to a historic process through which peace and cooperation can replace war and hate." It was the first time that the award was given to more than two persons.

---

### ALSO NOTEWORTHY

Courtesy of *The Jewish Week*, New York

**MADELINE MAY KUNIN**

▲ KUNIN, MADELINE MAY (originally Madeline May; born September 28, 1933, in Zurich, Switerland). The first Jewish, and first woman, governor of Vermont (elected 1984, served 1985–91). Married in 1959 to a Vermont physician, Arthur S. Kunin.

▲ LA GUARDIA, FIORELLO HENRY (born December 11, 1882, in New York City; died September 20, 1947, in New York City). New York City's most popular and successful mayor (1934–45). Son of a lapsed-Catholic father and Jewish mother, he was raised an Episcopalian.

# NEGOTIATING PALESTINIAN SELF-RULE
## Yitzhak Rabin

&

PRIME MINISTER YITZHAK RABIN OF ISRAEL, along with Foreign Minister Shimon Peres of Israel and Palestine Liberation Organization (PLO) Chairman Yasser Arafat, won the Nobel Peace Prize in 1994. They were so honored because "in a situation marked by war and hatred, they had to take the risk of showing their opposite numbers at least a minimum of trust" and of "confidence that if they offered an outstretched hand, there would be someone there to take it."

Rabin had decided that he had to defuse the PLO time bomb ticking away in Israel. He and his foreign minister, Peres, secretly engaged in negotiations with the PLO that culminated in the September 1993 accords in which Israel recognized the PLO and agreed to implement limited Palestinian self-rule. Many Israelis denounced Rabin for his peace initiative, but he went forward. On May 4, 1994, Rabin and Arafat signed an agreement for Palestinian self-rule in the Gaza Strip and the West Bank enclave of Jericho.

In October 1994 the three principals—Rabin, Peres, and Arafat—were awarded the Nobel Peace Prize for making "substantial contributions to a historic process through which peace and cooperation can replace war and hate." It marked the first time that the award was given to more than two persons. In 1995 Rabin and Arafat were still in conflict about the details of implementing the plan, but Rabin reaffirmed his commitment to the peace initiative that had won him his Nobel Prize.

Later that year, he was shot and killed by a Jewish right-wing extremist who opposed Rabin's efforts to make peace with the PLO.

*Yitzhak Rabin was born in Jerusalem on March 1, 1922. He was early influenced in his outlook by his parents, ardent Zionists from Russia. In 1941 he joined the Palmach, the commando unit of the Jewish Defense Forces. He rose in the military establishment and eventually served as Israel's chief of staff (1964–68). After retiring from the army, he was the ambassador to the United States (1968–73), Israel's first native-born prime minister (1974–77), and the defense minister (1984–90). In 1992 he once again became prime minister. On November 4, 1995, he was assassinated in Tel Aviv.*

◄ U.S. President Bill Clinton (*center*) presides over the famous handshake between Yitzhak Rabin (*left*) and Yasser Arafat (*right*).

State of Israel Government Press Office

### ALSO NOTEWORTHY

▲ MINOW, NEWTON NORMAN (born January 17, 1926, in Milwaukee, Wisconsin). Lawyer who, as chairman of the Federal Communications Commission (1961–63), made the famous 1961 speech in which he called television programming a "vast wasteland."

# DEVELOPING THE FIRST NUCLEAR SUBMARINE
## Hyman Rickover

❧

*Hyman Rickover was born in Makov, Russia, on January 27, 1900. He came to America as a small child; graduated from the United States Naval Academy (1922); earned an M.S. at Columbia University (1929); received submarine training at New London, Connecticut; fulfilled several naval assignments in the 1930s; headed the electrical section of the Navy Department's Bureau of Ships during World War II; and earned promotions to rear admiral (1953), vice admiral (1959), and full admiral (1973). He died in Arlington, Virginia, on July 8, 1986.*

HYMAN RICKOVER, NAVAL OFFICER AND ENGINEER, developed the world's first nuclear-powered engines and the first atomic-powered submarine. He also led the way in harnessing nuclear energy for peaceful purposes.

In 1946 he received special instruction in nuclear physics at Oak Ridge, Tennessee. After that experience, Rickover pressed the navy to build an atomic submarine. "The more you sweat in peace, the less you bleed in war," he argued.

In 1947 he began to manage the navy's nuclear-propulsion program. His energy and abilty to inspire strong loyalties among his team of specialists were the key factors in his development and early delivery of the U.S.S. *Nautilus* (begun in 1952, finished in 1954), the first atomic-powered submarine.

Later he headed the research team that the Atomic Energy Commission set up to develop a reactor for the peaceful use of nuclear energy. Rickover led the production of the first United States full-scale, civilian-use nuclear power plant, at Shippingport, Pennsylvania (1956–57).

As much as for his achievements, Rickover was known for his outspoken manner and unorthodox methods. But his manner and methods helped him achieve his position as the father of the nuclear submarine and of nuclear power plants.

### ALSO NOTEWORTHY

▲ NETANYAHU, BENJAMIN (or Binyamin; "Bibi"; born October 21, 1949, in Jerusalem, Israel). The youngest prime minister of Israel and the first to be elected (in late May 1996) by ballots directly for that office, not for parliament. Brother of Jonathan Netanyahu.

▲ NETANYAHU, JONATHAN (or Yonatan; "Yoni"; born March 13, 1946, in New York City; died July 3, 1976, in Entebbe, Uganda). Symbol of Israel's elite commandos. He was the field commander of the successful Israeli rescue of over one hundred hostages held by terrorists at Entebbe. Wounded during the mission, he died on the plane before leaving for home. Brother of Benjamin Netanyahu.

▲ REILLY, SIDNEY GEORGE (originally Sigmund Georgievich Rosenblum; born March 24, 1874, in Odessa, Ukraine; died probably November 24, 1925, in or near Moscow). England's most successful spy.

# SERVING AS THE FIRST PRESIDENT OF ISRAEL
## Chaim Weizmann

ᘓ

FOR DECADES BEFORE THE STATE OF ISRAEL WAS BORN, Chaim Weizmann was the guiding spirit of the World Zionist Organization. When the Jewish homeland finally came into being, Weizmann had the distinction of serving as the nation's first president.

Weizmann played an important part in prodding the British government into issuing the Balfour Declaration (November 1917), which stated the government's backing of a Jewish national home in Palestine. He served as president of the World Zionist Organization (1920–29) and of its expanded group, the Jewish Agency for Palestine (1929–31, 1935–46). Weizmann played a leading role in the events leading to the establishment of the state of Israel. His 1948 negotiations with President Truman led to American recognition of the newly proclaimed nation.

*State of Israel Government Press Office*

In 1948 he became president of the provisional government of Israel, and in 1949 the first president of the nation. His frail health affected his tenure in office, but his greatest achievement was his simple presence in stabilizing and symbolizing the new country. He held office till his death.

*Chaim Azriel Weizmann was born in Motol, near Pinsk, Russian-ruled Poland, on November 27, 1874. As a youth, he received Jewish nationalist culture and ideals from his father, a lumber transporter. Young Weizmann took a Ph.D. in chemistry at the University of Fribourg in 1900. In 1904 he went to England, where he worked as a chemist, teacher, and active Zionist. In 1948 he became president of Israel. He died in Rehovot, Israel, on November 9, 1952.*

## ALSO NOTEWORTHY

▲ ROSENBERG, ANNA (originally Anna Marie Lederer; born June 19, 1902, in Budapest, Hungary; died May 9, 1983, in New York City). American public official who, as assistant secretary of defense (1950–53), attained the highest Pentagon position ever held by a woman. She married Julius Rosenberg (not the Julius Rosenberg of the famous spying case) in 1919 and divorced him in 1962 to marry Paul Hoffman, whose surname she used in her later years.

▲ ROSENMAN, SAMUEL IRVING (born February 13, 1896, in San Antonio, Texas; died June 24, 1973, in New York City). Lawyer, judge, and presidential advisor who drafted most of Franklin Delano Roosevelt's speeches, including his "New Deal" acceptance speech at the 1932 Democratic Convention.

▲ ROTHSCHILD, LIONEL NATHAN DE (born November 22, 1808, in London, England; died June 3, 1879, in London). The first professed Jew to sit in the British Parliament (elected in 1847 but not seated till 1858). Grandson of the banker Mayer Amschel Rothschild and father of Nathaniel Mayer de Rothschild.

▲ ROTHSCHILD, NATHANIEL MAYER DE (sometimes recorded as Nathan Meyer Rothschild; born November 8, 1840, in London, England; died March 31, 1915, in London). The first Jewish peer in England (created Baron Rothschild in 1885). He was a member of the House of Commons (1865–85) and sat in the House of Lords (1885–1915). Son of Lionel Nathan de Rothschild, great-grandson of the banker Mayer Amschel Rothschild, and grandfather of the scientist Miriam Louisa Rothschild.

▲ SALOMONS, DAVID (born November 22, 1797, in London, England; died July 18, 1873, in London). The first Jewish lord mayor of London (1855–56).

▲ SALVADOR, FRANCIS (born 1747 in London, England; died August 1, 1776, in South Carolina). The first Jew to serve in a legislative body in America (as a delegate to the Revolutionary Provisional Congress of South Carolina, 1775–76) and possibly the first Jew in the modern world to hold such a public office. He was also the first Jew to die in the struggle for American independence, killed by Native Americans who had been encouraged by the invading British.

▲ STRAUS, OSCAR SOLOMON (born December 23, 1850, in Otterberg, Bavaria; died May 3, 1926, in New York City). The first Jewish United States Cabinet member, as secretary of commerce and labor (1906–1909). Brother of the businessmen Isidor and Nathan Straus.

HELEN SUZMAN

▲ SUZMAN, HELEN (originally Helen Gavronsky; born November 7, 1917, in Germiston, Transvaal, South Africa). A founder of the Progressive party of South Africa (1959) and for many years (1961–74) the only antiapartheid member of Parliament. Married in 1937 to Mosie Suzman, a physician.

▲ TRUMPELDOR, JOSEPH (born 1880 in Pyatigorsk, Caucasia, Russia; died March 1, 1920, between Tel Hai and Kefar Giladi, Palestine). The first Jewish officer in the Russian army (1906); the highest-ranking Jewish officer, a captain, in the British army's Zion Mule Corps (1915), which was the first official Jewish army unit in nearly two thousand years; and the principal symbol of the pioneering kibbutz ("communal settlement") movement and of the armed defense of the Land of Israel, being killed by Arabs while he was defending the settlement of Tel Hai. His grave at Tel Hai is a goal of pilgrims, and his attributed last words—"It is good to die for our country"—are virtually a motto for bravery in Israel.

SIMONE VEIL

▲ VEIL, SIMONE (originally Simone Annie Jacob; born July 13, 1927, in Nice, France). The most prominent Jewish politician in France, and president of the European Parliament from 1979 to 1982. Married in 1946 to Antoine Veil, a member of the French civil service.

# 2

# CIVIL RIGHTS, FEMINISM, AND JEWISH ACTIVISM

❧

MANY PIONEERING CIVIL RIGHTS LEADERS *in American history have been Jewish. The most notable example was Arthur Garfield Hays, the first important civil rights lawyer to defend clients from the richest to the poorest.*

*Modern feminism was created by a Jew. Betty Friedan sparked the feminist movement with her book* The Feminine Mystique.

*Among those with unique achievements as Jewish activists were Rebecca Gratz, founder of the Jewish Sunday school; Theodor Herzl, father of modern political Zionism; and Henrietta Szold, who established Hadassah. Simon Wiesenthal earned a place of special distinction in the history of Jewish activism by becoming the world's most successful Nazi hunter. The best-known war criminal whom he captured was Adolf Eichmann.*

# LAUNCHING THE MODERN AMERICAN FEMINIST MOVEMENT

## Betty Friedan

ᗄᓂ

*Betty Friedan was born in Peoria, Illinois, on February 4, 1921. Her original name was Betty Naomi Goldstein. She graduated from Smith College with a major in psychology in 1942, married Carl Friedan in 1947 (they divorced in 1969), and had three children. Feeling unfulfilled, she turned to writing and feminine activism.*

BETTY FRIEDAN, FOR MANY YEARS an apparently typical suburban housewife and mother, gradually allowed long-suppressed feelings to surface and in her early forties published *The Feminine Mystique,* the book that led to the current feminist movement in America.

Susan Wood

Anger and frustration motivated her. She was angry at discrimination and frustrated with her lifestyle. Her sensitivity to discrimination was at least partly due to her experiences as a young Jew in Peoria. "When you're a Jewish girl who grows up on the right side of the tracks in the Midwest," she later explained, "you're marginal. You're in, but you're not, and you grow up an observer." As an adult, she tired of "years of trying to be a kind of woman I wasn't, of too many lonesome, boring, wasted hours."

Those feelings led her to research and write her book *The Feminine Mystique* (1963). The title refers to the myth that a woman can only be fulfilled by being a wife, mother, and consumer. Friedan challenged that myth and exhorted women to seek personal fulfillment. The book was a best-seller and had a tremendous influence on American women and on society at large. In 1966 she became the founding president of the National Organization for Women (NOW), whose goal was to achieve equal rights and job opportunities for women. In 1970 she left NOW to concentrate on other projects, such as helping to form the National Women's Political Caucus (1971) and the First Women's Bank (1973). Since then she has continued to write and lecture on women's liberation, a movement to which, in its modern form, Friedan herself gave birth.

# FOUNDING THE JEWISH SUNDAY SCHOOL
## Rebecca Gratz

❦

REBECCA GRATZ WAS ACTIVE in many Jewish social-welfare programs and was the foremost Jewish-American woman of her day. She is now best remembered as the founder of the first permanent Jewish Sunday school.

Gratz became the first secretary of the pioneering Female Association for the Relief of Women and Children in Reduced Circumstances (1801), helped found the Philadelphia Orphan Asylum (1815), served as its secretary for forty years (1819–59), founded the Female Hebrew Benevolent Society (1819), and established the Jewish Foster Home and Orphan Asylum (1855).

As early as 1818 she acted on her desire to improve the religious education of Jewish children. In that year, she opened a short-lived school for eleven children in her own home. Later she became acquainted with the Christian Sunday school movement, and in 1838 she organized a Jewish counterpart. Her Hebrew Sunday School Society of Philadelphia began on March 4, 1838, her own birthday. Gratz served as its president till 1864. Much of the financial support, and most of the teaching staff, came from the congregation of Mikveh Israel, but the Sunday school was open free of charge to boys and girls from all Philadelphia Jewish communities. The society lasted into the twentieth century and served as a model for similar groups throughout the United States.

The Hebrew Sunday School Society was Gratz's most enduring achievement in a life filled with accomplishments.

> *Rebecca Gratz was born in Philadelphia, Pennsylvania, on March 4, 1781. There is a tradition that she loved a non-Jew, Samuel Ewing, but would not marry outside her faith. To drown her sorrow, according to the tradition, she devoted herself to charitable works. It is also believed that she was the prototype for the admirable character Rebecca in Sir Walter Scott's* Ivanhoe. *Both stories may be inventions, but they reflect the esteem in which she was held in her time. She died in Philadelphia on August 27, 1869.*

### ALSO NOTEWORTHY

▲ **GOLDMAN, MAYER CLARENCE** (born September 2, 1874, in New Orleans, Louisiana; died November 24, 1939, in New York City). Lawyer who was the most outspoken early advocate of the public defender for poor people accused of crimes.

▲ **KAHANE, MEIR** (originally Martin David Kahane; born August 1, 1932, in Brooklyn, New York; assassinated November 5, 1990, in New York City). Rabbi who founded the controversial Jewish Defense League in 1968.

# PIONEERING CIVIL RIGHTS ACTIVISM
## Arthur Garfield Hays

e/o

*Arthur Garfield Hays was born in Rochester, New York, on December 12, 1881. After earning his LL.B. at Columbia University (1905), he began his law career. He died in New York City on December 14, 1954.*

ARTHUR GARFIELD HAYS WAS THE FIRST GREAT LAWYER to expand the range of civil rights activism to include clients from the richest to the poorest. His purpose in taking cases never varied—to protect the personal liberties of individuals.

The fortune he earned by defending financiers, brokers, and merchants gave him the freedom to take on nonpaying clients in cases that he thought were important. But he never sacrificed his idealism just for money. Bankers, too, he said, have civil rights, and he "hated censorship of business as well as of books." His rich clients included brokers who argued that the Security and Exchange Commission was trampling their rights. He defended the publishing tycoon William Randolph Hearst when his private telegrams were subpoenaed and Henry Ford when he was engaged in a freedom-of-speech dispute.

At the same time, he spent many years as an unpaid general counsel for the American Civil Liberties Union. In the Scopes trial in Tennessee (1925), he assisted Clarence Darrow in defending the right of a teacher to teach evolution in a public school. In the Sacco-Vanzetti murder case (1927), he defended two men who, he felt, were accused simply because of their political views. He also aided striking coal miners and textile workers. Hays represented not only the fascist German-American Bund but also the communist John Strachey. He even made, at great personal risk to himself, an inquiry into violations of civil liberties in Puerto Rico.

In his honor, New York University established the Arthur Garfield Hays Memorial, the nation's first integrated teaching and research program in civil liberties.

---

### ALSO NOTEWORTHY

▲ NASI, DOÑA GRACIA (full Jewish name, Gracia Hannah Nasi; Christian name, Beatrice de Luna; born 1510 in Lisbon, Portugal; died 1569, possibly in Palestine). A Marrano who openly espoused Judaism and became the best-known Jewish-rights leader of her time by operating an underground railroad for the flight of other Marranos out of Portugal; giving financial aid to Jews; confronting the anti-Semitic Pope Paul IV; and establishing a Jewish settlement in Tiberias, Palestine.

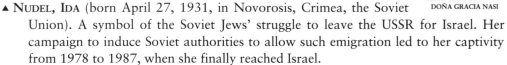

DOÑA GRACIA NASI

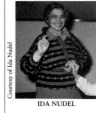

Courtesy of Ida Nudel

IDA NUDEL

▲ NUDEL, IDA (born April 27, 1931, in Novorosis, Crimea, the Soviet Union). A symbol of the Soviet Jews' struggle to leave the USSR for Israel. Her campaign to induce Soviet authorities to allow such emigration led to her captivity from 1978 to 1987, when she finally reached Israel.

# FOUNDING POLITICAL ZIONISM
## Theodor Herzl

ℰℛ

THEODOR HERZL WAS THE founder of the political form of Zionism, a movement to establish a Jewish homeland.

In spite of the anti-Semitism he encountered in Austria (which he attributed to peculiarities in the Austrian and German peoples), Herzl believed in assimilation till the mid-1890s when, in his capacity as a journalist, he visited Paris. There, in the heart of the liberal French Revolution, he still found anti-Semitism, exemplified in the Alfred Dreyfus affair, in which a French Jew had been framed for treason and publicly vilified.

State of Israel Government Press Office

*Theodor Herzl was born in Budapest, Hungary, on May 2, 1860. He studied law at the University of Vienna, but he decided to work as a journalist and playwright. In the 1890s he became an active Zionist. He died in Edlach, Austria, on July 3, 1904.*

Herzl reacted by writing the pamphlet *The Jewish State* (published in 1896). In it, he proposed that the Jewish issue was a political question that should be settled by a world council of nations. He organized a world congress of Zionists who met at Basel, Switzerland, in August 1897. The result was the World Zionist Organization, of which he became the first president.

Herzl was certainly not the first to conceive of a Jewish state, but because of his abilities as an organizer and propagandist, he was the most important figure in the development of Zionism as a political movement of worldwide significance. Over forty years after his death, his efforts finally resulted in the establishment of the state of Israel.

# CREATION OF HADASSAH
## Henrietta Szold

დ

*Henrietta Szold was born in Baltimore, Maryland, on December 21, 1860. Her father was Rabbi Benjamin Szold, a leader in the Baltimore Jewish community. He taught her Hebrew, the Bible, the Talmud, and Jewish history. Henrietta became a strong Jewish activist and Zionist. She died in Jerusalem on February 13, 1945.*

HENRIETTA SZOLD WAS THE PRINCIPAL FOUNDER OF HADASSAH, the Women's Zionist Organization of America.

The Russian pogroms of the 1880s resulted in a flood of Jewish immigrants into the Baltimore area. Witnessing their plight motivated Szold to become a Jewish activist. She established a night school for Jewish immigrants and began writing and editing Jewish works, especially for the Jewish Publication Society. In 1920 she settled in Palestine, where she organized medical and social services.

Szold's lasting achievement was Hadassah, which she and a group of women founded in 1912 and which she headed as its first president. *Hadassah* is the Hebrew name for the biblical heroine Esther. Szold's interest in Zionism had increased during a 1909 visit to Palestine. "If not Zionism," she said, "then nothing...then extinction for the Jews." Upset at the suffering that she saw in Palestine—the illnesses and the lack of basic hygienic standards— Szold, after returning to the United States, poured out her feelings to a group

▶
**Henrietta Szold** *(left)* **plants first tree in Ma'ale Ha'amisha Forest at age 82.**

Central Zionist Archives, Israel

83

of Jewish women: "If we are Zionists, as we say we are, what is the good of meeting and talking and drinking tea? Let us do something real and practical—let us organize the Jewish women of America and send nurses and doctors to Palestine."

Thus began Hadassah, which became the largest of all Zionist groups in the United States and the largest Jewish women's organization in the world.

# HOLOCAUST SURVIVOR BECOMES THE WORLD'S GREATEST NAZI HUNTER
## Simon Wiesenthal

❧

SIMON WIESENTHAL TRACKED DOWN over one thousand war criminals, including Adolf Eichmann.

After Wiesenthal was liberated from a Nazi concentration camp at the end of World War II, he helped the United States Army gather evidence with which to prosecute Nazi war criminals. From 1947 to 1954, he headed the Jewish Historical Documentation Center in Linz, Austria, aiding Jewish victims of Nazi persecution and providing evidence for war-crimes trials. From 1954 to 1961, he worked on his own and with Israeli agents to search out former Nazis, his most notable success being the capture of Adolf Eichmann (chief administrator of the "final solution") in Argentina in 1959.

In 1961 Weisenthal founded the Jewish Documentation Center in Vienna, Austria. Again his main purpose was to track down former Gestapo agents, SS officers, and other Nazis for trial. He prepared careful dossiers on suspects and cooperated with Israeli, Austrian, West German, and other governments. Wiesenthal asserted that he searched in the spirit of justice, not vengeance. "When history looks back," he explained, "I want people to know that the Nazis weren't able to kill eleven million people and get away with it."

The Simon Wiesenthal Center for Holocaust Studies, a film and document archive headquartered in Los Angeles, is appropriately named after the world's most tireless and successful Nazi hunter.

> *Simon Wiesenthal was born in Buczacz, Austria-Hungary, on December 31, 1908. He practiced architecture till World War II, during which he was interned in a series of Nazi concentration camps. After the war he became the world's most famous Nazi hunter.*

---

### ALSO NOTEWORTHY

▲ **PAPPENHEIM, BERTHA** (born 1859 in Vienna, Austria; died 1936 in Neu-Isenburg, Germany). Founder of the German Jewish feminist movement in the early twentieth century. Famous as the hysteria patient "Anna O.," treated by Josef Breuer and discussed by Sigmund Freud. *Photo credit:* American Jewish Archives, Cincinnati Campus, Hebrew Union College, Jewish Institute of Religion.

▲ **ROSE, ERNESTINE LOUISE** (originally Siismondi Potowski; born January 13, 1810, in Piotrkow, Russian-ruled Poland; died August 4, 1892, in Brighton, England). Feminist whose eloquence led to her sobriquet Queen of the Platform.

ERNESTINE ROSE

BERTHA PAPPENHEIM

▲ SCHENIRER, SARAH (born 1883 in Kraków, Poland; died 1935 in Vienna, Austria). Founder of the Beth Jacob network of schools for young religious women (1918).

▲ SCHWIMMER, ROSIKA (born September 11, 1877, in Budapest, Hungary; died August 3, 1948, in New York City). Feminist and pacifist who helped found the Woman's Peace Party in America in 1915, became perhaps the first woman ambassador of modern times when she was appointed Hungarian minister to Switzerland in 1918, and cofounded the Campaign for World Government in 1937.

▲ SHARANSKY, NATAN (originally Anatoly Borisovich Shcharansky; born January 20, 1948, in Stalino, Ukraine, the Soviet Union). Human-rights advocate who linked the two previously separate strands of dissent in the Soviet Union—the Jewish emigration movement and the broader human-rights movement. He was imprisoned (1977–86) by the Soviet government and then allowed to go to Israel.

NATAN SHARANSKY

State of Israel Government Press Office

▲ SOLOMON, HANNAH G(REENEBAUM) (originally Hannah Greenebaum; born 1858 in Chicago, Illinois; died December 7, 1942, in Chicago). Founder of the National Council of Jewish Women, the first national Jewish women's organization in the world.

HANNAH SOLOMON

▲ SPINGARN, JOEL ELIAS (born May 17, 1875, in New York City; died July 26, 1939, in New York City). Educator and author who helped found the National Association for the Advancement of Colored People (NAACP) in 1909, served as its president from 1930 till his death, and, in 1913, established the NAACP's Spingarn Medal.

# 3

# LAW

჻

JEWS HAVE BROKEN PATHS THROUGH GREAT ACCOMPLISHMENTS *in the field of law in many parts of the world.*

*Tobias Asser was a Dutch lawyer who promoted the idea of compelling nations to arbitrate as an alternative to war. He won a Nobel Peace Prize for his pioneering work on international legal relations.*

*The first Jew on the United States Supreme Court was Louis D. Brandeis. By successfully overcoming anti-Semitic opposition to his appointment, he opened doors to high judical positions for other Jews.*

*René Cassin, a French lawyer, wrote the United Nation's Universal Declaration of Human Rights. For his work on that great document, he was awarded the Nobel Peace Prize.*

*Another Jewish justice of the United States Supreme Court was Felix Frankfurter. His unique achievement was his formulation of the principle of judicial self-restraint.*

*The first Jewish woman on the American Supreme Court was Ruth Bader Ginsburg. She won the support of liberals because of her record as a women's rights lawyer and of conservatives because of her record as a cautious appellate court judge.*

# PIONEERING INTERNATIONAL LEGAL RELATIONS
## Tobias Asser

*Tobias Michael Carel Asser was born in Amsterdam, Netherlands, on April 28, 1838. He earned a doctorate in law at the Amsterdam Athenaeum (1860, later called the University of Amsterdam), taught at his alma mater (1862–93), and then held government posts. He died in The Hague, Netherlands, on July 29, 1913.*

TOBIAS ASSER WON THE 1911 NOBEL PEACE PRIZE for being "a pioneer in the field of international legal relations." He shared the award with Alfred Fried, who worked separately.

Asser played a prominent role in the Dutch government's decision to convene a series of international law conferences beginning in 1893. In 1899 he led the formation of the Permanent Court of Arbitration at a peace conference in The Hague. He promoted the principle of compulsory arbitration as an alternative to armed conflict between nations. In 1900 he was appointed to the Permanent Court of Arbitration, which began to hear cases involving disputes between nations in 1902.

The modern world owes a debt of gratitude to Asser for his role in pioneering peaceful solutions to international problems.

## ALSO NOTEWORTHY

▲ **ABRAM, MORRIS BERTHOLD** (born June 19, 1918, in Fitzgerald, Georgia). Lawyer who was the first head of the legal department of the Peace Corps in 1961.

▲ **BEN-PORAT, MIRIAM** (born April 26, 1918, in Vitebsk, Lithuania). The first woman to serve on the Supreme Court of Israel (1976–88) and, since 1988, the first Israeli state comptroller publicly to criticize government bureaucracies at the highest levels.

*State of Israel Government Press Office*

MIRIAM BEN-PORAT

▲ **CARDOZO, BENJAMIN NATHAN** (born May 24, 1870, in New York City; died July 9, 1938, in Port Chester, New York). Associate justice of the United States Supreme Court (1932–38).

▲ **FORTAS, ABE** (born June 19, 1910, in Memphis, Tennessee; died April 6, 1982, in Washington, D.C.). Associate justice of the United States Supreme Court (1965–69). *Photo credit:* Library of Congress.

ABE FORTAS

# A Jew Is Appointed a United States Supreme Court Justice
## Louis D. Brandeis

❧

LOUIS D. BRANDEIS WAS THE FIRST JEW TO SERVE on the United States Supreme Court. An associate justice from 1916 to 1939, he had a profound impact on America between the two world wars.

In his private practice, from 1877 to 1916, Brandeis earned a reputation as a "people's attorney" by opposing big-business abuses and by representing groups that were traditionally powerless, such as laborers. In 1907 he created the "Brandeis brief," a new type of legal document in which economic and social data, historical experience, and expert opinions were marshaled to support the legal propositions. From 1912 to 1921 he led the American Zionist movement.

*Louis David Brandeis was born in Louisville, Kentucky, on November 13, 1856. He changed his middle name to Dembitz to honor an uncle, Louis Dembitz, a well-known Zionist. After earning his law degree at Harvard Law School (1877), Brandeis entered private practice. In 1916 he became a justice of the United States Supreme Court. He retired in 1939 and died in Washington, D.C., on October 5, 1941.*

When President Woodrow Wilson nominated Brandeis for the Supreme Court, business interests and anit-Semites voiced powerful opposition. But in 1916 Brandeis took his seat as the Court's first Jewish member.

American Jewish Archives, Cincinnati Campus, Hebrew Union College, Jewish Institute of Religion.

Opponents need not have feared. Brandeis was not a sentimental reformer. He not only distrusted big business for its abuses; he also distrusted big government as a way of stopping those abuses. Brandeis supported the constitutional validity of most, but not all, New Deal legislation. And he supported the freedom of speech, press, and assembly, but not when it resulted in a clear and present danger of inciting illegal acts.

Brandeis University, in Waltham, Massachusetts, was named after Justice Brandeis, the pathbreaking Supreme Court jurist.

# WRITING THE DECLARATION OF HUMAN RIGHTS

## René Cassin

❧

*René-Samuel Cassin was born in Bayonne, France, on October 5, 1887. He took a doctorate at the University of Paris (1914), worked as a lawyer and teacher, attended disarmament conferences (1924–38), served as a member of the French government in exile during World War II, and held high legal offices in his later years, notably as the president of the European Court of Human Rights (1965–68). He died in Paris, France, on February 20, 1976.*

RENÉ CASSIN WON THE 1968 NOBEL PEACE PRIZE for his work as the principal author of the Universal Declaration of Human Rights issued by the United Nations in 1948.

Cassin was an ardent Zionist, and he campaigned for Jewish rights. That experience laid the foundation for his work on behalf of human rights for everyone. During 1947–48 he served on the United Nations Commission on Human Rights. For that body, he drew up the Universal Declaration of Human Rights, which was formally adopted on December 10, 1948. The document declared that all citizens were entitled to the rights of life, liberty, and personal security; equality before the law; freedom of conscience, religion, expression, and assembly; the right to work, equal compensation for equal work, and reasonable working hours; and a free education.

Many nations that have come into existence since 1948 have incorporated these provisions into their constitutions.

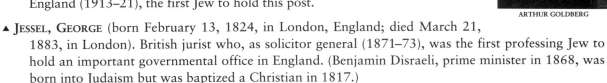

### ALSO NOTEWORTHY

▲ GOLDBERG, ARTHUR J(OSEPH) (born August 8, 1908, in Chicago, Illinois; died January 19, 1990, in Washington, D.C.). Labor lawyer who served as associate justice of the United States Supreme Court (1962–65) and as the United States representative to the United Nations (1965–68). *Photo credit:* Library of Congress.

▲ HEILBRON, ROSE (born 1914 in Liverpool, England). The first woman in Great Britain to be appointed a recorder (chief criminal judge, 1956) and the first woman barrister to argue a case in the House of Lords (1987).

▲ ISAACS, RUFUS DANIEL (first Marquess of Reading; born October 10, 1860, in London, England; died December 30, 1935, in London). Lord chief justice of England (1913–21), the first Jew to hold this post.

ARTHUR GOLDBERG

▲ JESSEL, GEORGE (born February 13, 1824, in London, England; died March 21, 1883, in London). British jurist who, as solicitor general (1871–73), was the first professing Jew to hold an important governmental office in England. (Benjamin Disraeli, prime minister in 1868, was born into Judaism but was baptized a Christian in 1817.)

# CHAMPIONING JUDICIAL SELF-RESTRAINT
## Felix Frankfurter

ℰℐ

DURING HIS TENURE AS AN ASSOCIATE JUSTICE of the United States Supreme Court (1939–62), Felix Frankfurter was the Court's leading exponent of judicial self-restraint.

Harris and Ewing/Collection of the Supreme Court of the United States

His political view was generally liberal (in 1920 he helped found the American Civil Liberties Union), and he defended personal liberties. But his principal concern was for the integrity of government, not for the victims of legal injustice. "Even where the social undesirability of a law may be convincingly urged," he wrote in a 1949 case, "invalidation of the law by a court debilitates popular democratic government." So he tended to uphold existing state and federal legislative action. He held that judges should closely adhere to precedent, disregarding their own opinions, and decide only "whether legislators could in reason have enacted such a law."

His policy of judicial self-restraint often put him at odds with his liberal supporters, but his integrity and judicial skill were never questioned.

> *Felix Frankfurter was born in Vienna, Austria, on November 15, 1882. In 1894 he immigrated to the United States. After receiving his law degree from Harvard Law School (1906), he served as an assistant United States attorney in New York City (1906–1909), an assistant in the War Department (1911–13), and a teacher at Harvard Law School (1914–39). From 1939 to 1962, he was an associate justice of the United States Supreme Court. Frankfurter retired in 1962 and died in Washington, D.C., on February 22, 1965.*

---

### ALSO NOTEWORTHY

▲ **LEVY, MOSES** (born 1757 in Philadelphia, Pennsylvania; died 1826 in Philadelphia). The first Jew to qualify as a lawyer in the United States, being admitted to the Pennsylvania bar in 1778.

# A Jewish Woman Is Appointed to the United States Supreme Court

## Ruth Bader Ginsburg

*Ruth Bader Ginsburg was born in Brooklyn, New York, on March 15, 1933. Her original name was Ruth Joan Bader. In 1954 she married Martin D. Ginsburg, a fellow law student. After she received her law degree from Columbia Law School (1959), she was turned down by all of the New York City law firms because she was a woman. Ginsburg went on to work as a law clerk (1959–61), a research associate at Columbia (1961–62), a teacher at Rutgers University (1963–72), a teacher at Columbia (1972–80), and a judge with the United States Court of Appeals in the District of Columbia (1980–93). In 1993 she was appointed to the United States Supreme Court.*

On August 10, 1993, Ruth Bader Ginsburg became the first Jewish woman to be a member of the highest court in the land. On that day, she was sworn in as an associate justice of the United States Supreme Court.

"I did not go into law with the purpose of becoming an advocate of equal rights," she said. "I became a lawyer for personal, selfish reasons. I thought I could do a lawyer's job better than any other" kind of job. But when she saw the problems that many women were having, she took action. In the 1970s she directed the Women's Rights Project of the American Civil Liberties

U.S. President Bill Clinton and Ruth Bader Ginsburg.

Union, for which she argued six cases before the United States Supreme Court, winning five and firmly establishing the unconstitutionality of unequal treatment for women.

Her efforts were so remarkable that she won an appointment as a federal appellate court judge. During her tenure in that capacity, she changed her image from that of a pioneering women's rights activist to that of a cautious, restrained, moderate judge. When she was nominated for the Supreme Court in 1993, she was approved by liberals because of her advocacy of women's rights and by conservatives because of her judicial restraint.

Ginsburg gave credit to her late mother for having stressed to the young Ruth that she should strive for achievement and independence. "I pray that I may be all that she would have been," Ginsburg said when President Bill Clinton selected her in June 1993, "had she lived to an age when women could aspire and achieve and daughters are cherished as much as sons." The mother's hope was more than fulfilled when her daughter became the first Jewish woman on the United States Supreme Court.

# 4

# RELIGION

஧

JEWS HAVE FOUNDED A WIDE VARIETY *of religious movements. Among the most notable founders were Baal Shem Tov (Hasidism) and Isaac Mayer Wise (Reform Judaism in America).*

*Other Jews made unique contributions to Jewish law and thought. Joseph Caro, for example, was the last great codifier of Jewish law. Moses Maimonides wrote the Thirteen Articles of Faith and other works of great importance in the history of Judaism.*

*Women, too, have made their mark in the Jewish faith. Lilian Montagu was the first Jewish woman lay minister. Sally Priesand was America's first woman rabbi.*

*Other unique religious achievements included Leo Baeck's spiritual unification of German Jewry during the Nazi period and Nehama Leibowitz's revolutionary approach to Bible teaching.*

# FOUNDING HASIDISM
## Baal Shem Tov

cx/3

*Baal Shem Tov was born about 1700, probably in Tluste, Podolia, Poland. His original name was Israel ben Eliezer. After holding various minor jobs, he retired to the Carpathian Mountains for mystical speculation, earning his living as a lime digger. Later he worked as an innkeeper and a ritual slaughterer. His last years were devoted entirely to spiritual pursuits. He died in Miedzboz, Podolia, in 1760.*

BAAL SHEM TOV FOUNDED HASIDISM, a spiritual movement characterized by mysticism and opposition to secular studies and Jewish rationalism.

Early in his career, he developed a reputation as a miracle healer who worked with talismans and other objects inscribed with God's name. He was therefore called Baal Shem Tov ("Master of the Good Name") or Besht (an acronym derived from the Hebrew name).

Baal Shem Tov taught three principal points. First, he emphasized direct personal communion with God. Second, he renounced mortification of the flesh and claimed that ordinary bodily existence was holy; every deed done "for the sake of heaven," including working and eating, was equal in value to observing formal commandments. Third, he exhorted his followers to rescue the "sparks" of divinity trapped in the material world; redemption did not require retreat. These teachings endeared him to the common folk, with whom he mixed freely (in a "descent for the sake of ascent"), contrary to the usual practice of holy men of his time.

The Hasidic movement soon conquered a major part of eastern European Jewry. It added a new dimension to the Jewish religion—an atmosphere of joy and ecstasy. After his death, Baal Shem Tov became a legendary figure.

# UNIFYING GERMAN JEWRY UNDER THE NAZIS
## Leo Baeck

cx

WHEN THE NAZIS CONTROLLED GERMANY in the 1930s and 1940s, Leo Baeck served as the spiritual leader of German Jewry.

In 1933, when the Nazis came to power, Baeck and Otto Hirsch (1885–1941) founded the National Agency of Jews in Germany, a

Courtesy of *The Jewish Week*, New York

unification of all of German Jewry's organizations. Through the agency, Baeck provided Jews with economic aid, emigration assistance, and educational and cultural opportunities. He personally negotiated with the Nazis on various issues, providing moral resistance and hoping to stall for time till their control in Germany dissipated. In 1939 he took a trainload of children to England and then, instead of staying there for his own safety, returned to Germany to help the Jews who remained.

After suffering five arrests, he was finally put into the Theresienstadt concentration camp. Of the 140,000 Jews placed there, fewer than 9,000 survived. Baeck set up classes inside the camp and gave lectures on philosophy. On May 8, 1945, the day before he was to be executed, the Russians liberated Theresienstadt, and Baeck stopped the inmates from killing the guards.

After the war, he taught and lectured in England and the United States. His life summarized both the greatness and the flaws of the German Jews, who had committed themselves to assimilating with western European civilization, which ultimately nearly destroyed them.

*Leo Baeck was born in Lissa, Posen, Prussia, on May 23, 1873. He earned a doctorate in philosophy at the University of Berlin (1895) and was ordained by the Berlin Hochschule (1897). His book* The Essence of Judaism *(1905) helped make him the leading liberal Jewish theologian of the era. He held positions as a rabbi in various German cities, notably Berlin (1912–42). Baeck died in London, England, on November 2, 1956.*

# CODIFYING JEWISH LAW
## Joseph Caro

cro

*Joseph ben Ephraim Caro (sometimes spelled Karo or Qaro) was born in Spain, probably in Toledo, in 1488. In 1492 the Jews were expelled from Spain, an experience that affected Caro for the rest of his life. In 1536 he settled in Safed, Palestine, a center for students of the Talmud. He died there on March 24, 1575.*

JOSEPH CARO WAS THE AUTHOR of the last great codification of Jewish law.

Because of the partial disintegration of Jewish life after the Spanish expulsion and because of the diversity of Talmudic authorities in different countries, Caro saw a need to standardize Jewish laws. He decided to write not an independent work but a commentary "in order to avoid having to repeat what my predecessors have already written."

In 1542 he finished *Bet Yoseph* ("House of Joseph," published 1555–59), a commentary on Jacob ben Asher's *Arba'ah turim* ("Four Rows"). Caro systematized a vast body of material, concentrating on bringing together the legal decisions of three important Talmudists: Moses Maimonides, Isaac Alfasi, and Asher ben Jehiel. Because of the length and complexity of *Bet Yoseph*, Caro prepared a condensed version, *Shulhan 'arukh* ("Prepared Table," published 1565), which is still authoritative for Orthodox Jewry throughout the world.

---

### ALSO NOTEWORTHY

▲ **ABOAB, ISAAC DA FONSECA** (born 1605 in Castrodaire, Portugal; died 1693 in Amsterdam, Holland). The first rabbi and the first Jewish author in the New World (1642–54, in Brazil).

▲ **FRANK, RAY** (born 1865 in California; died 1948). Writer and teacher who was probably the first American woman to preach from a Jewish pulpit (though never formally employed as a rabbi). Also the first female student (for one semester only) at Hebrew Union College in Cincinnati.

▲ **FRANKEL, ZACHARIAS** (born September 30, 1801, in Prague, Bohemia; died February 13, 1875, in Breslau, Germany). Rabbi who led the Conservative movement in Europe.

▲ **GEIGER, ABRAHAM** (born May 24, 1810, in Frankfurt am Main, Germany; died October 23, 1874, in Berlin, Germany). Theologian who led the early development of Reform Judaism in Europe.

# Development of a New Approach to Bible Teaching
## Nehama Leibowitz

❧

NEHAMA LEIBOWITZ, A LEGENDARY FIGURE in the Jewish world, taught biblical commentary to all sectors of Israeli society for over sixty years. She taught the Bible at the Mizrachi Women Teachers' Seminar in Jersualem (1930–55) and traveled the country, teaching, as well. In

Scoop 80

1957 she began to teach at Tel Aviv University. In addition, she conducted correspondence courses for thousands of Jews around the world and published books that have been valuable aids for teachers and rabbis.

The traditional approach to teaching her subject was simply to cite what biblical commentators had written about a text. Leibowitz, on the other hand, urged her students to ask *why* a commentator had made a particular comment. She encouraged them to examine problematic sections of text, to understand the role of commentary on that text, and to confront differences among the commentators and the implications of those differences.

Her methods have been tremendously successful. Many teachers and rabbis are passing her ideas along to new generations of students. She is certainly Judaism's most famous Bible teacher.

> *Nehama Leibowitz was born in Riga, Latvia, in 1905. Her father taught her the Torah, and from an early age she knew that she wanted to be a biblical scholar. In 1914 her family went to Berlin. She earned a doctorate in Bible studies at the University of Berlin and, in 1930, immigrated to Palestine, where she embarked on a long career as a Bible teacher.*

### ALSO NOTEWORTHY

▲ HILDESHEIMER, AZRIEL (or Israel Hildesheimer; born 1820 in Halberstadt, Germany; died 1899 in Berlin, Germany). Rabbi who founded the wing of Neo-Orthodoxy that led to modern "centrist" Orthodoxy.

# CREATION OF THE GREATEST POSTBIBLICAL JEWISH SCHOLARSHIP
## Moses Maimonides

ຂ໑

*Moses Maimonides was born in Córdoba, Spain, on March 30, 1135. His original name was Moses ben Maimon. Later he became known as Rambam, an acronym for Rabbi Moses ben Maimon. After Córdoba fell to an Islamic sect, he and his family wandered for many years before settling in Egypt, where he earned a living as a physician. He died in Fostat, near Cairo, Egypt, on December 13, 1204.*

MOSES MAIMONIDES is widely regarded as the greatest post-biblical figure in Judaism.

During his years of wandering, "while," he wrote, "my mind was troubled, and amid divinely ordained exiles, on journeys by land and tossed on the tempests of the sea," he laid the foundations of his vast learning and began his literary work. One of his earliest writings was a commentary on the Mishnah, in which he formulated his Thirteen Articles of Faith, later imcorporated into the daily Prayer Book. His *Mishneh Torah* (completed in 1168) was a monumental codification of Talmudic law. In his *Guide for the Perplexed,* published in Arabic in 1190, he sought to reconcile the contradictions between biblical doctrines and rationalist-scientific philosophy.

Maimonides held some views that were regarded as radical during his lifetime, such as his idea of the incorporeality of God. But his creed has become part of the Orthodox liturgy, and he is universally regarded as the pillar of traditional faith.

## ALSO NOTEWORTHY

▲ HIRSCH, SAMSA RAPHAEL (born June 20, 1808, in Hamburg, Germany; died December 31, 1888, in Frankfurt am Main, Germany). Rabbi who was the principal founder of Neo-Orthodoxy.

▲ ISAAC BEN MOSES (or Isaac Or Zaru'a; born about 1180 in Bohemia; died about 1250 in Vienna, Austria). Codifier of Jewish law in the monumental *Or Zaru'a* ("Light Is Sown").

# A JEWISH WOMAN BECOMES A LAY MINISTER
## Lilian Montagu

✑

LILIAN MONTAGU WAS THE DOMINANT SPIRITUAL FIGURE in social work in England and a leader in the Liberal Jewish movement. But her most pathbreaking achievement was to become the first woman formally recognized as a Jewish lay minister.

Montagu was determined to cultivate piety in the Jewish community, yet her experiences as a London social worker convinced her that she must somehow adapt the ritual of Jewish tradition to modern life. Influenced by the writings of Claude Goldsmid Montefiore, she became active in the Liberal Jewish movement, a British analogue of American Reform Judaism. On June 15, 1918, she preached at the Liberal Jewish Synagogue, a history-making event because it was the first time that a woman had been officially granted the status of a Jewish lay minister. She went on to preach regularly at the synagogue, and in 1926 she became a lay minister of the West Central Congregation. In 1928 she became the first woman to preach from a rabbinic pulpit in Germany, at the Reform Synagogue in Berlin. Montagu also preached and advocated Liberal Judaism throughout the United Kingdom, the United States, and elsewhere.

In her role as the first female Jewish lay minister, Montagu not only opened doors for countless women who have followed but also enriched the Jewish experience for the communities nurturing those women.

American Jewish Archives, Cincinnati Campus, Hebrew Union College, Jewish Institute of Religion

*Lilian Helen Montagu was born in London, England, on December 22, 1873. She learned piety from her parents, wealthy Orthodox Jews. As a teenager, she saw that the children of immigrant Jews were losing their interest in religion, so, at seventeen, she began to hold Sabbath services for those children. At about the same time, she started engaging in social work for Jewish working girls, an activity that led, in 1893, to the West Central Jewish Day Settlement, which she ran for the rest of her life. She died in London on January 22, 1963.*

# BECOMING AMERICA'S FIRST WOMAN RABBI
## Sally Priesand

ɕ

*Sally Priesand was born in Cleveland, Ohio, on June 27, 1946. As a child, she attended a Conservative synagogue. After earning a B.A. in English at the University of Cincinnati (1968), she studied Hebrew letters at the Hebrew Union College-Jewish Institute of Religion (M.A., 1972). She was the only woman student at the school. Later she worked as a rabbi.*

ON JUNE 3, 1972, SALLY PRIESAND WAS ORDAINED a Reform rabbi. She was the first female rabbi in the United States.

"I didn't do this so that I would be the first woman rabbi or to carry a torch for the feminist movement," Priesand explained. "I had always wanted to teach, and simply realized that what I wanted to teach was Judaism."

When she was ordained in 1972, she became not only the first woman rabbi in America but also the first woman ever ordained by a

*The Jewish Week, New York*

theological seminary. Other women who had served as rabbis were privately ordained by other rabbis, not by a seminary. "For thousands of years," she thought to herself at the ceremony, "women in Judaism had been second-class citizens. They were not permitted to own property. They could not serve as witnesses. They did not have the right to initiate divorce proceedings.... Even in Reform Judaism, they were not permitted to participate fully in the life of the synagogue. With my ordination, all that was going to change."

She served as an assistant rabbi at the Stephen Wise Free Synagogue in New York City, took the pulpit at Congregation Beth El in Elizabeth, New Jersey, and then, in 1981, began a long tenure as the full-time rabbi at the Monmouth, New Jersey, Reform Temple.

Priesand's ordination has had a profound effect on the rabbinate in the United States. Her success helped the Conservative movement decide, in 1981, to ordain women rabbis. By the early 1990s, the Hebrew Union College-Jewish Institute of Religion had entering classes that were 50 percent female students.

# ORGANIZING REFORM JUDAISM IN AMERICA
## Isaac Mayer Wise

cx

ISAAC MAYER WISE, MORE THAN ANYONE ELSE, established Reform Judaism in the United States.

The atmosphere of freedom in the United States profoundly affected Wise's approach to the rabbinate. He felt that Judaism should adapt to meet the needs of a pioneer people. In Cincinnati he instituted such changes as mixed pews, organ music, choral singing, and prayers in English. His ideal was to unite in Reform Judaism the best of the Jewish tradition with the best of modern Western culture.

In 1855 Wise called a conference of rabbis to organize the Reform congregations of the United States into a nationwide movement. In 1857 he published a Reform prayer book, *Minhag America* ("American Usage"). In 1873 he organized the Union of American Hebrew Congregations, still the only organization of Reform Jewish communities in the United States. In 1875 he founded in Cincinnati the Hebrew Union College, the Reform rabbinic seminary of the United States (in 1950 it merged with the Jewish Institute of Religion). In 1889 he established the Central Conference of American Rabbis, which united all Reform rabbis in the United States.

> *Isaac Mayer Wise was born in Steingrub, Bohemia, on March 29, 1819. His original surname was Weis. He immigrated to the United States in 1846. After serving as a rabbi in Albany, New York, for eight years, he moved to Cincinnati, Ohio, where he was a rabbi for the rest of his life. He died in Cincinnati on March 26, 1900.*

American Jewish Archives, Cincinnati Campus,
Hebrew Union College, Jewish Institute of Religion

Isaac Mayer Wise, through these many activities, firmly rooted the Reform movement in his adopted homeland and permanently affected its direction.

## ALSO NOTEWORTHY

▲ KAPLAN, MORDECAI MENAHEM (born June 11, 1881, in Švenčionys, Lithuania; died November 8, 1983, in New York City). Rabbi who founded the Reconstructionist movement in Judaism.

▲ LEESER, ISAAC (born December 12, 1806, in Neuenkirchen, Westphalia, Prussia; died February 1, 1868, in Philadelphia, Pennsylvania). Rabbi who was the first to introduce a regular English sermon into an American synagogue service (beginning June 2, 1830, at Congregation Mikveh Israel in Philadelphia); founded the first successful Jewish periodical in the United States, *The Occident and American Jewish Advocate* (1843); prepared the first American translation of the Bible (published 1845); and founded Maimonides College (1867), the first American Jewish rabbinical school.

MORDECAI MENAHEM
KAPLAN

▲ LICHTENSTEIN, TEHILLA (originally Tehilla Hirschensohn; born 1893 in Jerusalem, Palestine; died 1973). Cofounder, with her husband, Morris Lichtenstein, of the Society for Jewish Science (1922), and, after his death in 1938, director of the organization, thus becoming the first woman formally to assume a position of religious leadership in the United States.

▲ LIPKIN, ISRAEL BEN ZE'EV WOLF (or Israel Salanter, after his spiritual mentor, Joseph Salent; born 1810 in Zhagory, Kovno, Lithuania; died 1883 in Königsberg, Germany). Talmudist who founded the Musar movement.

▲ LURIA, ISAAC BEN SOLOMON (known as Ha-Ari ["The Lion"], an acronym for the Hebrew words for "the divine rabbi"; born 1534 in Jerusalem, Palestine; died August 5, 1572, in Safed, Palestine). Founder of the Lurianic school of Cabala (Jewish esoteric mysticism), which had a profound influence on Hasidim.

▲ MOSES DE LEÓN (originally Moses ben Shem Tov; born 1250 in Spain [León]; died 1305 in Arévalo, Avila, Spain). The presumed author of the *Sefer ha-Zohar* ("Book of Splendor"), the most important book of Jewish mysticism.

▲ RACHEL, HANNAH (born 1815 in Ludomir, Poland; died 1892). The most famous of the Hasidic women rebbes and the first Hasidic leader to settle in the Holy Land.

▲ RAPHALL, MORRIS JACOB (born October 3, 1798, in Stockholm, Sweden; died June 23, 1868, in New York City). The first rabbi to open a session of the United States House of Representatives with prayer (February 1, 1860), and the first rabbi in New York City to present regular weekly sermons in English.

▲ RICE, ABRAHAM JOSEPH (born 1802 in Gochshein, Bavaria; died 1862 in Baltimore, Maryland). The first traditionally ordained rabbi in the United States (Baltimore Hebrew Congregation, 1840).

▲ ROSENZWEIG, FRANZ (born December 25, 1886, in Kassel, Germany; died December 10, 1929, in Frankfurt am Main, Germany). Theologian who created a form of Jewish religious existentialism.

▲ SCHECHTER, SOLOMON (born December 7, 1847, in Focsani, Romania; died November 19, 1915, in New York City). Theologian and scholar who, in 1896, discovered priceless ancient manuscripts in Cairo, including a fragment of the Hebrew text of Ecclesiasticus, and, in the early 1900s, crystallized the philosophy of Conservative Judaism in America.

Library of Congress

**MENACHEM MENDEL SCHNEERSON**

▲ SCHNEERSON, MENACHEM MENDEL (born April 18, 1902, in Nikolayev, Ukraine; died June 12, 1994, in New York City). Rabbi who transformed the Lubavitch Hasidic sect into the fastest-growing segment of Orthodox Judaism.

▲ VOLOZHINER, HAYYIM BEN ISAAC (born 1749 in Volozhin, Poland; died 1821 in Volozhin). Founder, in 1802, of a yeshiva in Volozhin, the prototype of, and inspiration for, similar schools throughout the rest of the world.

▲ WISE, STEPHEN SAMUEL (born March 17, 1874, in Budapest, Hungary; died April 19, 1949, in New York City). Reform rabbi who founded the influential Free Synagogue (1907) and the Jewish Institute of Religion (1922, later merged, in 1950, with Hebrew Union College), both in New York City.

# 5

# BIOLOGICAL SCIENCES

☙

JEWS HAVE HAD A PROFOUND EFFECT *on the biological sciences. The first effective polio vaccine by injection was developed by Jonas Salk, and the first oral polio vaccine came through the efforts of Albert Sabin.*

*A staggering number of Jews have won the Nobel Prize in physiology or medicine for their original research. Their unique achievements included the founding of modern ear medicine by Robert Bárány, the development of transplant immunology by Baruj Benacerraf, the discovery of cholesterol formation by Konrad Bloch, the purification of penicillin by Ernst B. Chain, the discovery of "magic bullets" by Paul Ehrlich, the invention of the electrocardiogram by Willem Einthoven, the development of a better way to create new drugs by Gertrude B. Elion, the creation of artificial DNA by Arthur Kornberg, the discovery of blood typing by Karl Landsteiner, the laying of the foundation for genetic engineering by Joshua Lederberg, the discovery of X-ray-caused mutations by Hermann J. Muller, the first genetic mapping by Daniel Nathans, the first translation of the genetic code by Marshall W. Nirenberg, the discovery of cortisone by Tadeus Reichstein, and the development of streptomycin by Selman A. Waksman.*

# UNDERSTANDING NERVE IMPULSE TRANSMISSION
## Julius Axelrod

෧

*Julius Axelrod was born in New York City on May 30, 1912. He wanted to become a physician, but because of Jewish quota limits, he was unable to enter medical school. As a result of that frustrated ambition, he turned his attention to medical research, obtained his Ph.D. at George Washington University (1955), and took a long-term position at the National Institutes of Health in Maryland.*

JULIUS AXELROD SHARED THE 1970 NOBEL PRIZE in physiology or medicine with Bernard Katz and Ulf von Euler "for their discoveries concerning the humoral transmitters in the nerve terminals and the mechanism for their storage, release, and inactivation." Axelrod, a biochemist and pharmacologist, opened the door for many potential cures through his research on nerve impulses and nerve-muscle connections.

His Nobel Prize-winning research focused on noradrenaline, which is a neurotransmitter—that is, a chemical released by a nerve cell to stimulate or inhibit adjacent neurons or other excitable cells. While studying noradrenaline, Axelrod proved that drugs achieve their effect by causing changes in the storage of neurotransmitters. This discovery provided insight into how existing psychoactive drugs worked and how similar drugs might be produced to treat a wide range of nervous-system disorders.

### ALSO NOTEWORTHY

▲ BARUCH, SIMON (born July 29, 1840, in Schwersen, Germany; died June 3, 1921, in New York City). Physician who performed the first appendectomy in the United States (1888) and was the leading American exponent of hydrotherapy. Father of the public official Bernard Mannes Baruch.

▲ COHN, FERDINAND JULIUS (born January 24, 1828, in Breslau, Lower Silesia; died June 25, 1898, in Breslau). Botanist who discovered bacterial spores and was the first scientist to treat bacteria as plants.

▲ FRANKLIN, ROSALIND ELSIE (born July 25, 1920, in London, England; died April 16, 1958, in London). Chemist whose X-ray photographs, and description of the probable structure, of DNA paved the way for the later discovery of that substance.

▲ FUNK, CASIMIR (born February 23, 1884, in Warsaw, Poland; died November 20, 1967, in New York City). Biochemist who, in 1912, coined the term *vitamine* (Latin for "life-amine"). (Later, when it was discovered that the type of substance referred to was not always an amine, the *e* was dropped to distance the term from the original error.)

# DISCOVERY OF REVERSE TRANSCRIPTASE
## David Baltimore

ॐ

SCIENTISTS HAVE LONG KNOWN THAT GENETIC INFORMATION can be transformed from DNA into RNA, but the reverse process, from RNA into DNA, was believed to be impossible. In 1970 the microbiologist David Baltimore and his friend Howard M. Temin each independently discovered that such a process does occur. They found that some RNA viruses can make DNA copies of themselves through the action of an enzyme that Baltimore and Temin named the RNA-directed DNA polymerase, now called the reverse transcriptase. This discovery was crucial to medical research in certain diseases, such as cancer and AIDS, now known to be associated with such viruses (called retroviruses because they reproduce themselves in ways unlike those of most other viruses).

Baltimore and Temin met as high-school students during a summer class at a scientific research laboratory. Early in their careers, they both became interested in RNA virus replication, and both faced the same hostility from the scientific establishment when, in 1964, Temin proposed, and Baltimore accepted, the unorthodox theory that some RNA viral genes can duplicate themselves in the DNA of a cell. "My motivating force," Baltimore explained, "is not that I will find a 'cure' for cancer. There may never be a cure as such. I work because I want to understand." Within days of each other in 1970, Baltimore and Temin announced that they had isolated the enzyme that controls the RNA-into-DNA transformation.

In 1975 Baltimore, Temin, and Renato Dulbecco, who had developed many of the scientific techniques used by the two other men, shared the Nobel Prize in physiology or medicine for "discovering the interaction between tumor viruses and the genetic material of the cell."

> *David Baltimore was born in New York City on March 7, 1938. He earned his Ph.D. at the Rockefeller Institute for Medical Research (now Rockefeller University, 1964), served for many years on the faculty at the Massachusetts Institute of Technology, directed the Whitehead Institute of Biomedical Research, and taught at Rockefeller University.*

### ALSO NOTEWORTHY

▲ GOLDBERGER, JOSEPH (born July 16, 1874, in Austria; died January 17, 1929, in Washington, D.C.). Physician who discovered that pellagra was caused by a deficiency of a nutritional factor now known as niacin, or nicotinic acid.

▲ GOLDSCHMIDT, RICHARD BENEDICT (born April 12, 1878, in Frankfurt am Main, Germany; died April 24, 1958, in Berkeley, California). Zoologist and geneticist who discovered that genetics is the cause of geographical variation among animals.

# FOUNDING MODERN EAR MEDICINE
## Robert Bárány

❧

*Robert Bárány was born in Vienna, Austria, on April 22, 1876. A childhood attack of tuberculosis left him with a strong interest in medicine. After earning his M.D. at the University of Vienna (1900), he worked in an ear clinic and served as a professor and researcher in Austria before moving to Sweden, where he was on the faculty at the University of Uppsala (1917–36). He died in Uppsala, Sweden, on April 8, 1936.*

ROBERT BÁRÁNY WAS THE FOUNDER OF MODERN MEDICINE of the ear. In 1914 he received the Nobel Prize in physiology or medicine "for his work on the physiology and pathology of the vestibular apparatus" (the organ of balance in the inner ear).

At an ear clinic, Bárány flushed a subject's ear with water above and below body temperature, noticed the subject's dizziness and rapid rhythmic eye movement, and concluded that those symptoms were caused by movement of the ear-canal fluid, which in turn resulted from the fluid's specific gravity changing as the fluid was warmed or cooled by the water. With this experiment as a starting point, Bárány developed methods for diagnosing inflammations of the inner ear.

Bárány went on to make pioneering studies in other kinds of ear diseases, such as otosclerosis, an important cause of deafness.

### ALSO NOTEWORTHY

▲ GRUBY, DAVID (born August 20, 1810, in Kis-Kér, Hungary; died November 14, 1898, in Paris, France). Physician and parasitologist who founded an important branch of modern medicine, discovering the dermatomycoses, a group of skin diseases caused by parasitic lower plants.

▲ HAFFKINE, WALDEMAR MORDECAI WOLFE (born March 15, 1860, in Odessa, Ukraine, Russia; died October 25, 1930, in Lausanne, Switzerland). Bacteriologist who developed a cholera vaccine.

# ESTABLISHING THE FIELD OF TRANSPLANT IMMUNOLOGY
## Baruj Benacerraf

೮೨

Courtesy of Baruj Benacerraf

BARUJ BENACERRAF, an immunologist, won the 1980 Nobel Prize in physiology or medicine for his contribution to the understanding of the mechanisms and genetic basis of the immunologic response and especially of its role in the autoimmune diseases. He shared the award with George Snell and Jean Dausset, who had independently performed related research.

While studying antigens (protein or carbohydrate substances capable of stimulating immune responses), Benacerraf made important discoveries about how the body's immunological system works. In particular, his research led to the development of rules for the transplantability of human organs. His work lies at the core of the field of transplant immunology.

When he won the Nobel Prize in physiology or medicine, he expressed pride at being "the first Sephardic Jew" to win the award.

*Baruj Benacerraf was born in Caracas, Venezuela, on October 29, 1920. He immigrated to the United States in 1939, earned an M.D. at the Medical College of Virginia (1945), and served on the faculties at New York University (1956–68) and Harvard University (1970–91).*

---

### ALSO NOTEWORTHY

▲ HENLE, JACOB (full name, Friedrich Gustav Jacob Henle; born July 1809 in Fürth, near Nuremberg, Germany; died May 13, 1885, in Göttingen, Germany). Anatomist and pathologist who gave the first detailed description of epithelial tissue, identified a kidney structure now known as Henle's loop, confirmed the cell theory, and anticipated the germ theory of disease.

▲ KANTROWITZ, ADRIAN (born October 4, 1918, in New York City). Surgeon who developed and, in 1966, used the first artificial heart pump completely implanted inside the human body, and who, in 1967, performed the world's second, and America's first, heart transplant.

# DEVELOPMENT OF RECOMBINANT-DNA TECHNOLOGY
## Paul Berg

*Paul Berg was born in New York City on June 30, 1926. He earned a Ph.D. at Western Reserve University (1952), and in 1959 he began a long association with Stanford University.*

PAUL BERG, A BIOCHEMIST, WON THE 1980 NOBEL PRIZE in chemistry "for his fundamental studies of the biochemistry of nucleic acids, with particular regard to recombinant DNA." He shared the award with Walter Gilbert and Frederick Sanger, who performed related research.

While studying the actions of isolated genes, Berg developed techniques for splitting a DNA molecule at selected sites and attaching segments of the molecule to the DNA of a virus or plasmid, which could then enter bacterial or animal cells. The foreign DNA was incorporated into the host and caused the synthesis of proteins not usually found there. The DNA prepared by breaking up and splicing together DNA from different sources is called recombinant DNA.

Berg's recombinant-DNA technology profoundly affected biochemistry. One early practical result was the development of a strain of bacteria containing the gene for producing the hormone insulin.

❧

# UNDERSTANDING HOW CHOLESTEROL IS FORMED
## Konrad Bloch

*Konrad Emil Bloch was born in Neisse, Germany, on January 21, 1912. He earned the equivalent of a B.S. from a technical university in Munich (1934), moved to the United States (1936), received a Ph.D. from Columbia University (1938), and then worked on various college faculties, notably for many years at Harvard University.*

KONRAD BLOCH, A BIOCHEMIST, MADE IMPORTANT CONTRIBUTIONS to the understanding of how cholesterol is synthesized in a living organism. In 1964 he and Feodor Lynen (who worked separately on similar issues) shared the Nobel Prize in physiology or medicine for their studies in "the mechanisms and regulation of cholesterol and fatty acid metabolism."

In the early 1940s he helped to show that acetic acid is the major precursor of cholesterol in rats. That proved to be the first in a long series of discoveries tracing the numerous fat and carbohydrate metabolic changes leading to the synthesis of cholesterol. Eventually he showed that the overall conversion of acetic acid into cholesterol requires thirty-six distinct chemical transformations. Bloch discovered that cholesterol is a necessary constitutent of all body cells, and he laid the groundwork for future research to fight diseases related to cholesterol.

# DISCOVERY OF THE HEPATITIS B ANTIGEN
## Baruch S. Blumberg

ひ

BARUCH S. BLUMBERG, A VIROLOGIST, DISCOVERED THE HEPATITIS B antigen, a substance capable of stimulating an immune response. He and Daniel Carleton Gajdusek shared the 1976 Nobel Prize in physiology or medicine for their "discoveries concerning new mechanisms for the origin and dissemination of infectious diseases."

Blumberg made his great discovery by accident. "Science is not as scientific as most people think it is," he says. "Direct, cold logic is not the only method scientists use. Individual intuition and style are very important." While traveling the world to find out why people of different backgrounds react differently to various diseases, Blumberg happened to test antibodies from a New York patient's blood with blood samples from people of many different ethnic backgrounds.

The New Yorker's antibodies reacted against only one serum—that of an Australian aborigine. Blumberg's further research showed that he had discovered a chemical marker—called the Australian antigen—revealing the presence of hepatitis B, the most severe and often fatal form of the liver inflammation known as viral hepatitis. Blumberg paved the way not only for programs to screen blood donors who have this disease but also for later research on hepatitis B vaccines.

> *Baruch Samuel Blumberg was born in New York City on July 28, 1925. After earning an M.D. at Columbia University (1951) and a Ph.D. at Oxford University (1957), he worked as a physician and biochemical researcher.*

## ALSO NOTEWORTHY

▲ LEVINE, PHILIP (born August 10, 1900, in Kletsk, Russia; died October 18, 1987, in New York City). Immunologist who, in 1927, codiscovered the blood factors M, N, and P, and who, in 1939, was the first to recognize the connection between the Rh factor and erythroblastosis fetalis, a disease characterized by jaundice in the fetus and newborn.

▲ REMAK, ROBERT (born July 1815 in Posen, Germany; died August 29, 1865, in Kissingen, Germany). Embryologist and neurologist who discovered and named the three germ layers of the early embryo (the ectoderm, the mesoderm, and the endoderm); discovered the nerve cells in the heart (Remak's ganglia); and pioneered the use of electrotherapy for the treatment of nervous diseases.

▲ ROTHSCHILD, MIRIAM LOUISA (born August 5, 1908, near Peterborough, England). Naturalist who became the world's leading authority on fleas, of which there are about eleven thousand species. Granddaughter of the government official Nathaniel Mayer de Rothschild.

# UNDERSTANDING CHOLESTEROL METABOLISM
## Michael S. Brown

> *Michael Stuart Brown was born in New York City on April 13, 1941.*
> *After receiving his M.D. at the University of Pennsylvania (1966), he*
> *worked as a physician at Massachusetts General Hospital, did research*
> *at the National Institutes of Health, and had a long career at the*
> *University of Texas Health Science Center.*

MICHAEL S. BROWN, A GENETICIST, SHARED THE 1985 NOBEL PRIZE in physiology or medicine with Joseph L. Goldstein for their combined work that "revolutionized our knowledge about the regulation of cholesterol metabolism and the treatment of diseases caused by abnormally elevated cholesterol levels in the blood."

At the University of Texas, Brown joined Goldstein, a friend from earlier in their careers, in an investigation into the problem of high blood cholesterol levels. Goldstein initiated the research because he had encountered patients suffering from that dangerous condition. Cholesterol is a fat molecule present in the membranes of all animal cells; when excessive cholesterol accumulates in the walls of blood vessels, it can block the blood flow, causing heart attacks and strokes.

Brown and Goldstein discovered that "receptor" molecules on cells function to control the level of blood cholesterol. They found that people with inherited high blood cholesterol are deficient in these cell receptors, and they described the mechanisms of cholesterol extraction from the blood. Brown and Goldstein helped shape the medical consensus that cholesterol causes heart disease; their work gave direction to research in prevention and treatment methods.

❧

# THE ANTIBIOTIC ERA BEGINS
## Ernst B. Chain

> *Ernst Boris Chain was born in Berlin, Germany, on June 19, 1906.*
> *After earning a Ph.D. at Friedrich-Wilhelms University (1930), he*
> *moved to England (1933), where he worked as a teacher and researcher.*
> *He died in Mulranny, County Mayo, Ireland, on August 12, 1979.*

THE BIOCHEMIST ERNST B. CHAIN, WITH ALEXANDER FLEMING AND HOWARD W. FLOREY, shared the 1945 Nobel Prize in physiology or medicine "for the discovery of penicillin and its curative effects in various infectious diseases." Chain's role in this discovery was crucial.

In 1928 Fleming first described penicillin, but he had difficulty in purifying it. That difficulty "only increased my interest in Fleming's penicillin," Chain claimed. In the late 1930s and early 1940s, Chain, working with Florey and others, extracted and purified penicillin and demonstrated for the first time its chemotherapeutic properties. This success marked the beginning of the modern antibiotic era.

# DISCOVERY OF THE EPIDERMAL GROWTH FACTOR

## Stanley Cohen

✌

STANLEY COHEN, A BIOCHEMIST AND ZOOLOGIST, shared the 1986 Nobel Prize in physiology or medicine with Rita Levi-Montalcini for "their discoveries which are of fundamental importance for our understanding of the mechanisms which regulate cell and organ growth." Specifically, they explored a substance known as the nerve growth factor (NGF).

In 1953 Cohen was asked to assist Levi-Montalcini, who had already discovered NGF—a protein that promotes development of the sensory and sympathetic nervous systems—but needed help in isolating and identifying it. Other scientists had already rejected the position because of its great difficulty. Cohen accepted because, he explained, "I might as well go down in flames on some important problem as on a trivial one." With his knowledge of biochemistry and hers of neuroembryology, they succeeded in their project and began to produce NGF in large quantities.

Moving on to Vanderbilt, Cohen worked independently on the epidermal growth factor (EGF), which he had discovered in Saint Louis while working on the NGF project. EGF stimulates the growth of cells in the skin, cornea, liver, and other organs.

Knowledge of these two factors is being applied to medical studies. NGF has a therapeutic value in the repair of damaged nerve tissues and sheds light on various diseases, including Alzheimer's. EGF stimulates the healing of wounds and provides insight into the action of viruses.

> *Stanley Cohen was born in Brooklyn, New York, on November 17, 1922. After earning a Ph.D. at the University of Michigan (1948), he worked at several schools, notably with Levi-Montalcini at Washington University in Saint Louis during the 1950s and, from 1959, at Vanderbilt University.*

---

### ALSO NOTEWORTHY

▲ SACHS, BERNARD (born January 2, 1858, in Baltimore, Maryland; died February 8, 1944, in New York City). Neurologist who described a genetically caused disease characterized by the arrest of cerebral development, later known as Tay-Sachs disease.

▲ SCHICK, BÉLA (born July 16, 1877, in Boglár, Hungary; died December 6, 1967, in New York City). Pediatrician who developed the Schick test for determining susceptibility to diphtheria.

# UNDERSTANDING GLYCOGEN CONVERSION
## Gerty Cori

> *Gerty Cori was born in Prague, Bohemia, on August 15, 1896. Her original name was Theresa Radnitz. In 1920 she married Carl F. Cori, and in the same year they both earned medical degrees at the University of Prague. They immigrated to the United States (1922), worked together at the Institute for the Study of Malignant Diseases in Buffalo, New York (1922–31), and both served on the faculty at the Washington University medical school in Saint Louis, Missouri (1931–57). She died in Saint Louis on October 26, 1957.*

GERTY CORI, A BIOCHEMIST, SHARED THE 1947 NOBEL PRIZE in physiology or medicine with her non-Jewish husband, Carl F. Cori, "for their discovery of the course of the catalytic conversion of glycogen." Another recipient of the same award that year, Bernardo Houssay, performed separate research.

During the 1930s and 1940s, they discovered the biochemical steps through which glycogen, or stored sugar, is converted into glucose, which cells can use for the production of energy. The various pathways of the process is known as the Cori cycle. Their discovery led to many scientific benefits, including the identification of the biochemical defects that cause glycogen-storage disease.

∽

# DISCOVERY OF THE CHEMICAL STRUCTURE OF ANTIBODIES
## Gerald M. Edelman

> *Gerald Maurice Edelman was born in New York City on July 1, 1929. After earning an M.D. at the University of Pennsylvania (1954) and a Ph.D. at the Rockefeller Institute for Medical Research (now Rockefeller University, 1960), he stayed at the latter institution as a researcher and faculty member.*

GERALD M. EDELMAN, A BIOCHEMIST, WON THE 1972 NOBEL PRIZE in physiology or medicine for his "discoveries concerning the chemical structure of antibodies." He shared the award with Rodney R. Porter, on whose earlier work Edelman based his own research.

Edelman focused on immunology because "it provokes unusual ideas, some of which are not easily come upon through other fields of study." To understand how antibodies are structured, he cleaved immunoglobulin molecules. Edelman examined the molecules and found two different component polypeptides as well as different kinds of antigen-binding properties. This new knowledge about antibodies stimulated much further related research that helps in fighting many diseases. Edelman himself went on to determine the structure of human myeloma protein (cancer of the immunoglobulin-producing cells).

# PIONEERING THE FIELDS OF HEMATOLOGY, IMMUNOLOGY, AND CHEMOTHERAPY
## Paul Ehrlich

ભ

PAUL EHRLICH PERFORMED PIONEERING STUDIES IN HEMATOLOGY, immunology, and chemotherapy. In 1908 he shared the Nobel Prize in physiology or medicine with Élie Metchnikoff (who worked separately) for their work on the theory of immunity.

Ehrlich was greatly influenced by Carl Weigert, his cousin, a bacteriologist who used dyes to stain various tissues for study. In his own doctoral dissertation (1878), Ehrlich reported his development of dyes by which he could distinguish different types of white blood cells, thus initiating the modern science of hematology.

Later other researchers created a diphtheria antitoxin, but they encountered problems in administering it because dosages tended to be too strong or too weak for individual patients. Ehrlich perfected a method for standardizing the dose strength and, in the process, developed a theory of immunity.

His side-chain theory held that specific receptors in the body could combine with toxic substances and stimulate the production of antibodies, called "magic bullets" because they attack specific bacteria while not harming the rest of the body. His most famous "magic bullet" was salvarsan, which was aimed at syphilis microorganisms. Salvarsan, an arsenic compound, played a major role in establishing the new field of chemotherapy.

> *Paul Ehrlich was born in Strehlen, Silesia, on March 14, 1854. After taking an M.D. at the University of Leipzig (1878), he worked as a physician and researcher at various institutions, notably as director of the Royal Institute for Experimental Therapy in Frankfurt, Germany (1899–1915). Ehrlich died in Bad Homburg, Hesse, Germany, on August 20, 1915.*

Courtesy of German Information Center

# DESIGNING THE ELECTROCARDIOGRAM
## Willem Einthoven

❧

*Willem Einthoven was born in Semarang, Java, Dutch East Indies, on May 21, 1860. He earned a doctorate in medicine at the University of Utrecht (1885) and taught at the University of Leiden for the rest of his career. He died in Leiden, Netherlands, on September 29, 1927.*

WILLEM EINTHOVEN, A PHYSIOLOGIST, WON THE 1924 NOBEL PRIZE in physiology or medicine for "his discovery of the mechanism of the electrocardiogram."

Though trained in medicine, Einthoven had a special interest in physics. By the 1880s, other scientists already knew that there were electrical charges involved with the contracting of the heart, but the methods for recording those charges were crude. Taking advantage of his expertise in physics, Einthoven, in 1903, designed the first string galvanometer, an apparatus with a delicate conducting thread stretched across a magnetic field. A current flowing through the thread would cause the thread to deviate at right angles to the direction of the magnetic lines of force. The machine could thus monitor the varying electrical potentials of the heart and record them graphically.

Einthoven called the tracing produced by the instrument an electrocardiogram, known as an EKG because in German -*cardio* is spelled with a *k*. By 1906 he could correlate the recordings with various types of heart diseases.

His instrument developed into the modern electrocardiograph, an invaluable aid in detecting heart diseases.

### ALSO NOTEWORTHY

▲ STERN, LINA SOLOMONOVNA (born 1878 in Irany, Lithuania, Russia; died March 8, 1968, in the Soviet Union). The first woman admitted to the Soviet Academy of Sciences; the discoverer of the hematoencephalic barrier, a filtering membrane that protects human nerves and spinal fluid from harmful substances; and a pioneer in the use of brain injections to cure many illnesses.

# REVOLUTIONARY RESEARCH IN DRUG DEVELOPMENT

## Gertrude B. Elion

ɞ

GERTRUDE B. ELION, A BIOCHEMIST, REVOLUTIONIZED MEDICINE by changing the way new drugs are discovered. In 1988 she shared the Nobel Prize in physiology or medicine with George Hitchings and James W. Black, not for developing a specific drug but for demonstrating a new way of developing drugs. "While drug development had earlier mainly been built on chemical modifications of natural products," the Nobel announcement explained, "they introduced a more rational approach based on the understanding of basic biochemical and physiolgical processes."

Elion had a personal motivation to fight disease. As a teenager, she visited her beloved grandfather in the hospital as he was dying slowly and painfully of stomach cancer. "That was the turning point," she later said. "It was as though the signal was there: 'This is the disease you're going to have to work against.'" Her resolve was reinforced when her fiancé died of heart disease and her mother died of cervical cancer, both ailments later curable.

Elion and Hitchings abandoned the traditional trial-and-error method of searching for new drugs. Instead, they studied the subtle differences between normal and abnormal cell reproduction; then they developed drugs that would block the life cycle of abnormal cells while leaving the healthy cells unharmed. Using that procedure, Elion developed many effective drugs, including the first drug to attack viruses, one to fight childhood leukemia, and a drug to prevent transplant rejection. Her research laid the foundation for azidothymidine (AZT), for many years the only drug approved by the Food and Drug Administration for AIDS patients.

> Gertrude Belle Elion was born in New York City on January 23, 1918. After graduating from Hunter College (1937), she held several jobs as a research assistant and then spent many years as a senior research chemist at Burroughs Wellcome Research Laboratories.

Courtesy of Burroughs Wellcome

# FOUNDING MODERN NEUROPHYSIOLOGY
## Joseph Erlanger

> *Joseph Erlanger was born in San Francisco, California, on January 5, 1874. He earned his M.D. at Johns Hopkins School of Medicine (1899) and served on the faculty for many years at Washington University in Saint Louis, Missouri. He died in Saint Louis on December 5, 1965.*

JOSEPH ERLANGER, A PHYSIOLOGIST, WON THE 1944 NOBEL PRIZE in physiology or medicine for his "discoveries regarding the highly differentiated functions of single nerve fibers." He shared the award with his colleague Herbert S. Gasser.

Erlanger had a dual concern for physiology and medicine. He hoped that by investigating how the body works, he would lay the groundwork for fighting diseases.

In the 1920s he and Gasser used the cathode-ray oscillograph to study the transmission of nerve impulses under varying temperature and chemical conditions. They found that the speed at which a nerve impulse is transmitted along a nerve fiber varies with the thickness of the fiber: the thicker the fiber, the faster the speed. The two scientists went on to study the differences between sensory and motor nerves, the perception of pain, and other nerve-related topics. Together, they virtually created modern neurophysiology.

გ

# FOUNDING MODERN NEUROPHYSIOLOGY
## Herbert S. Gasser

> *Herbert Spencer Gasser was born in Platteville, Wisconsin, on July 5, 1888. After earning his M.D. at Johns Hopkins (1915), he worked for many years at Washington University in Saint Louis, Missouri, and in 1935 began a long term as director of the Rockefeller Institute for Medical Research. He died in New York City on May 11, 1963.*

HERBERT S. GASSER, A PHYSIOLOGIST, WON THE 1944 NOBEL PRIZE in physiology or medicine for his "discoveries regarding the highly differentiated functions of single nerve fibers." He shared the award with his colleague Joseph Erlanger.

Like Erlanger, Gasser studied physiology to help medical research. "When one looks at the diseases that are decreasing and those that are increasing," he observed, "one finds that those that are lethal because of deterioration of organs are increasing."

Gasser and Erlanger pioneered the use of the cathode-ray oscillograph for studying the electric potential of nerve fibers. Their principal discovery was that a nerve impulse is transmitted faster along a thicker nerve fiber, and slower along a thinner one. With that finding and their studies on sensory and motor nerves, pain, and other nerve-related subjects, Gasser and Erlanger founded modern neurophysiology.

# DETERMINING SEQUENCES IN NUCLEIC ACIDS
## Walter Gilbert

✑

WALTER GILBERT, A MOLECULAR BIOLOGIST, SHARED THE 1980 NOBEL Prize in chemistry with Paul Berg and Frederick Sanger "for their contributions concerning the determination of base sequences in nucleic acids." Gilbert's work was separate from, but related to, that of Berg, while Sanger used methods of Gilbert's devising.

When he was a doctoral candidate in mathematics at Cambridge University, Gilbert became acquainted with James D. Watson and Francis Crick, who in 1953 had jointly discovered the structure of DNA, the cell's master blueprint for the production of proteins. Watson and Crick found that a strand of DNA consists of a chain of structural units called nucleotides.

In 1960 Watson joined Gilbert on the faculty at Harvard University. Renewing their friendship, Watson asked Gilbert to assist in further DNA studies. The young mathematician agreed, and his interest in the new subject grew to such an extent that in 1964 he transferred from the physics department to the biophysics.

Gilbert developed a method for determining the sequence of nucleotide links in the chainlike molecules of nucleic acids (DNA and RNA). This work provided new fundamental knowledge at the molecular level. It also yielded important technical applications, as in the production of human hormones with the aid of bacteria.

> *Walter Gilbert was born in Boston, Massachusetts, on March 31, 1932. He earned a Ph.D. in mathematics at Cambridge University in England (1957), and in 1958 he began a long career on the faculty at Harvard University, where his interests grew to include biochemistry and molecular biology. In 1979 he helped found Biogen, Inc., a commercial genetic-engineering corporation.*

---

### ALSO NOTEWORTHY

▲ WASSERMANN, AUGUST PAUL VON (born February 21, 1866, in Bamberg, Germany; died March 16, 1925, in Berlin, Germany). Bacteriologist who led the development of the Wassermann test for the diagnosis of syphilis. He also contributed an antitoxin treatment for diphtheria; inoculations against typhoid, cholera, and tetanus; and a serum for diagnosing a predisposition to tuberculosis.

# Understanding Cholesterol Metabolism
## Joseph L. Goldstein

&

*Joseph Leonard Goldstein was born in Sumter, South Carolina, on April 18, 1940. After earning an M.D. at the Southwestern Medical School of the University of Texas (1966), he worked as a physician at Massachusetts General Hospital, did research at the National Institutes of Health, and then joined the faculty at the University of Texas.*

JOSEPH L. GOLDSTEIN, A MEDICAL GENETICIST, SHARED THE 1985 NOBEL Prize in physiology or medicine with Michael S. Brown for their combined work that "revolutionized our knowledge about the regulation of cholesterol metabolism and the treatment of diseases caused by abnormally elevated cholesterol levels in the blood."

While he was at the National Heart Institute in Bethesda, Maryland, Goldstein attended to patients with a disease called familial hypercholesterolemia, in which a genetic defect causes an error of metabolism that results in high blood cholesterol levels and heart attacks, sometimes in very young people. When he moved to the University of Texas, he teamed up with his friend Michael S. Brown to study this disease.

Goldstein and Brown discovered that a "receptor" molecule on the surface of a cell controls the blood cholesterol level. They also found that people who inherit high blood cholesterol are deficient in cell receptors for cholesterol, and they described the mechanisms of cholesterol extraction from the blood.

Coronary heart disease kills more people in Western countries than any other disease. Goldstein and Brown helped shape a medical consensus that excessive cholesterol causes heart disease, and their work showed the way toward possible prevention and treatment.

# DEVELOPMENT OF EQUATIONS FOR CRYSTAL STRUCTURES
## Herbert A. Hauptman

ભૂ

HERBERT A. HAUPTMAN, A BIOPHYSICIST, SHARED THE 1985 NOBEL Prize in chemistry with his coworker Jerome Karle "for their outstanding achievements in the development of direct methods for the determination of crystal structures."

Hauptman and Karle worked together for many years, beginning in 1947, at the Naval Research Laboratory in Washington, D.C. Their great achievement was to improve the use of X-ray crystallography, a method, discovered in the early 1900s, of determining the

Courtesy of Herbert A. Hauptman

three-dimensional configurations of molecules by directing an X-ray beam at a pure crystal of a substance; some X rays pass through the crystal, while others are diffracted. Hauptman and Karle developed a mathematical method (published in 1949) for determining the three-dimensional crystal structures of important molecules in such substances as hormones, antibodies, and vitamins. Specifically, the scientists devised mathematical equations to describe the arrangements of the spots that appear on photographic film as a result of the diffraction that occurs in X-ray crystallography.

Before Hauptman and Karle, it generally took about two years to deduce the structure of a simple biological molecule. By the 1980s, using Hauptman and Karle's equations, scientists could perform the same function in two days.

> *Herbert Aaron Hauptman was born in New York City on February 14, 1917. He earned a Ph.D. in mathematics at the University of Maryland (1955), specializing in a mathematical approach to the study of organic molecules. In 1972 he began a long career as director of the Medical Foundation of Buffalo in Buffalo, New York.*

# Discovering How Genetic Information Transforms into Chemical Activity
## François Jacob

> *François Jacob was born in Nancy, France, on June 17, 1920.*
> *He studied at the University of Paris, where he earned an M.D.*
> *(1947) and a D.Sc. (1954). In 1950 he began a long association*
> *with the Pasteur Institute, and in 1964 he was named a professor*
> *at the Collège de France.*

FRANÇOIS JACOB, A BIOLOGIST, HELPED EXPLAIN how genes act. In 1965 he shared the Nobel Prize in physiology or medicine with Jacques Monod and André Lwoff for contributing "to our knowledge of the fundamental processes in living matter which forms the bases for such phenomena as adaptation, reproduction, and evolution."

Jacob and Monod made key discoveries in understanding how genetic information is transformed into chemical activity. In 1961 they first suggested the existence of messenger RNA—that is, RNA molecules that carry genetic messages from the DNA in the nucleus to the ribosomes (sites of protein synthesis) in a cell. They also reported finding two kinds of genes: structural genes, which synthesize proteins and serve in the production of RNA; and regulatory genes (called operators), which regulate the activity of the structural genes. Furthermore, a group of protein-synthesizing genes plus their regulating gene form a unit called an operon. Jacob's work opened new areas of research into possible genetic origins of cancer.

❧

# Understanding Nerve Impulse Transmission
## Bernard Katz

> *Bernard Katz was born in Leipzig, Germany, on March 20, 1911. In*
> *1934 he took his medical degree at the University of Leipzig, and in*
> *1935 he moved to England, where he studied neurophysiology and*
> *earned a doctorate at the University of London in 1938. For many years*
> *he was a member of the faculty at the University College of London.*

BERNARD KATZ SHARED THE 1970 NOBEL PRIZE for physiology or medicine with Julius Axelrod and Ulf von Euler "for their discoveries concerning the humoral transmitters in the nerve terminals and the mechanism for their storage, release, and inactivation." Katz, a biophysicist, opened the door for many potential cures through his research on nerve impulses and nerve-muscle connections.

Katz made his greatest impact by studying the chemistry of nerve impulse transmission. He investigated the chemical acetylcholine—its storage, release from nerve endings during impulse transmission, and inactivation. This research aided the development of the whole field of neurophysiology, particularly the search for drugs that act on the nervous system.

# DEVELOPMENT OF CRYSTALLOGRAPHIC ELECTRON MICROSCOPY
## Aaron Klug

> *Aaron Klug was born in Zelvas, Lithuania, on August 11, 1926. When he was a toddler, he moved with his parents to South Africa. In 1953 he earned a doctorate at Trinity College of Cambridge University in England, and in 1962 he began a long career as a researcher at Cambridge.*

AARON KLUG, A BIOCHEMIST, WON THE 1982 NOBEL PRIZE in chemistry "for his development of crystallographic electron microscopy and his structural elucidation of biologically important nucleic acid-protein complexes."

As a student, Klug "developed a strong interest...in the structure of matter, and how it was organized." His Nobel Prize-winning research involved his investigation of the three-dimensional structure of viruses and other particles that are combinations of nucleic acids and proteins. In the course of that research, he developed the techniques of crystallographic electron microscopy, in which a series of electron micrographs (graphic reproductions of images formed by a microscope), taken from different angles, can be combined to produce three-dimensional images of particles.

Klug's methods are now widely used by other scientists to study proteins and viruses.

❧

# SYNTHESIZING ARTIFICIAL DNA
## Arthur Kornberg

> *Arthur Kornberg was born in Brooklyn, New York, on March 3, 1918. In 1941 he received his M.D. at the University of Rochester. During the 1950s he worked at Washington University in Saint Louis, Missouri, and in 1959 he began a long-term association with the Stanford School of Medicine.*

ARTHUR KORNBERG, A BIOCHEMIST, SHARED THE 1959 NOBEL PRIZE in physiology or medicine with Severo Ochoa "for their discovery of the mechanisms in the biological synthesis of ribonucleic acid and deoxyribonucleic acid." Specifically, Kornberg discovered the way in which an enzyme replicates DNA.

Kornberg's Nobel Prize-winning work began with his desire to produce a giant molecule of artificial DNA. To do so, he needed preexisting DNA as a template to be copied; a set of the nucleotides A, T, G, and C; and an enzyme that would select and arrange the nucleotides according to the directions from the template and would link them together into the DNA chain. The main problem was the enzyme. Kornberg's great contribution was to isolate and purify the enzyme DNA polymerase, which he then combined with the other ingredients to produce a large molecule of artificial DNA. This DNA was a chemically exact but genetically inert replica of natural DNA. In 1967 he synthesized, for the first time in history, biologically active DNA in a test tube.

# Discovery of the Citric Acid Cycle

## Hans Krebs

ଏ୬

*Hans Adolf Krebs was born in Hildesheim, Germany, on August 25, 1900. In 1925 he earned his medical degree at the University of Hamburg. In 1933 he fled the Nazis and moved to England, where he served on several university faculties. He died in Oxford, England, on November 22, 1981.*

HANS KREBS WON THE 1953 NOBEL PRIZE IN PHYSIOLOGY OR medicine "for his discovery of the citric acid cycle." He shared the award with Fritz Lipmann, who worked on a related topic. Krebs, a biochemist, made a major contribution to understanding how the body converts food into energy.

In 1937 he discovered the citric acid cycle, also known as the Krebs cycle. This cycle is the process by which the two-carbon fragments produced by the metabolism of fats, proteins, and carbohydrates are converted into water and carbon dioxide, releasing energy in the process. The discovery of this cycle was a landmark in biochemistry because it provided scientists with a deeper understanding of metabolic pathways and it stimulated more experiments.

The cycle also had broader implications. "The presence of the same mechanism of energy production [the citric acid cycle] in all forms of life suggests two other references," Krebs believed: "firstly, that the mechanism of energy production has arisen very early in the evolutionary process, and secondly, that life, in its present form, has arisen only once."

# Discovery of Human Blood Groups

## Karl Landsteiner

❧

KARL LANDSTEINER IS OFTEN CALLED THE FATHER OF IMMUNOLOGY. But he is best known for winning the 1930 Nobel Prize in physiology or medicine "for his discovery of human blood groups."

In 1900, while studying blood for immunology purposes, Landsteiner found that blood serums from one person mixed with those from another person sometimes agglutinated (clumped). The following year he reported that he had used agglutination to divide human blood into three groups: A, B, and C (later changed to O). Soon other researchers added a fourth type: AB.

This process of typing blood into groups provided physicians and scientists with countless benefits. For example, before Landsteiner's discovery, doctors rarely performed blood trasfusions, because if the blood from the donor did not match that of the patient, the results could be disastrous. By showing how to type blood, Landsteiner paved the way for the safe transfusion of blood from one individual to another.

*Karl Landsteiner was born in or near Vienna, Austria, on June 14, 1868. Both of his parents were of Jewish origin; but his father died when Karl was six, and his mother, a convert to Christianity, raised him as a Roman Catholic. Landsteiner received his medical degree from the University of Vienna in 1891; worked as a physician, teacher, and researcher in Europe; and, in 1922, moved to the United States, where he performed research at the Rockefeller Institute for Medical Research. He died in New York City on June 26, 1943.*

# BIRTH OF GENETIC RECOMBINATION
## Joshua Lederberg

ॐ

*Joshua Lederberg was born in Montclair, New Jersey, on May 23, 1925. After earning a Ph.D. at Yale University in the late 1940s, he served on the faculties at the University of Wisconsin and Stanford University before taking over the presidency of Rockefeller University in 1978.*

JOSHUA LEDERBERG, A GENETICIST, WON THE 1958 NOBEL PRIZE in physiology or medicine "for his discoveries concerning genetic recombination and the organization of the genetic material of bacteria." He shared the award with Edward L. Tatum, with whom he was closely associated in his research, and with George W. Beadle.

During his student years, Lederberg had begun medical school at Columbia University, but Tatum invited him to help with some research. Lederberg planned to spend only three months with Tatum, but the work was so fascinating that he never returned to medical school.

With Tatum, Lederberg discovered a process they called genetic recombination, a process of sexual fertilization in bacteria, which usually reproduce by simple cell division. The scientists found that when two different biochemical mutants of bacteria are mixed, their genes recombine and the recombination is present in the offspring.

Extending this work, Lederberg artificially introduced new genes into bacteria, making it easier to investigate hereditary material. He also examined a process called bacterial transduction, in which a bacterial virus carries a gene from one bacterial cell to another, where it becomes part of the genetic makeup of the second cell.

Lederberg's work laid the foundation for genetic engineering.

# DISCOVERY OF NERVE GROWTH FACTOR
## Rita Levi-Montalcini

ᘓ

RITA LEVI-MONTALCINI SHARED THE 1986 NOBEL PRIZE in physiology or medicine with Stanley Cohen for "their discoveries which are of fundamental importance for our understanding of the mechanisms which regulate cell and organ growth." Levi-Montalcini, a neurobiologist, discovered the nerve growth factor (NGF), a protein instrumental in the growth and differentiation of cells in the nervous system.

Courtesy of Rita Levi-Montalcini

In 1947 she experienced a breakthrough in her research when she examined silver-salt-impregnated chicken-embryo sections. She compared what she saw with a battlefield: groups of cells were advancing, retreating, being killed, and being cleared away. "It struck me that the discovery of great migratory and degenerative processes affecting nerve cell populations at the early stages of their development might offer a tenuous yet valid path to follow into the fascinating and uncharted labyrinth of the nervous system."

In the early 1950s, she and a colleague, Giuseppe Levi, grafted cancer tumors from mice onto chicken embryos, where, in 1951, bundles of nerve fibers started to grow, apparently in response to the tumors' release of a chemical that the two scientists called the nerve growth factor. From 1953 to 1959, with Cohen, Levi-Montalcini developed techniques for extracting large quantities of NGF. Researchers have used NGF as an aid in shedding light on many human disorders, including cancer, Alzheimer's, Parkinson's, and birth defects.

> Rita Levi was born in Turin, Italy, on April 22, 1909. As an adult, she added her mother's maiden name, Montalcini, to her surname. When Rita was twenty, her beloved governess, Giovanna, died of cancer and Rita vowed to become a doctor. She earned a medical degree at the Turin School of Medicine in 1936. However, as a Jew she was forbidden by the Fascist government from teaching or practicing medicine, so she began neurological research. In 1946 she started a long-term association with Washington University in Saint Louis, Missouri.

# DISCOVERY OF COENZYME A
## Fritz Lipmann

ℰℐ

*Fritz Albert Lipmann was born in Königsberg, Germany, on June 12, 1899. At the University of Berlin, he earned a medical degree (1924) and a doctorate in chemistry (1927). In 1939 he immigrated to the United States, where he served on the staffs at Cornell Medical School, Massachusetts General Hospital, Harvard Medical School, and, beginning in 1957, the Rockefeller Institute for Medical Research (now Rockefeller University). He died in Poughkeepsie, New York, on July 24, 1986.*

FRITZ LIPMANN, A BIOCHEMIST, WON THE 1953 NOBEL PRIZE in physiology or medicine "for his discovery of coenzyme A and its importance for intermediary metabolism." He shared the award with Hans Krebs, who worked on a similar topic.

"You have to follow your nose," Lipmann said of his research. "You try one experiment, then another, and bring some sense to it." While investigating energy metabolism in the mid-1940s, he isolated coenzyme A, a compound involved in the transfer of two-carbon units from one molecule to another, an important step in sugar metabolism.

Eventually Lipmann showed that coenzyme A plays a major role in the metabolism of fats, carbohydrates, sterols, and proteins. His discovery of this essential factor in the transfer of energy in living tissues greatly aided all future research into living cells.

# BREAKTHROUGH IN NERVE IMPUSLE RESEARCH

## Otto Loewi

୧୨

OTTO LOEWI, A PHARMACOLOGIST, won the 1936 Nobel Prize in physiology or medicine for his "discoveries relating to chemical transmission of nerve impulses." He shared the award with Henry H. Dale.

Before 1921, there was a theory among some scientists that nerve impulses were carried by chemical transmitters, but no one had been able to prove it. In that year, Loewi, on two successive nights, had the same dream about how to prove the theory, and he immediately carried out the experiment that had come to him in the dream. He set up two test tubes. In one he put a frog's heart whose beat had been inhibited by the stimulation of its vagus nerve. Loewi took fluid from that test tube and transferred it to the second test tube, in which he had placed a second, unstimulated frog's heart. The fluid caused a similar beat inhibition in the second heart. The experiment showed that chemical substances were released when the nerve to the first heart was stimulated, and those same chemicals, transferred to the second test tube, caused a similar effect in the second heart. The theory of chemical transmission of nerve impulses had finally been proven.

Loewi's discovery revolutionized neurophysiology. The concept of chemical transmission had tremendous clinical implications, especially regarding the causes and treatments of neurological disorders.

> Otto Loewi was born in Frankfurt am Main, Germany, on June 3, 1873. He earned a medical degree at the University of Strasbourg (1896), taught at the University of Graz (1909–1938), fled the Nazis, and immigrated to the United States, where he served on the faculty at the New York University College of Medicine. He died in New York City on December 25, 1961.

# UNLOCKING THE SECRET OF VIRUS GROWTH
## Salvador E. Luria

> *Salvador Edward Luria was born in Turin, Italy, on August 13, 1912.*
> *He earned a medical degree at the University of Turin (1935), worked at*
> *the Radium Institute in Paris (1938–40), and then immigrated to the*
> *United States, where he served on the faculties of Indiana University, the*
> *University of Illinois, and, from 1959, at the Massachusetts Institute of*
> *Technology. He died in Lexington, Massachusetts, on February 6, 1991.*

SALVADOR E. LURIA, A BIOLOGIST, HELPED LAY THE FOUNDATION for molecular biology through his studies of bacterial resistance to bacteriophages (viruses that attack bacteria). In 1969 he shared the Nobel Prize in physiology or medicine with Max Delbrück and Alfred Hershey "for their discoveries concerning the replication mechanism and the genetic structure of viruses."

Luria isolated a phage-resistant variant of bacteria. He showed that a phage (virus) particle is basically DNA with a protein shell; when it invades a bacterial cell, the DNA sheds its protein coating, takes over the genetic mechanism of the host, and reproduces new viruses instead of new cells. Unlocking this secret of virus growth in bacteria aided research in combating viral diseases and paved the way for research into how more complex organisms reproduce.

❧

# UNDERSTANDING LYSOGENY
## André M. Lwoff

> *André Michel Lwoff was born in Ainay-le-Château, France, on*
> *May 8, 1902. At the University of Paris, he earned a medical degree*
> *(1927) and an academic doctorate (1932). Lwoff worked for many*
> *years at the Pasteur Institute and, from 1959, at the University of Paris.*
> *He died in Paris on September 30, 1994.*

ANDRÉ M. LWOFF SHARED THE 1965 NOBEL PRIZE IN PHYSIOLOGY or medicine with François Jacob and Jacques Monod "for their discoveries concerning genetic control of enzyme and virus synthesis." Lwoff, a biologist, particularly contributed to an understanding of lysogeny, the process by which bacteriophages (viruses that attack bacteria) bring about the destruction of infected bacteria.

Early in his career, Lwoff described a previously misclassified genus of bacterium, which came to be known as *Moraxella lwoffii* in his honor. Jacob and Monod, two of his colleagues at the Pasteur Institute, recognized his ability and encouraged him to study lysogenic bacteria (bacteria that contain a bacteriophage and can lyse, or break open, to release the virus).

In 1950 Lwoff discovered that lysogenic bacteria retain a dormant capacity for lysis through many generations. This capacity is inherited through a noninfective virus that, in the presence of ultraviolet light, becomes infective and causes lysis. His work greatly helped to establish the field of molecular biology and led to important research into viral causes of cancer.

# Uncovering the Role of Phagocytes in Fighting Infection
## Élie Metchnikoff

⌘

ÉLIE METCHNIKOFF SHARED THE 1908 NOBEL PRIZE in physiology or medicine with Paul Ehrlich "for their work on immunization." Metchnikoff, an embryologist and immunologist, was especially noted for his discovery of the role of white blood cells in combating infection.

"It was in Messina [Italy] that the great event of my scientific life took place," he reported. "A zoologist until then, I suddenly became a pathologist." The event, in the 1880s, was his observation of mobile cells surrounding and engulfing foreign bodies in transparent starfish larvae. He was not the first to witness this kind of engulfing, but other scientists believed that the process served merely as a way for the blood system to spread the foreign material throughout the body. Metchnikoff was the first to deduce that the mobile cells were policing or sanitizing the foreign objects.

He named these policing cells phagocytes, from Greek *phagein* ("to eat"), and he explored the whole process of phagocytosis, the engulfing of foreign bodies by a cell and the role of this process in the body's defense against disease. Phagocytosis explains the ability of white blood cells to help control bacterial infections by absorbing bacteria in the bloodstream. His cellular theory of immunity, in which phagocytic cells capture and destroy invading bacteria, profoundly influenced the development of immunology.

> *Élie Metchnikoff was born in Ivanovka, Kharkov province, Russia, in May 1845. His original name was Ilya Ilich Mechnikov, and his mother was Jewish but his father was not. After earning a doctorate at the University of Saint Petersburg (1868), he worked at several universities before serving as an administrator at the Pasteur Institute in Paris (1888–1916). He died in Paris on July 15, 1916.*

# DISCOVERY OF CHEMICAL REACTIONS DURING MUSCLE CONTRACTION
## Otto Meyerhof

ের

*Otto Meyerhof was born in Hannover, Germany, on April 12, 1884. After earning a medical degree at the University of Heidelberg (1909), he worked at universities and institutes in Germany till 1938, spent 1938–40 in Paris, and in 1940 immigrated to the United States, where he was on the faculty at the University of Pennsylvania from 1940 to 1951. He died in Philadelphia, Pennsylvania, on October 6, 1951.*

OTTO MEYERHOF, A BIOCHEMIST AND PHYSIOLOGIST, won the 1922 Nobel Prize in physiology or medicine "for his discovery of the fixed relationship between the consumption of oxygen and the metabolism of lactic acid in the muscle." He shared the award with Archibald V. Hill, who had done earlier work in this field.

Meyerhof chose muscle for study because he believed that he could describe the dynamics of biological processes in the language of chemistry and physics. He set about to prove this theory by investigating the chemical reactions that occur during muscle contraction, especially the origin and fate of lactic acid during contraction. He found that glycogen is broken down into lactic acid, which, in turn, is converted back to glycogen. This series of reactions came to be known as the Pasteur-Meyerhof cycle. His findings provided a chemical basis for the earlier ideas of Archibald V. Hill regarding heat changes that occur during muscle contraction and during the subsequent recovery of the muscle. Meyerhof was the first person to apply thermodynamic concepts to the analysis of cell reactions.

# DISCOVERY OF X-RAY MUTATIONS
## Hermann J. Muller

HERMANN J. MULLER, A BIOLOGIST AND GENETICIST, won the Nobel Prize in 1946 in physiology or medicine "for the discovery of the production of mutations by X-ray irradiation." This discovery had far-reaching implications, not only scientifically but also politically.

He developed an early interest in genetics when he learned of Charles Darwin's theory of natural selection and when he observed a sequence of pictures showing the evolution of the horse.

In 1926 he subjected eggs of the fruit fly to X-ray treatment. The result was startling. The X rays increased the natural mutation rate of the insect hundreds or thousands of times. Muller observed a variety of radical mutations, including alterations in eye and wing shapes and in the general structure of the fly. The mutations resulted from changes within individual genes and from chromosome breakage.

This discovery produced at least two profound effects. First, using this technique, scientists could now create large numbers of mutations for important research in genetics and biochemistry. Second, since most of the mutations were harmful, Muller and others urged the minimizing of exposure to ionizing radiation of any kind. His discovery entered the political arena when many people backed up their protests against nuclear testing by drawing on Muller's data to show how dangerous the testing could be.

*Hermann Joseph Muller was born in New York City on December 21, 1890. His father was of Catholic background, his mother Jewish. After receiving his Ph.D. at Columbia University (1916), Muller worked at many campuses, notably the University of Texas and Indiana University. He died in Indianapolis, Indiana, on April 5, 1967.*

# CREATION OF THE FIRST GENETIC MAP OF A DNA MOLECULE
## Daniel Nathans

❧

*Daniel Nathans was born in Wilmington, Delaware, on October 30, 1928. After earning his medical degree at Washington University (1954) in Saint Louis, Missouri, he practiced medicine for a short time and then, in 1962, began a long-term stay on the faculty at Johns Hopkins University.*

DANIEL NATHANS, A PHYSICIAN AND BIOLOGICAL RESEARCHER, shared the 1978 Nobel Prize in physiology or medicine with Werner Arber and Hamilton O. Smith for "the discovery of restriction enzymes and their application to problems of molecular genetics." Nathans was the first to map out the genetic components of a DNA molecule.

Like many other researchers, Nathans sought a better understanding of cancer. He knew that in 1968 Arber had found that bacteria cells produce special substances called restriction enzymes, which prohibit the growth of attacking bacteriophages (viruses). In 1970 Nathans became the first to apply restriction enzymes to the study of cancer-virus DNA molecules. He used the enzymes to cleave DNA at various sites in the interior of the molecule so that he could identify the location and function of specific genes. He thus created the first genetic map of a DNA molecule.

This new knowledge of genetic information opened the door to much further research into cancer. Later other scientists used his methods for genetic mapping of more complex molecules, as well as in recombinant DNA techniques for the production of DNA "factories" that synthesize medically useful compounds, such as insulin and growth hormones.

# TRANSLATING THE GENETIC CODE
## Marshall W. Nirenberg

> *Marshall Warren Nirenberg was born in New York City on April 10, 1927. After earning a Ph.D. at the University of Florida (1957), he began a long career as a researcher and administrator at the National Institutes of Health in Bethesda, Maryland.*

MARSHALL W. NIRENBERG, A BIOCHEMIST, PROVIDED AN IMPORTANT KEY to how genes determine all functions. In 1968 he shared the Nobel Prize in physiology or medicine with Har Gobind Khorama and Robert W. Holley "for their interpretation of the genetic code and its function in protein synthesis."

Nirenberg believed that the practical medical implications of research must be based on the long-term building of basic biological knowledge. To help lay that basic foundation, he sought, and in 1961 found, a procedure for deciphering the genetic code in living cells. He mixed a batch of chemicals containing all the amino acids, excluding from them the DNA, RNA, and other components. Then he added an artificial RNA made up only of uracil. By adding radioactive carbon 14 to one amino acid at a time in each mixture, he found that the amino acid directed into protein by uracil is phenylalanine. This was the first "word" translated from the genetic code. He further developed this technique to decipher more information from genetic material.

Because the genetic code controls not only the production of all proteins in the body but also the transmission of inherited characteristics, Nirenberg's techniques provide basic knowledge that may eventually enable scientists to control heredity and eliminate diseases caused by genetic defects.

❦

# ISOLATION OF CORTISONE
## Tadeus Reichstein

> *Tadeus Reichstein was born in Włodawek, Poland, on July 20, 1897. In 1905 he moved to Switzerland, where he took a Ph.D. at the Federal Institute of Technology in 1922. In 1933, while working at the Institute, he synthesized ascorbic acid (vitamin C), the first laboratory preparation of any vitamin. In 1938 he began a long career at the University of Basel.*

TADEUS REICHSTEIN, A CHEMIST, SHARED THE 1950 NOBEL PRIZE in physiology or medicine with Philip S. Hench and Edward C. Kendall "for their discoveries relating to the hormones of the adrenal cortex, their chemical structure, and biological effects." One of those hormones was cortisone.

Between 1934 and 1946 Reichstein isolated, and determined the chemical structure of, hormones produced by the adrenal cortex, a gland located near the kidney. In 1937 he and Kendall independently isolated a hormone later called cortisone. Eventually cortisone became well known for its use in the treatment of rheumatoid arthritis and other ailments.

# DEVELOPMENT OF THE ORAL POLIO VACCINE

## Albert Sabin

‿

*Albert Bruce Sabin was born in Białystok, Russia, on August 26, 1906. He immigrated to the United States in 1921. After earning his M.D. degree at New York University (1931), he served on the staffs at many medical institutions, including the medical school at the University of Cincinnati and the Children's Hospital Research Foundation in the same city. He died in Washington, D.C., on March 3, 1993.*

ALBERT SABIN, A VIROLOGIST, DEVELOPED VACCINES against several virus diseases, including encephalitis and dengue. He also investigated possible links between viruses and some forms of cancer. But he is best known for creating an oral vaccine against poliomyelitis (or polio).

In the early 1950s, Jonas Salk developed a dead-virus polio vaccine, made from polio viruses that were killed by formaldehyde. Sabin opposed Salk's vaccine because, he felt, a dead-virus serum would have only a short-term effect. Sabin set out to develop a live-virus vaccine. The difficulty was to find virus strains of each of the three types of polio (each producing its own variety of antibody) that were too weak to produce the disease itself. In the late 1950s he succeeded in making a vaccine from living polio viruses that were "attenuated" (weakened) from the disease-causing strains. He tested it on himself first, then on prison volunteers. In the late 1950s it was widely used in Russia and Europe, and in the early 1960s it was generally distributed in the United States.

Sabin's vaccine had two advantages over Salk's: it was taken orally, not by injection; and its effectiveness lasted much longer.

# CREATION OF THE FIRST EFFECTIVE POLIO VACCINE

## Jonas Salk

❧

POLIO (IN FULL, POLIOMYELITIS) IS an acute infectious virus disease that can cause paralysis, deformity, and death. In 1952 it struck over 57,000 Americans and killed 3,300 of them. Dr. Salk's polio vaccine, announced in 1953, extensively tested on children in 1954, and licensed for manufacture in 1955, was the first effective preventive developed for the disease.

*Jonas Edward Salk was born in New York City on October 28, 1914. After earning his medical degree at New York University (1939), he interned at New York's Mount Sinai Hospital (1940–42); worked as a researcher at the University of Michigan (1942–47), where he helped develop influenza vaccines; headed the Virus Research Laboratory at the University of Pittsburgh (1947–63), where he created his polio vaccine; and, in 1963, founded the Salk Institute for Biological Studies, a research center near San Diego, California, where, in the 1980s and 1990s, he worked on a vaccine for AIDS. Salk died in La Jolla, California, on June 23, 1995.*

In 1949 the National Foundation for Infantile Paralysis asked Salk to become one of the directors of a study, funded by the March of Dimes, for identifying the various strains of polio virus. He accepted because the program would allow him to run his own laboratory, something he had not previously been able to do. However, he soon realized that simply gathering knowledge about various types of polio was not enough for him. A perfectionist, he felt compelled to seek ways to help the body fight off the polio virus, just as he had earlier worked on successful influenza vaccines.

Salk's special skill was his ability to apply the technical achievements of many scientists to the development of a polio vaccine. Among those techniques were methods of growing polio virus, killing it with formaldehyde, and whipping the vaccine with mineral oil to increase the stimulation of antibodies by the virus. In 1952 he successfully tested the vaccine on a small number of children. However, he resisted pressure from others to make large-scale field tests, explaining that he wanted to perfect the vaccine. When those tests finally took place in 1954, the vaccine showed an overall 80–90 percent effectiveness in preventing the various types of polio.

Salk objected to the use of the term "Salk vaccine" because, he said, many people contributed to its development. He made no profit from the vaccine. When asked who held the patent for the drug, he replied, "There is no patent. Could you patent the sun?" The *New York Times* hailed the serum as "one of the greatest triumphs in the history of medicine."

# ISOLATION OF HYPOTHALAMUS HORMONES
## Andrew Schally

> *Andrew Victor Schally was born in Wilno, Poland, on*
> *November 30, 1926. He earned a Ph.D. at McGill University (1957)*
> *in Montreal, Canada, and in 1962 began a long association with*
> *Tulane University of Louisiana.*

ANDREW SCHALLY, A BIOCHEMIST, SHARED THE 1977 NOBEL PRIZE IN PHYSIOLOGY OR MEDICINE with Roger Guillemin "for their discoveries concerning the peptide hormone production of the brain." A cowinner of the award that year was Rosalyn S. Yalow, who also did research on hormones.

Schally, working at first with Guillemin and later competitively against him, isolated and synthesized hormones that the hypothalamus (in the brain) produces to control the activities of other hormone-producing glands. Two brain hormones that he identified were TRH (thyrotropin-releasing hormone) and GRH (growth-hormone-releasing hormone). TRH was later used for the diagnosis and treatment of certain hormone-deficiency diseases. GRH led to a treatment for infertility.

જી

# DISCOVERY OF REVERSE TRANSCRIPTASE
## Howard M. Temin

> *Howard Martin Temin was born in Philadelphia, Pennsylvania, on*
> *December 10, 1934. After earning his Ph.D. at the California Institute of*
> *Technology (1959), he joined the faculty at the University of Wisconsin.*
> *He died in Madison, Wisconsin, on February 9, 1994.*

IN 1975 HOWARD M. TEMIN, A VIROLOGIST, SHARED THE NOBEL PRIZE in physiology or medicine with David Baltimore and Renato Dulbecco "for their discoveries concerning the interaction between tumor viruses and the genetic material of the cell." Temin and Baltimore isolated an enzyme that led to a new understanding of how viruses act upon DNA, while Dulbecco had developed many of the techniques used by the two other scientists.

Temin met Baltimore when both of them were high-school students attending a summer course in a scientific laboratory. They became lifelong friends. In 1964 Temin proposed, and Baltimore accepted, the unorthodox theory that some RNA viral genes can duplicate themselves in the DNA of a cell. The accepted belief in the scientific community was that genetic information could be transformed only from DNA into RNA, never from RNA into DNA. Both men encountered great hostility from their colleagues till 1970, when, within days of each other, Temin and Baltimore independently isolated the enzyme that controls the RNA-into-DNA transformation in some viruses. The two scientists called the enzyme RNA-directed DNA polymerase, later known as reverse transcriptase.

Viruses that possess such an enzyme are called retroviruses, which are now known to cause AIDS and certain cancers. Temin's work led to the creation of a new branch of virology to combat retroviruses.

# DISCOVERY OF STREPTOMYCIN
## Selman A. Waksman

എ

SELMAN A. WAKSMAN, A MICROBIOLOGIST, won the 1952 Nobel Prize in physiology or medicine "for his discovery of streptomycin, the first antibiotic effective against tuberculosis."

Waksman lectured on soil microbiology at Rutgers and also served as a microbiologist at the New Jersey Agricultural Experiment Station. Observing that certain soil microbes won over others in the struggle to survive, he thought he might be able to find a way for such microbes to destroy germs in humans. In 1939 he began his search. After he found that streptomyces, a type of soil bacteria, survived under conditions where other species perished, he embarked on a long, systematic search for a strain that would kill disease microorganisms without poisoning a human patient or injuring animal tissue. In 1943 he finally succeeded when he derived streptomycin, which proved to be the first real cure for tuberculosis.

Later streptomycin was also found to be effective in fighting certain kinds of pneumonia, influenza, dysentery, and other diseases. Streptomycin led to the development of related forms for which Waksman himself coined the term *antibiotics* (Latin for "against life").

*Selman Abraham Waksman was born in Priluki, Ukraine, Russia, on July 22, 1888. He came to the United States in 1910, earned a Ph.D. at the University of California (1918), and taught for many years at Rutgers University. He died in Hyannis, Massachusetts, on August 16, 1973.*

# UNDERSTANDING CHEMICAL PROCESSES IN THE EYE
## George Wald

ॐ

*George Wald was born in New York City on November 18, 1906. Wald was introduced to the study of vision by his Columbia University teacher Selig Hecht. "I left Hecht's laboratory," he said, "with a great desire to lay hands on the molecules" involved in vision. After earning his Ph.D. at Columbia (1932), he studied for one year in Europe, where he discovered that vitamin A is one of the major chemical constituents of retinal pigments. Returning to the United States, he taught for many years at Harvard University.*

GEORGE WALD, A BIOLOGIST, SHARED THE 1967 NOBEL PRIZE in physiology or medicine with Ragmar Granit and H. Keffer Hartline "for their discoveries concerning the primary physiological and chemical visual processes in the eye." Wald's research focused on the chemical processes that allow pigments in the retina of the eye to convert light into vision.

Wald found that the pigment of the eye rods (receptors on the retina used for night vision) is made up of a protein and a vitamin A compound. Light striking the pigment separates the two components and produces an energy burst that moves along the retina's nerve network. "The vitamin A in every visual pigment we know is bent and twisted," he reported. "What light does in vision is to straighten out the vitamin A molecule into its natural form. This is all that light does—everything else that happens in the eye could happen in the dark." He also proved that there are three retinal pigments in human color vision, all made up by a combination of vitamin A and one of three different proteins; color blindness results when one of the three proteins is lacking.

Wald singlehandly formed the basic knowledge that science has concerning the chemical process by which retinal pigments in the human eye transmute light into sight.

# DEVELOPMENT OF RADIOIMMUNOASSAY
## Rosalyn S. Yalow

ɞ

Rosalyn S. Yalow was born in New York City on July 19, 1921. Her original name was Rosalyn Sussman. In 1943 she married a fellow physics student, A. Aaron Yalow. After earning her Ph.D. in physics at the University of Illinois (1945), she taught at Hunter College and then worked for many years as a researcher and administrator at a Veterans Administration (VA) hospital in New York City.

IN 1977 ROSALYN S. YALOW, A MEDICAL PHYSICIST, became the first American-born woman to win a Nobel Prize in science, sharing the award in physiology or medicine with Roger Guillemin and Andrew Schally. All three had done research on hormones. Yalow's recognition came specifically "for the development of radioimmunoassays of peptide hormones." Radioimmunoassay (RIA) is a procedure that employs radioisotopes and immunologic methods to measure substances in the blood or other body fluids.

She and her VA colleague Solomon A. Berson (who died in 1972 and thus did not receive a Nobel Prize) became part of a program to investigate the possible use of radioactive substances in the diagnosis and treatment of diseases. Yalow and Berson, to find out how long insulin remained in a diabetic's system, injected patients with radioactively tagged insulin; the tagged insulin took longer to disappear from diabetics than from nondiabetics who had never had insulin. Following up on that discovery, they developed radioimmunoassay, a way of using radioisotopic tracers to measure the concentration of hundreds of different pharmacologic and biologic substances in the blood and other fluids in the human body, as well as in lower animals and even in plants. Previously, these substances had often been impossible to measure because their quantities had been too small or their chemical properties had been too similar to those of other substances.

Courtesy of Rosalyn Yalow

RIA revolutionized the study of ductless glands and hormones, and the treatment of hormonal disorders, such as diabetes. Doctors can now diagnose conditions caused by minute changes in hormones. Dwarf children can be treated with human growth hormones. Blood banks can be screened for diseases. Fetuses and newborns can be tested for diseases. People can be tested for drug abuse and poisons. Yalow's RIA has had a profound effect on the world of medicine.

# 6

# PHYSICAL SCIENCES

ॐ

JEWS HAVE MADE MANY UNIQUE ACHIEVEMENTS *in the physical sciences.
Probably the greatest scientist of the twentieth century was the physicist
Albert Einstein, the Nobel laureate who changed humankind's perception
of the universe with his theory of relativity.*

*Other Nobel Prize–winning physicists included Hans A. Bethe, who explained
the energy production in stars; Neils Bohr, who founded the modern theory of
atomic structure; Max Born, who established quantum mechanics; Murray Gell-
Mann, who described and named the quarks; Donald A. Glaser, who invented
the bubble chamber; Gabriel Lippmann, who pioneered color photography; Arno
A. Penzias, who discovered the cosmic radioactivity that supports the "big bang"
theory of creation; and Otto Stern, who developed the molecular beam. Among
the Nobel Prize winners in chemistry were Adolf von Baeyer, who laid the
foundation for the modern dye industry; Fritz Haber, whose synthetic ammonia
prevented food shortages in the Western world; George de Hevesy, who
developed tracer chemistry; Henri Moissan, who isolated the element fluorine;
Otto Wallach, who laid the foundation for the modern perfume industry; and
Richard Willstätter, who discovered the structure of chlorophyll.*

# FOUNDING THE MODERN DYE INDUSTRY

## Adolf von Baeyer

ભ

*Johann Friedrich Wilhelm Adolf Baeyer was born in Berlin, Germany, on October 31, 1835. His mother was born Jewish but converted to the Evangelical faith. He earned a doctorate at the University of Berlin (1858) and held posts at many institutions, notably the University of Munich (1875–1917). In 1885 he was granted nobility, at which point he added* von *to his name. He died in Starnberg, near Munich, Germany, on August 20, 1917.*

ADOLF VON BAEYER, AN ORGANIC CHEMIST, won the 1905 Nobel Prize in chemistry "for the services he has rendered to the development of organic chemistry and the chemical industry through his work concerning organic dyes and hydrocarbon hydroaromatic compounds."

Early in his career, Baeyer discovered barbituric acid, the parent compound of the modern drugs known as barbiturates, but his Nobel Prize-winning research was on dyes. In 1865 he began working on the organic dye indigo, a commercially valuable blue dye from the plant of the same name. Baeyer developed a process for making synthetic indigo. In 1883 he formulated the structure (later revised) of the dye. He also discovered phthalein dyes, which are aniline dyes and hydroaromatic compounds.

His synthetic indigo had little commercial impact, but it stimulated the chemical dye industry. In fact, Baeyer's research helped lay the foundation for the entire science of biochemistry.

## ALSO NOTEWORTHY

▲ BEER, WILHELM (born January 4, 1797, in Berlin, Germany; died March 27, 1850, in Berlin). Amateur astronomer who, with Johann Mädler, constructed the most complete map of the moon of his time (1836). Half brother of the composer Giacomo Meyerbeer.

▲ CARO, HEINRICH (born February 1834 in Posen, Germany; died October 11, 1910, in Dresden, Germany). Chemist who discovered the dye induline, was responsible for the growth of the dye industry in Germany, and led Germany's world domination of industrial chemistry for many years.

▲ DREYFUS, CAMILLE EDOUARD (born November 11, 1878, in Basel, Switzerland; died September 27, 1956, in New York City). Chemist who, with his brother Henry, perfected cellulose acetate fiber in Basel just before World War I. In 1918 Camille Dreyfus founded an American company that, in 1925, became the Celanese Corporation of America.

▲ FRISCH, OTTO ROBERT (born October 1, 1904, in Vienna, Austria; died September 22, 1979, in Cambridge, England). Physicist who, with Lise Meitner, his aunt, was the first, in 1939, to describe the division of neutron-bombarded uranium into lighter elements. Frish named the process fission.

# PIONEERING STUDY OF ENERGY PRODUCTION IN STARS
## Hans A. Bethe

> *Hans Albrecht Bethe was born in Strassburg, Germany, on July 2, 1906. He earned a doctorate at the University of Munich (1928), fled the Nazis to England and then the United States, and taught for many years at Cornell University.*

HANS A. BETHE, A PHYSICIST, WON THE 1967 NOBEL PRIZE IN PHYSICS "for his contributions to the theory of nuclear reactions, especially his discoveries concerning the energy production in stars."

In 1938, at a conference on theoretical physics in Washington, D.C., his attention was drawn to the unsolved question of what mechanism supplies the energy of the sun and other stars. Bethe investigated the problem and developed the theory that solar energy comes from a series of thermonuclear reactions, known as the carbon cycle because carbon and nitrogen are involved in the process. The end result of the thermonuclear reactions is the fusion of hydrogen nuclei to form helium nuclei. He provided calculations to show that the carbon cycle could account for the energy output of stars, including the sun. Bethe was the first scientist to give an acceptable explanation of how the stars are powered.

☙

# DEVELOPMENT OF NUCLEAR INDUCTION
## Felix Bloch

> *Felix Bloch was born in Zurich, Switzerland, on October 23, 1905. He earned a Ph.D. at the University of Leipzig (1928), fled the Nazis to the United States in 1933, and taught for many years at Stanford University (1934–71). He died in Zurich on September 10, 1983.*

FELIX BLOCH, A PHYSICIST, SHARED THE 1952 NOBEL PRIZE in physics with Edward M. Purcell "for their development of new methods for nuclear magnetic precision instruments and discoveries in connection therewith." Bloch created a technique that he called nuclear induction, a way of measuring the magnetic field of atomic nuclei.

During World War II, Bloch worked on radar countermeasures. His resulting familiarity with radio techniques suggested to him a way of detecting, he said, "nuclear moments through the normal methods of radio reception. The signals to be detected would be due to the electromagnetic induction caused by nuclear reorientation and should appear as a voltage difference between the terminals of an external electric circuit." He therefore called the method nuclear induction (also known as nuclear magnetic resonance). This technique was later applied to research in astronomy, chemistry, and diagnostic medicine.

# FOUNDING THE MODERN THEORY OF ATOMIC STRUCTURE
## Niels Bohr

*Niels Henrik David Bohr was born in Copenhagen, Denmark, on October 7, 1885. He earned a Ph.D. at the University of Copenhagen (1911) and directed the Institute of Theoretical Physics in his homeland (1920–62), except for a period in the United States when he helped with the atomic bomb project during World War II. He died in Copenhagen on November 18, 1962.*

NIELS BOHR, A PHYSICIST, WON THE 1922 NOBEL PRIZE IN PHYSICS "for his services in the investigation of the structure of atoms and of the radiation emanating from them."

Shortly after receiving his doctorate, Bohr began to examine the existing, recently discovered model of the atom. Under classical law, the atom would be expected to decay quickly because of the radiation of energy by the moving electrons. Bohr's great achievement was to apply to this problem another new idea—quantum theory, based on the concept that radiant energy is subdivided into tiny particles called quanta (singular, quantum). He postulated that the atom is capable of existing in a series of stationary states; in each state, the electrons have certain orbits in which they do not radiate energy (quanta). The atom radiates energy only when an electron jumps from one orbit to another, thus making a transition from one stationary state to another. He published his theory in 1913, and his atomic model came to be called the "Bohr atom."

In the 1920s, his model was superceded by a more complex one, but he had already established himself as the founder of the modern theory of atomic structure.

### ALSO NOTEWORTHY

▲ GOLDSCHMIDT, VICTOR MORITZ (born January 27, 1888, in Zurich, Switzerland; died March 20, 1947, in Oslo, Norway). Mineralogist and petrologist who laid the foundation of inorganic crystal chemistry and founded modern geochemistry.

▲ GOMPERTZ, BENJAMIN (born March 5, 1779, in London, England; died July 14, 1865, in London). Mathematician who developed a mathematical law of human mortality long used in actuarial calculations.

▲ HADAMARD, JACQUES-SALOMON (born December 8, 1865, in Versailles, France; died October 17, 1963, in Paris, France). Mathematician who proved the prime-number theorem (1896) and helped to lay the foundation for the modern theory of functional analysis (1910), in connection with which he introduced the term *functional*.

▲ JACOBI, KARL GUSTAV JACOB (born December 10, 1804, in Potsdam, Germany; died February 18, 1851, in Berlin, Germany). Mathematician who contributed to many branches of mathematics and founded, with Niels Abel, the theory of elliptic functions in 1829.

# Founding Quantum Mechanics
## Max Born

cx

Max Born, a physicist, won the 1954 Nobel Prize in physics "for his fundamental research in quantum mechanics, especially for his statistical interpretation of the wave function." He shared the award with Walther Bothe, who had done related work.

In the mid-1920s, Born's assistant at Göttingen, Werner Heisenberg, stated the "uncertainty principle"—the idea, with respect to subatomic particles, that the laws of classical mechanics could not be applied and that only probabilities could be calculated. Born picked up the problem and explained and refined Heisenberg's idea. The system that emerged from their work showed that an electron wave is a wave of probability, the presence of the wavelike manifestation indicating the probable presence of the electron to be associated with it.

> Max Born was born in Breslau, Germany, on December 11, 1882. He earned his doctorate from the University of Göttingen (1907) and taught at many institutions, including the University of Göttingen and, after leaving Germany during the Nazi era, the University of Edinburgh (1936–53). He died in Göttingen, West Germany, on January 5, 1970.

Courtesy of German Information Center

Through these investigations, Born virtually founded quantum mechanics, a general mathematical theory in which he tried to tie together many ideas to account for various kinds of quantum effects.

# BREAKTHROUGH RESEARCH IN BORON DERIVATIVES
## Herbert C. Brown

> *Herbert Charles Brown was born in London, England, on May 22, 1912. His original name was Herbert Brovarnik. He moved to the United States (1914), earned a Ph.D. at the University of Chicago (1938), and taught at Purdue University (1947–78).*

HERBERT C. BROWN, AN ORGANIC CHEMIST, shared the 1979 Nobel Prize in chemistry with Georg Wittig "for their development of boron- and phosphorus-containing compounds, respectively, into important reagents in organic synthesis."

Brown made many fundamental contributions to physical and synthetic organic chemistry, most of which involved the chemistry and synthetic utility of boron derivatives. During World War II, while he was part of the Manhattan Project (which developed the atomic bomb), he worked with borohydrides. His efforts had little effect on the creation of the bomb, but he developed techniques that had a major impact on organic chemistry by revolutionizing the methods of reduction, one of the two most basic chemical processes. He provided new synthetic routes in the production of important compounds. Later, in the 1950s, he discovered the organoboranes, which revealed a wide range of powerful reagents for organic synthesis. Brown's work with boron-derived reagents led to many practical applications, as in the synthesis of pheromones for use in pest control.

୶

# SOLVING THE RIDDLE OF PHOTOSYNTHESIS
## Melvin Calvin

> *Melvin Calvin was born in Saint Paul, Minnesota, on April 8, 1911. He earned his Ph.D. at the University of Minnesota (1935) and from 1937 was associated for many years as a teacher and researcher at the University of California at Berkeley.*

MELVIN CALVIN, A CHEMIST, WON THE 1961 NOBEL PRIZE IN CHEMISTRY for "his research on the carbon dioxide assimilation in plants." His work led to the first true understanding of the chemical reactions involved in plant photosynthesis.

One of the most important factors in sustaining life on earth is photosynthesis, the process in which chlorophyll (the green pigment in plants) uses sunlight, carbon dioxide, and water to form foods, such as carbohydrates, and to release oxygen. Before Calvin, the chemical steps involved in photosynthesis were uncertain. Using radioactive carbon, he traced the complete path of carbon dioxide through the complex series of intermediate compounds to the end products. His discovery provided a new understanding of living organisms on a molecular level. He also used his new knowledge as a basis for theories on the chemical evolution of life.

# REVOLUTIONIZING MODERN THEORETICAL PHYSICS
## Albert Einstein

ɔ

ALBERT EINSTEIN, A PHYSICIST, won the 1921 Nobel Prize in physics "for his services to theoretical physics, and especially for his discovery of the law of the photoelectric effect." Though the Nobel Prize committee specified only his work on the theory of light, he is best remembered today for his special and general theories of relativity, which revolutionized human perception of the universe.

In his childhood, when he read popular science books, Einstein developed what came to be a lifelong belief that the universe is orderly. He also developed, from the beginning, an independent way of thinking. Those qualities, together with his genius, exploded in four scientifically revolutionary papers that he published in 1905 (a fifth paper that year served as his Ph.D. dissertation).

In the first paper, he worked out an equation to explain Brownian motion, a long-known but never-understood irregular motion of microscopic particles suspended in a liquid or gas. He proved that Brownian motion can be used as direct evidence for the existence of molecules, which had previously been only theoretical.

In his second 1905 paper, Einstein provided a revolutionary theory of light. He argued that light is a stream of quanta (energy packets later called photons). His theory explained many phenomena, such as the photoelectric effect, in which an electric current is formed by electrons that are released when a bright beam of light strikes a metal object; Einstein showed that when quanta of light energy strike atoms in a metal, the quanta force the atoms to release electrons.

In his third 1905 paper, Einstein answered a question that he had posed to himself when he was a teenager: if one were to travel through space with the same velocity as a beam of light, how would one describe the beam? His answer has come to be called the special theory of relativity. It is "relativity" because velocity is relative to an observer, there being no absolute rest against which an absolute motion can be measured. Furthermore, there is no absolute space or absolute time, because both depend on velocity and both have meaning only relative to a viewer. The theory is "special" because it confines itself to the special case of objects that are moving at a constant velocity. It does not take into account the effects of gravitation, which are everywhere pre-

*Albert Einstein was born in Ulm, Germany, on March 14, 1879. He worked at the Swiss patent office in Bern (1902–1908), received a doctorate from the University of Zurich (1905), served on the faculties at several European institutions till the rise of the Nazis, and held a post at the Institute for Advanced Study in Princeton, New Jersey (1933–45). In 1939 he wrote the famous letter encouraging President Franklin D. Roosevelt to embark upon the development of the atomic bomb before the Nazis built one. Einstein supported Zionism and, after World War II, initiatives to control nuclear energy and protect world peace. He died in Princeton on April 18, 1955.*

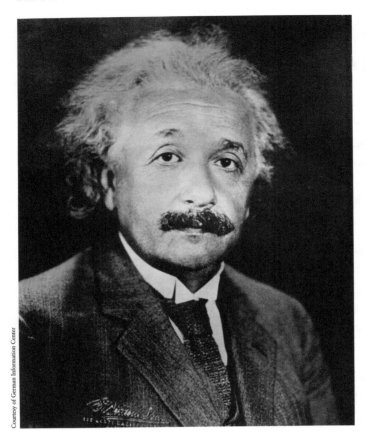

Courtesy of German Information Center

sent. Traditional Newtonian mechanics still hold for small distances and velocities; Einstein's equations hold for large distances and velocities.

His fourth 1905 paper was a footnote to the third. In it, Einstein proclaimed mass and energy to be different manifestations of the same thing. The energy of a quantity of matter equals the mass of that matter times the square of the velocity of light: $E = mc^2$.

In a 1916 paper he extended the special theory to systems moving relative to each other at any velocity, however changing. This was his general theory of relativity. He proposed that space is curved in the presence of mass and that gravitation is not a force but merely the result of moving objects following the shortest possible path in curved space. Einstein predicted that light rays from a distant star would be bent if they passed close to the gravitaional field of the sun on their way to the earth. During a total solar eclipse in 1919, tests proved that his prediction was correct. He virtually founded the science of cosmology.

Through these and other findings, Einstein became the principal architect of twentieth-century theoretical physics.

# REFORMATION OF QUANTUM ELECTRODYNAMICS AND INVENTION OF FEYNMAN DIAGRAMS
## Richard P. Feynman

ᥱᢖ

RICHARD P. FEYNMAN, A PHYSICIST, SHARED THE 1965 NOBEL Prize in physics with Julian S. Schwinger and Sinitiro Tomonaga "for their fundamental work in quantum electrodynamics, with deep-ploughing consequences for the physics of elementary particles." All three men had worked independently to develop equivalent theories. Feynman, in particular, remade the field of quantum electrodynamics (the theory of the interaction between light and matter) and invented one of the most useful tools in theoretical physics, the Feynman diagrams.

Feynman, dissatisfied with existing methods of predicting electron and electromagnetic interactions, used the quantum theory to work out equations governing such interactions. In the process, he changed the way science understands the nature of waves and particles. He tied together all the varied phenomena at work in light, radio, electricty, and magnetism. His problem-solving tools included pictorial representations of particle interactions, known as Feynman diagrams. Feynman's diagrams later entered use in many other areas of theoretical physics.

> *Richard Phillips Feynman was born in New York City on May 11, 1918. He earned his Ph.D. at Princeton University (1942), worked on the atomic bomb project at Los Alamos during World War II, and, from 1950 on, held a long-term position at the California Institute of Technology. He died in Los Angeles on February 15, 1988.*

## ALSO NOTEWORTHY

The Library of Congress

**LISE MEITNER**

▲ MEITNER, LISE (born November 7, 1878, in Vienna, Austria; died October 27, 1968, in Cambridge, England). Physicist who, with Otto Hahn, discovered the chemical element protactinium (1917); with Otto Robert Frisch, her nephew, was the first to recognize that the unusual results of a 1938 Berlin uranium experiment had been caused by the splitting of the atom; and, with Frisch, was the first, in 1939, to calculate the energy released by splitting the uranium atom, thus providing the theoretical groundwork for the atomic bomb.

▲ MEYER, VIKTOR (born September 8, 1848, in Berlin, Germany; died August 8, 1897, in Heidelberg, Germany). Chemist who developed a method for determining the density of vapors (1876–78), discovered the series of organic compounds known as oximes (1882), discovered the sulfur compound thiophene (1883), coined the term *stereochemistry* (1888), and introduced the concept of steric hindrance (1894).

# Providing the First Confirmation of the Quantum Theory
## James Franck

> *James Franck was born in Hamburg, Germany, on August 26, 1882. He took his doctorate at the University of Berlin (1906); taught in Germany, notably at the University of Berlin (1906–1918), till the rise of the Nazis in 1933; immigrated to the United States in 1935; and served on the faculty at the University of Chicago (1938–47). He died in Göttingen, West Germany, on May 21, 1964.*

JAMES FRANCK, A PHYSICIST, SHARED THE 1925 NOBEL PRIZE IN PHYSICS with his coworker Gustav Hertz "for their discovery of the laws governing the impact of an electron upon an atom."

In 1914 Franck bombarded mercury vapor with electrons of various energies. He found that atoms bombarded by electrons both absorb and emit energy in indivisible units, or quanta. This was the clearest demonstration to date of the existence of energy quanta, theorized in 1900 by Max Planck. The experiments also supported Niels Bohr's recently proposed model of the atom as a series of discrete energy states.

Franck provided the first solid confirmation of the quantum theory.

છ૭

# Introduction of Quarks
## Murray Gell-Mann

> *Murray Gell-Mann was born in New York City on September 15, 1929. He earned his Ph.D. at the Massachusetts Institute of Technology (1951) and, in 1955, began a long association with the California Institute of Technology.*

MURRAY GELL-MANN, A PHYSICIST, won the 1969 Nobel Prize in physics "for his contributions and discoveries concerning the classification of elementary particles and their interactions." He is best known for naming the subatomic particles called quarks.

In 1953 he developed the concept of "strangeness" to account for the relatively slow decay of certain particles in the atomic nucleus. In 1961 he described the "eightfold way," a scheme for classifying particles into a simple, orderly arrangement of families; some particles were grouped into families having eight members (the name is a reference to the eight attributes of right living in Buddhism). Within a couple of years, he refined this system by introducing the concept of quarks (he borrowed the term from a fanciful word in James Joyce's *Finnegans Wake*), which are fundamental particles, or building blocks, that help explain certain properties of known particles; quarks are fractionally charged particles that help account for the groupings in the eightfold way.

Through his many contributions to the study of elementary particles, especially quarks, Gell-Mann has assured himself of a permanent place in the history of science.

# FORMULATION OF A THEORY OF UNIFIED WEAK AND ELECTROMAGNETIC INTERACTION
## Sheldon Glashow

> *Sheldon Lee Glashow was born in New York City on December 5, 1922. He earned a Ph.D. at Harvard University (1959) and, after several years of teaching at the University of California at Berkeley, joined the faculty at his alma mater.*

SHELDON GLASHOW, A PHYSICIST, SHARED THE 1979 NOBEL PRIZE in physics with Abdus Salam and Steven Weinberg "for their contributions to the theory of the unified weak and electromagnetic interaction between elementary particles, including, inter alia, the prediction of the weak neutral current." Glashow's research formed the basis of this theory, which Salam and Weinberg developed.

Glashow's main interest from early in his career was the problem of unifying all the forces observed in nature. His principal achievement in that direction was his formulation of a theory that encompasses both the electromagnetic interaction and the weak interaction (which tends to break apart the atomic nucleus) of elementary particles.

"In 1956, when I began doing theoretical physics," Glashow explained, "the study of elementary particles was like a patchwork quilt. Electrodynamics, weak interactions, and strong interactions were clearly separate disciplines, separately taught and separately studied. There was no coherent theory that described them all. Things have changed....The theory we now have is an integral work of art: the patchwork quilt has become a tapestry."

෫ఇ

# INVENTION OF THE BUBBLE CHAMBER
## Donald A. Glaser

> *Donald Arthur Glaser was born in Cleveland, Ohio, on September 21, 1926. He earned his Ph.D. at the California Institute of Technology (1950) and taught at the University of Michigan and the University of California at Berkeley.*

DONALD A. GLASER, A PHYSICIST, WON THE 1960 Nobel Prize in physics "for the invention of the bubble chamber."

Dissatisfied with the available instruments for detecting nuclear particles, Glaser decided to invent his own instrument. The result was his bubble chamber, a device that enables scientists to photograph the trail of gas bubbles left in the path of speeding atomic particles passing through a superheated liquid under pressure. The bubble chamber has proved to be an important tool for discovering new particles and experimenting with the behavior of known particles. Glaser's bubble chamber has given him a uniquely valuable place in today's scientific community.

# CREATION OF SYNTHETIC AMMONIA
## Fritz Haber

*Fritz Haber was born in Breslau, Germany, on December 9, 1868. He earned his doctorate in organic chemistry at the technical university in Berlin (1891), taught himself physical chemistry, and codirected the Kaiser Wilhelm Insitute near Berlin (1911–33). He died in Basel, Switzerland, on January 29, 1934.*

FRITZ HABER, A CHEMIST, WON THE 1918 NOBEL PRIZE IN CHEMISTRY "for the synthesis of ammonia from its elements."

In the early years of the twentieth century, the world's farmlands were running into trouble. Nitrogen must be replaced in farmland for continued growth of good crops. But while the need for nitrogen-rich fertilizers was growing rapidly (because of the rising population and consequent need for more food production), natural sources of fertilizer, such as animal excrement, were not increasing.

In 1905 Haber became aware of this problem. From 1907 to 1909 he combined and altered existing techniques to create the first economical method of synthesizing ammonia from nitrogen and hydrogen. The ammonia was in turn processed into nitrates for fertilizer.

Haber's technique was later supplanted by other methods, but in his time he played a major role in preventing food shortages in the Western world.

ᘓ

# PIONEERING MOLECULAR SPECTROSCOPY
## Gerhard Herzberg

*Gerhard Herzberg was born in Hamburg, Germany, on December 25, 1904. He earned a doctorate in engineering at the Darmstadt Institute of Technology (1928), fled the Nazis in 1935 and settled in Canada, and, from 1948, performed research for many years at the National Research Council in Ottawa.*

GERHARD HERZBERG, A PHYSICIST, WON THE 1971 NOBEL PRIZE IN CHEMISTRY for "his contributions to the knowledge of electronic structure and geometry of molecules, particularly free radicals."

Herzberg early singled out spectroscopy as his main interest. Eventually he came to be regarded as the father of molecular spectroscopy, the science that, by measuring the light emitted or absorbed by molecules, provides precise information on molecular energies, vibrations, and electronic structure. With this method, he discovered the spectra of certain free radicals (groups of atoms that contain odd numbers of electrons) that are intermediate stages in many chemical reactions. He was also the first to identify the spectra of certain radicals in interstellar gas.

Herzberg's studies of free radicals contributed to an understanding how chemcial reactions proceed. His work also added important information to quantum mechanics.

# BIRTH OF TRACER CHEMISTRY
## George de Hevesy

❧

GEORGE DE HEVESY, A CHEMIST, won the 1943 Nobel Prize in chemistry "for his work on the use of isotopes as tracers in the study of chemical processes."

Early in his career, Hevesy tried to separate radium D from lead. That goal proved to be chemically impossible, but through this struggle, he learned about radioactive lead. It occurred to him that radioactive lead could be substituted in all chemical reactions for ordinary lead and could be traced by its radioactivity through the most complex chemical operations. This idea marked the birth, in 1912, of tracer chemistry.

Hevesy's first metabolic study using radioactive lead came in 1923, when he used it to examine the metabolism of bean plants. Beginning in 1934, he used radioactive isotopes of phosphorus to study animal and human metabolisms.

Hevesy's work opened large new areas of biological research.

*George Charles de Hevesy was born in Budapest, Hungary, on August 1, 1885. His name was also recorded in Hungarian as György Hevesy and in German as Georg Karl Hevesy. He often signed his surname in German as von Hevesy because his father's family was ennobled by Franz Joseph I. He earned his doctorate from the University of Freiburg (1908) and later held posts at many institutions, including the universities of Budapest (1912–20) and Freiburg (1926–34). With the rise of the Nazis, he moved to Scandinavia. He died in Freiburg, Germany, on July 5, 1966.*

### ALSO NOTEWORTHY

▲ SAGAN, CARL (born November 9, 1934, in Brooklyn, New York). Astronomer whose television documentary series *Cosmos* (1980) was a landmark in the popularization of science.

▲ SYLVESTER, JAMES JOSEPH (originally James Joseph; born September 3, 1814, in London, England; died March 15, 1897, in London). Mathematician who, with Arthur Cayley, created the theory of algebraic invariants, and, by himself, founded the *American Journal of Mathematics* (1878). He adopted the surname Sylvester as an adult.

▲ SZILARD, LEO (born February 11, 1898, in Budapest, Hungary; died May 30, 1964, in La Jolla, California). Physicist who contributed a paper (1929) that became the foundation for information theory and the development of modern computers; drafted the letter (1939) that Albert Einstein sent to President Franklin D. Roosevelt and that resulted in the Manhattan Project for the development of the atomic bomb; with Enrico Fermi, conducted the first sustained nuclear chain reaction (1942); and led the fight (1945) against the actual use of the atomic bomb.

# FORMULATION OF THE WOODWARD-HOFFMANN RULES
## Roald Hoffmann

> *Roald Hoffman was born in Zloczow, Poland, on July 18, 1937.*
> *His original name was Roald Safran. After his natural father was killed*
> *in a labor camp during World War II, his mother married a man named*
> *Paul Hoffmann. Roald Hoffmann immigrated to the United States*
> *(1949), took a Ph.D. at Harvard University (1962), and, in 1965,*
> *began a long association with Cornell University.*

ROALD HOFFMAN, A CHEMIST, SHARED THE 1981 NOBEL PRIZE in chemistry with Kenichi Fukui "for their theories, developed independently, concerning the course of chemical reactions." Hoffmann's achievement was the Woodward-Hoffmann rules, which explain why certain chemical reactions do *not* take place.

In 1965 he sought to explain an unexpected reaction observed by the chemist R.B. Woodward in the latter's synthesis of vitamin $B_{12}$. The two men worked out a theory, the Woodward-Hoffman rules, to account for the failure of certain cyclic compounds to form from apparently appropriate starting materials. The theory was the most important theoretical advancement in organic chemistry since World War II. The Woodward-Hoffmann rules have had practical applications in medicine and industry.

❦

# UNDERSTANDING THE STRUCTURE OF NUCLEONS
## Robert Hofstadter

> *Robert Hofstadter was born in New York City on February 5, 1915.*
> *He earned his Ph.D. at Princeton University (1938) and taught*
> *at Stanford University (1950–85). He died in Stanford, California,*
> *on November 17, 1990.*

ROBERT HOFSTADTER, A PHYSICIST, WON THE 1961 NOBEL PRIZE IN PHYSICS "for his pioneering studies of electron scattering in atomic nuclei and for his thereby-achieved discoveries concerning the structure of the nucleons." He shared the award with Rudolf L. Mössbauer, who had done related work.

Hofstadter's researches were driven by his desire to know how the universe is composed. Using two machines, a linear accelerator (atom smasher) and a scattering machine (which he and his assistants had developed), Hofstadter discovered that the particles composing the atomic nucleus— protons and neutrons, together called nucleons—are not solid spheres. He made the first precise measurements of the sizes and shapes of nucleons and anatomized their internal structures.

Hofstadter's work stimulated the discovery of other particles essential for an understanding of the forces acting in atomic nuclei.

# DISCOVERY OF JOSEPHSON EFFECTS
## Brian D. Josephson

ري

BRIAN D. JOSEPHSON, A PHYSICIST, WON THE 1973 NOBEL PRIZE in physics "for his theoretical predictions of the properties of a super-current through a tunnel barrier, in particular those phenomena which are generally known as the Josephson effects." He shared the award with Leo Esaki and Ivar Giaever, who had done earlier related research.

Electron "tunneling" occurs when electrons cross (tunnel through) what should be insurmountable energy barriers. Esaki and Giaever had examined the tunneling of normal electrons in the late 1950s. In 1962, while a graduate student at Cambridge, Josephson published a prediction that superconducting electrons, known as Cooper pairs, also could tunnel. (Superconductivity is the phenomenon in which materials, when they are cooled below a critical temperature, lose all resistance to the flow of electricity.) The Josephson effect is an electric current resulting from the tunneling of electrons between two superconducting metals separated by a thin insulating barrier. This discovery permits very sensitive measurements of basic physical phenomena; it has led to the most sensitive detector of magnetic fields known, and it has been used for magnetic investigations of living organisms. The Josephson effect also promises faster and denser electronic circuitry for use in computers and scientific instruments.

> *Brian David Josephson was born in Cardiff, Wales, on January 4, 1940. He took his Ph.D. at Cambridge University (1964), where, in 1967, he began a long-held faculty position.*

---

### ALSO NOTEWORTHY

▲ TELLER, EDWARD (originally Ede Teller; born January 15, 1908, in Budapest, Hungary). Physicist who led the development of the world's first thermonuclear weapon, the hydrogen bomb (1952).

▲ WIENER, NORBERT (born November 26, 1894, in Columbia, Missouri; died March 18, 1964, in Stockholm, Sweden). Mathematician who established the science of cybernetics.

▲ ZACHARIAS, JERROLD REINACH (born January 23, 1905, in Jacksonville, Florida; died July 16, 1986, in Belmont, Massachusetts). Physicist who developed the first practical atomic clock (1956).

# PIONEERING RESEARCH IN MAGNETISM AND CRYOGENICS
## Pyotr Kapitsa

എ

*Pyotr Leonidovich Kapitsa (sometimes recorded in English as Peter Kapitza) was born in Kronshtadt, Russia, on July 8, 1894. His father was of old Russian stock, and his mother was Jewish. He graduated from the Polytechnic Institute in Petrograd (1918); worked in Cambridge, England (1921-34); returned to Russia for a conference (1934) and was detained by the Soviets; directed a scientific institute in Moscow (1935–46); was under house arrest (1946–54) for refusing to work on Soviet nuclear weapons development; and, after Josef Stalin's death, again directed the Moscow institute (1955–84). Kapitsa died in Moscow on April 8, 1984.*

PYOTR KAPITSA, A PHYSICIST, WON THE 1978 NOBEL PRIZE in physics for his pioneering work in magnetism and cryogenics (the physics of very low temperatures). He shared the award with Arno A. Penzias and Robert W. Wilson, who performed separate research.

In the 1920s Kapitsa worked on the generation and precise measurement of intense magnetic fields. He devised a method of obtaining magnetic fields six to eight times greater than ever before achieved. To study the reactions of metals in these intense fields, he needed to create extremely low temperatures so that the molecular action would be cut to a minimum. In the process of producing these low temperatures, he discovered, in 1937, the superfluidity (lack of resistance to flow) of helium II (the stable form of liquid helium cooled to near absolute zero).

# DEVELOPING MATHEMATICAL EXPLANATIONS OF SUPERFLUID
## Lev Landau

> *Lev Davidovich Landau was born in Baku, Azerbaijan, Russia, on January 22, 1908. He studied at several institutions in the Soviet Union and in Europe before the Soviet Academy of Sciences awarded him a doctorate (1934) without a dissertation. Later he was a researcher for many years at the Institute for Physical Problems in Moscow (1937–68). Landau died in Moscow in April 1968.*

LEV LANDAU, A PHYSICIST, won the Nobel Prize in 1962 "for his pioneering theories for condensed matter, especially liquid helium."

Pyotr Kapitsa, the director of the Institute for Physical Problems, was a low-temperature expert who had discovered the superfluidity of helium II in 1937. Helium I, ordinary liquid helium, is similar to other liquid gases. But when it is cooled to near absolute zero, it becomes helium II, the only known superfluid, a peculiar state of matter that is characterized by its apparently frictionless flow. Landau's achievement was to develop, in the early 1940s, mathematical physical theories to explain the behavior of superfluid. He described a "two-fluids" model in which extremely low temperature allows helium II to exhibit quantum effects, behaving like an ideal nonviscous fluid.

❧

# DISCOVERY OF THE MUON NEUTRINO
## Leon M. Lederman

> *Leon Max Lederman was born in New York City on July 15, 1922. He earned a Ph.D. at Columbia University (1951), where he remained as a faculty member for many years.*

LEON M. LEDERMAN, A PHYSICIST, SHARED THE 1988 NOBEL PRIZE in physics with his coworkers Melvin Schwartz and Jack Steinberger for their discovery of the muon neutrino.

In the years 1960 to 1962, Lederman and his two colleagues perfomed an experiment using a particle accelerator to produce the first laboratory-made beam of neutrinos (uncharged subatomic particles having no detectable mass). Scientists already knew that neutrinos seldom interact with matter, but when they do, either electrons or electronlike particles called muons are created. Lederman's group established that the neutrinos that produce muons are a distinct, and previously unknown, type of neutrino, which they named the muon neutrino. This discovery led to further refinements in the categorization of other subatomic particles, eventually resulting in the standard model, a scheme used to classify all known elementary particles.

# INNOVATIONS IN COLOR PHOTOGRAPHY
## Gabriel Lippmann

cs

*Gabriel Jonas Lippmann was born in Hollerich, Luxembourg, on August 16, 1845. He received his doctorate at the University of Paris (1875), with which he was associated for most of the rest of his career. He died at sea, en route from Canada to France, in July 1921.*

GABRIEL LIPPMANN, A PHYSICIST, won the 1908 Nobel Prize in physics "for his method of reproducing colors photographically based on the phenomenon of interference."

Lippmann was always interested in photography. Early in his career, he invented the coleostat, an instrument that allowed for long-exposure photographs of the sky.

Later he concerned himself with the old problem of color photography. A color-photography method had been tried as early as 1848, but the color in the pictures faded rapidly. In 1891 he developed a technique, later called the Lippmann process, that utilized natural colors of light wavelengths instead of using dyes and pigments. He placed a coat of mercury behind the emulsion of a panchromatic plate. The mercury reflected light rays back through the emulsion to interfere with the incident rays, forming a latent image that varied in depth according to each ray's color. The development process reproduced this image in accurate colors.

The process was slow and tedious because of the long exposure times necessary. Furthermore, no copies could be made of the original. Nevertheless, Lippmann's work provided an important stimulus for further experiments in color photography.

# WINNING AMERICA'S FIRST NOBEL PRIZE IN SCIENCE
## Albert A. Michelson

ALBERT A. MICHELSON, A PHYSICIST, WON THE 1907 NOBEL PRIZE in physics "for his optical precision instruments, and the spectroscopic and metrological investigations carried out with their aid." He was the first American to win a Nobel Prize in science.

During 1880–81, while still a postgraduate student in Europe, he conceived and tested his most famous instrument, later known as an interferometer. In 1887 he used it in the classic Michelson–Morley experiment, which was designed to detect differences in the apparent velocity of light caused by the earth's motion through the ether (at that time, believed to be the medium that carries light waves). The test showed that the velocity of light is constant, regardless of the earth's motion, thus implying that there is no ether. Later Albert Einstein praised Michelson's work, saying that it paved the way for his own ideas on relativity.

Michelson continued to refine his instruments, and in the 1920s he became the first to record an accurate measurement of the velocity of light. His profound achievements gave added luster to his position as America's first Nobel Prize–winning scientist.

*Albert Abraham Michelson was born in Strelno, Prussia, on December 19, 1852. His parents brought him to the United States when he was a child. He graduated from the United States Naval Academy at Annapolis (1873) and taught at several institutions, notably the University of Chicago (from the early 1890s to 1929). He died in Pasadena, California, on May 9, 1931.*

American Jewish Archives, Cincinnati Campus, Hebrew Union College, Jewish Institute of Religion

# DISCOVERY OF FLUORINE AND INVENTION OF THE MOISSAN FURNACE

## Henri Moissan

❧

*Ferdinand-Frédéric-Henri Moissan was born in Paris, France, on September 28, 1852. He earned his doctorate at the University of Paris (1880) and taught for many years at the School of Pharmacy in Paris before spending his last years at the Sorbonne (1900–1907). He died in Paris on February 20, 1907.*

HENRI MOISSAN, A CHEMIST, won the 1906 Nobel Prize in chemistry "in recognition of the great services rendered by him in his investigation and isolation of the element fluorine, and for the adoption in the service of science of the electric furnace called after him."

Moissan tackled a problem that had stumped scientists for generations. The similarity between hydrochloric acid and hydrofluoric acid implied the existence of fluorine, but fluorine resisted analysis. It was the most active element known, and nothing seemed capable of forcing it out of combination with other elements. It was also dangerous; other scientists who attempted to isolate it kept finding themselves involved with poisonous materials.

Moissan, however, used platinum for all of his equipment because it was one of the few substances that fluorine would not attack and combine with instantly. He placed a solution of potassium fluoride in hydrogen fluoride in his platinum equipment, chilled it, and passed an electric current through it on June 26, 1886. The result was a pale yellow gas—fluorine.

Moissan's Nobel Prize also honored him for his development of an electric furnace that he used to make calcium carbide. He claimed to have produced artificial diamonds in the furnace, but that claim was never verified. The furnace became an invaluable tool in industrial chemistry. Moissan, because of his furnace, is said to have founded the chemistry of high temperature.

As the discoverer of fluorine and the inventor of his furnace, Moissan made a lasting contribution to science.

# DISCOVERY OF VARIATIONS IN NUCLEAR SHAPES
## Ben R. Mottelson

കൗ

BEN R. MOTTELSON, A PHYSICIST, shared the 1975 Nobel Prize in physics with Aage Bohr and James Rainwater "for the discovery of the connection between collective motion and particle motion in atomic nuclei and the development of the theory of the structure of the atomic nucleus based on this connection." Mottelson and Bohr were coworkers, while Rainwater had done similar work earlier.

In the 1950s, Mottelson and Aage Bohr (son of Niels Bohr) performed some experiments and discovered that the motion of subatomic particles can distort the shape of the nucleus into an asymmetrical form. This finding challenged the widely accepted theory that all nuclei are perfectly spherical. Mottelson's work stimulated new research into a deeper understanding of the structure of the atomic nucleus.

*Ben Roy Mottelson was born in Chicago, Illinois, on July 9, 1926. He earned his Ph.D. at Harvard University (1950), started teaching at the Nordic Institute for Theoretical Atomic Physics in Copenhagen, Denmark, in 1957, and became a Danish citizen in 1971.*

# DEVELOPMENT OF THE ATOMIC BOMB
## J. Robert Oppenheimer

ა

J. ROBERT OPPENHEIMER, A PHYSICIST, directed the Los Alamos, New Mexico, laboratory that developed the atomic bomb during World War II.

In the late 1930s and early 1940s, Oppenheimer, like many other scientists, feared for the future of humanity if the Nazis developed the first atomic bomb. He did much research on the feasibility of military applications for atomic energy, and, as a consequence, in 1943 he was named director of the laboratory charged with the task of creating such a bomb for the United States. Oppenheimer himself chose the site of the lab—the plateau of Los Alamos, near Santa Fe, New Mexico, where he had spent part of his childhood at a boarding school—and supervised the erection of the complex equipment. He also had to persuade hundreds of scientists (later thousands would work there) to commit themselves to the assignment; he stressed that the world needed to be protected from the Nazis and that many nonmilitary applications would spin off from their efforts.

*AP/Wide World Photos*

Oppenheimer's great achievement was to provide leadership at Los Alamos. He had an incredible ability to absorb a wide range of information and to coordinate the activities of the various teams of scientists. He also showed thoughtfulness about the individual welfare of the people working on the project. As a result of Oppenheimer's leadership, the world's first nuclear explosion took place on July 16, 1945, at Alamogordo, New Mexico. Shortly thereafter, two atomic bombs were dropped on Japan (the Germans having already been defeated), thus bringing World War II to a sudden end.

He resigned from his position in October 1945, and in later years Oppenheimer, the father of the atomic bomb, became one of the strongest voices against the use of nuclear weapons.

*J. Robert Oppenheimer was born in New York City on April 22, 1904. As an adult, he claimed that the intitial J. stood for nothing, but the name Julius is on his birth certificate. He earned a Ph.D. at the University of Göttingen, Germany (1927), and taught at the University of California in Berkeley and at the California Institute of Technology before heading the Los Alamos atomic bomb project (1943–45). After the war, he served as director of the Institute for Advanced Study in Princeton, New Jersey (1947–66). In December 1953, he was stripped of his security clearance by the Atomic Energy Commission because of his past associations. The evidence, however, was ambiguous, and in 1963 the same organization gave him its coveted Enrico Fermi Award. He died in Princeton on February 18, 1967.*

# DISCOVERY OF COSMIC RADIATION
## Arno A. Penzias

❧

ARNO A. PENZIAS, AN ASTROPHYSICIST, shared the 1978 Nobel Prize in physics with Pyotr Kapitsa and Robert W. Wilson "for their discovery of cosmic microwave background radiation." Wilson was Penzias's coworker, while Kapitsa did separate research.

Penzias went to work at Bell Telephone Laboratories because, he said, "I liked the connection between the work and useful things. I always wanted to do something practical."

Consequently, when Bell gave him an opportunity to rebuild an old instrument into a radio telescope, he accepted readily. To test their new instrument, he and Wilson began monitoring radio signals from space. Unexpectedly, they detected uniform background static that suggested a residual thermal energy throughout the universe of about 3.5° K, widely accepted as the residual background radiation stemming from the primordial explosion billions of years ago from which the universe was created. Thus, Penzias, through his inadvertent discovery of cosmic background radiation, provided one of the most important supports for the "big bang" theory of creation.

*Arno Allan Penzias was born in Munich, Germany, on April 26, 1933. He immigrated to the United States as a youth, earned a Ph.D. at Columbia University (1962), and embarked on a long career at Bell Telephone Laboratories.*

# Uncovering the Secrets of Hemoglobin Structure
## Max Perutz

෴

*Max Ferdinand Perutz was born in Vienna, Austria, on May 19, 1914. He moved to England (1936), earned a Ph.D. at the University of Cambridge (1940), and, in 1947, began a long-term association with his alma mater as a researcher.*

MAX PERUTZ, A BIOCHEMIST, won the 1962 Nobel Prize in chemistry for his "studies of the structures of globular proteins," specifically hemoglobin (the substance that carries oxygen in the blood). He shared the award with John C. Kendrew, his coworker.

The principal reason that Perutz had selected the University of Cambridge for his studies was the work being done there in X-ray crystallography, a technique for determining the molecular structure of substances. While still a student, Perutz learned that the structure and physiological functions of hemoglobin, so vital to the life processes, were still unclear. In 1936 he began to use X-ray crystallography on the hemoglobin problem, and in 1946 Kendrew joined him.

However, progress was slow till 1953, when Perutz introduced a method of incorporating heavy atoms, such as mercury, into hemoglobin crystals. By comparing the X-ray patterns of the crystals with and without the heavy atoms, Perutz finally determined that hemoglobin consists of four myoglobinlike chains and four nonprotein groups. This information and later studies led to a much better understanding of oxygen transport in respiration and of certain diseases, such as anemia, related to structural malformations of hemoglobin.

# INVENTION OF THE MAGNETIC-RESONANCE METHOD OF OBSERVING ATOMS
## I. I. Rabi

> *Isidor Isaac Rabi was born in Rymanów, Austria–Hungary, on July 29, 1898. He was brought to the United States when he was an infant, earned his Ph.D. at Columbia University (1927), and served on the faculty at Columbia (1929-67). He died in New York City on January 11, 1988.*

I. I. RABI, A PHYSICIST, WON THE 1944 NOBEL PRIZE in physics "for his resonance method for recording the magnetic properties of atomic nuclei."

In the 1930s he invented his atomic- and molecular-beam magnetic-resonance method of observing and measuring the magnetic properties of atoms, atomic nuclei, and molecules. The technique was based on measuring the spin of the protons in the atom's core, a phenomenon known as nuclear magnetic moments. He used his method of magnetic resonance to deduce many mechanical and magnetic properties, as well as the shape, of an atomic nucleus. Other scientists have used the method as their central technique for atomic- and molecular-beam experimentation.

Rabi's work made possible the invention of the laser, the atomic clock, and the medical diagnostic technique of scanning the human body by resonance imaging.

❧

# DISCOVERY OF THE SUBATOMIC PARTICLE PSI
## Burton Richter

> *Burton Richter was born in Brooklyn, New York, on March 22, 1931. He earned his Ph.D. at the Massachusetts Institute of Technology (1956) and, in 1956, began a long association with Stanford University.*

BURTON RICHTER, A PHYSICIST, shared the 1976 Nobel Prize in physics with Samuel C.C. Ting "for their pioneering work in the discovery of a heavy elementary particle of a new kind." The two scientists had independently discovered the same particle at about the same time.

In 1973 Richter completed the construction of the Stanford Positron-Electron Asymmetric Ring, a colliding-beam accelerator. With it, he discovered a new subatomic particle that he called psi (the twenty-third letter of the Greek alphabet). It was the first of a whole new class of massive, long-lived mesons (a group of strongly interacting fundamental particles). Ting called the same particle J; sometimes the two names are combined: J/psi.

Richter pursued his research because he believed that "the more man learned about the universe, the more he could do. The significance" of J/psi, he said, "is that we have learned something more about the structure of the universe."

# DISCOVERY OF THE MUON NEUTRINO
## Melvin Schwartz

> *Melvin Schwartz was born in New York City on November 2, 1932.*
> *He earned his Ph.D. at Columbia University (1958), taught*
> *there (1958–66), and served many years (1966–83) on the faculty*
> *at Stanford University.*

MELVIN SCHWARTZ, A PHYSICIST, SHARED THE 1988 NOBEL PRIZE IN PHYSICS with his coworkers Leon M. Lederman and Jack Steinberger for their discovery of the muon neutrino.

In the years 1960 to 1962, Schwartz, Lederman, and Steinberger worked together on an experiment with neutrinos (subatomic particles having no electric charge and virtually no mass). Because neutrinos almost never interact with matter, they are difficult to detect. At Schwartz's suggestion, the team of scientists devised a way of producing a beam of billions of neutrinos and sending it through an aluminum detector in which some neutrinos interacted with the aluminum atoms. In analyzing those interactions, the scientists discovered a new type of neutrino, the muon neutrino.

The scientists' work led to the recognition of many different families of subatomic particles and eventually to the standard model, a scheme used to classify all known elementary particles.

એ

# REVISION OF QUANTUM ELECTRODYNAMICS
## Julian S. Schwinger

> *Julian Seymour Schwinger was born in New York City on February 12,*
> *1918. He took his Ph.D. at Columbia University (1939) and taught at*
> *Harvard University (1945–72) and UCLA (1972–94). Schwinger died*
> *in Los Angeles on July 16, 1994.*

JULIAN S. SCHWINGER, A PHYSICIST, shared the 1965 Nobel Prize in physics with Richard P. Feynman and Sinitiro Tomonaga "for their fundamental work in quantum electrodynamics, with deep-ploughing consequences for the physics of elementary particles." All three men worked separately.

In the 1940s, Schwinger saw that quantum mechanics, which had developed early in the twentieth century, had never been adequately updated to fit in with new ideas opened up by Einstein's special theory of relativity. In 1948 Schwinger published equations that finally brought quantum mechanics into line with relativity. His work enabled physicists to calculate the electromagnetic interaction of subatomic particles with a much higher degree of accuracy than was previously possible.

# DISCOVERY OF THE ANTIPROTON
## Emilio Segrè

❧

EMILIO SEGRÈ, A PHYSICIST, shared the 1959 Nobel Prize in physics with Owen Chamberlain "for their discovery of the antiproton." Chamberlain was a coworker.

In the 1950s, Segrè engaged in an effort to produce and detect a theoretically predicted particle called an antiproton, a negatively charged twin of the positive proton. In 1955, using a particle accelerator at the University of California, he accelerated a stream of protons and directed them at a copper block. When the protons struck the copper, the collision created many subatomic particles, a few of which were antiprotons.

Segrè's great achievement was the development of techniques for detecting and identifying these elusive particles. He also stimulated the discovery of many more antiparticles (subatomic particles identical to other subatomic particles in mass but opposite to them in electric and magnetic properties; when brought together with their counterparts, antiparticles produce mutual annihilation).

> *Emilio Segrè was born in Tivoli, Italy, on February 1, 1905. He earned his doctorate at the University of Rome (1928) and served on the faculties at his alma mater (1930–36), the University of Palermo (1936–38), and the University of California at Berkeley (1938–72). He died in Lafayette, California, on April 22, 1989.*

# Discovery of How Ribonuclease Catalyzes Digestion

## William H. Stein

❧

*William Howard Stein was born in New York City on June 25, 1911. He received his Ph.D. at the Columbia College of Physicians and Surgeons (1938) and soon joined the staff at the Rockefeller Institute for Medical Research (later called Rockefeller University). He died in New York City on February 2, 1980.*

William H. Stein, a biochemist, shared the 1972 Nobel Prize in chemistry with Christian Anfinsen and Stanford Moore "for their contribution to the understanding of the connection between chemical structure and catalytic activity of the active center of the ribonuclease molecule." Moore was Stein's coworker, while Anfinsen had done earlier related research.

From 1949 to 1963, Stein and Moore deciphered how ribonuclease (an enzyme discovered by Anfinsen) catalyzes the digestion of food. They developed methods for the analysis of amino acids and peptides obtained from proteins, and then they applied those procedures to determine the structure of ribonuclease. They became the first scientists to determine the complete structure of an enzyme and then to relate its catalytic mechanism to its structure.

In the process, they developed general principles to explain how nature designs catalysts for given purposes. Knowledge of those principles has led to many practical applications in other research, such as discoveries about hemogloblin.

# DISCOVERY OF THE MUON NEUTRINO
## Jack Steinberger

> *Jack Steinberger was born in Bad Kissigen, Germany, on May 25, 1921. He immigrated to the United States in 1934, earned a Ph.D. at the University of Chicago (1948), and taught at Columbia University (1950–71).*

JACK STEINBERGER, A PHYSICIST, SHARED THE 1988 NOBEL PRIZE in physics with his coworkers Melvin Schwartz and Leon M. Lederman for their discovery of the muon neutrino.

In the years 1960 to 1962, Steinberger and his two colleagues devised an experiment that would have far-reaching consequences for all nuclear physicists. The three scientists produced the first laboratory-made stream of neutrinos (subatomic particles having no electric charge and virtually no mass). They also discovered a new type of neutrino, which they called the muon neutrino. The high-energy beam of neutrinos they produced became a basic research tool in the study of nuclear forces, making possible, for example, the study of radioactive-decay processes involving the weak nuclear force, or weak interaction, one of the four fundamental forces in nature.

❦

# DEVELOPING THE MOLECULAR BEAM AND PROVING THE ATOMIC MAGNETIC MOMENT
## Otto Stern

> *Otto Stern was born in Sorau, Germany, on February 17, 1888. He took his doctorate at the University of Breslau (1912), taught in Germany till 1933, and then immigrated to the United States and served on the faculty at the Carnegie Institute of Technology (1933–45). He died in Berkeley, California, on August 17, 1969.*

OTTO STERN, A PHYSICIST, WON THE 1943 NOBEL PRIZE in physics "for his contribution to the development of the molecular-ray method and his discovery of the magnetic moment of the proton."

Stern developed the molecular beam as a tool for studying the characteristics of molecules and atoms. Using molecular beams, he proved that atomic magnetic moments (magnetic properties) exist, and he measured their magnitudes. In 1933 he measured the magnetic property of the proton and found that it was $2\frac{1}{2}$ times its theoretical value.

Stern's techniques and discoveries have had a profound effect on the study of molecules, atoms, and subatomic particles.

# INTERPRETATION OF THE CHERENKOV EFFECT
## Igor Tamm

> *Igor Yevgenyevich Tamm was born in Vladivostok, Siberia, on July 8, 1895. He earned a doctorate at the Crimean University in Simferopol (1918), and in 1924 he began a long association with the University of Moscow. Tamm died in Moscow on April 12, 1971.*

IGOR TAMM, A PHYSICIST, WON THE 1958 NOBEL PRIZE in physics for his work in interpreting the Cherenkov radiation effect, that is, the emission of light waves by electrically charged atomic particles moving in a medium faster than the speed of light for that same medium. He shared the award with Pavel A. Cherenkov, who had done earlier research on the subject, and Ilya M. Frank, Tamm's assistant.

In 1934 Tamm became involved with the work of Cherenkov, who had noticed a blue light emitted by water and other transparent substances when exposed to gamma radiation from radioactive material. No one could explain the blue light. In 1937 Tamm worked out a theory to account for the Cherenkov radiation. He based his explanation on the well-known electromagnetic interpretation that a charged particle traveling through a medium with a velocity greater that the velocity of light in the same medium gives out an electromagnetic shock-wave effect. Therefore, the Cherenkov radiation is analogous to the sonic boom made by airplanes traveling faster than the speed of sound in the air. His technique for interpreting the interaction of elementary nuclear particles came to be called the Tamm effect.

જી

# FOUNDING THE MODERN PERFUME INDUSTRY
## Otto Wallach

> *Otto Wallach was born in Königsberg, Prussia, on March 27, 1847. He received his doctorate at the University of Göttingen (1869), taught at the University of Bonn, and directed the Chemical Institute at Göttingen (1889–1915). Wallach died in Göttingen, Germany, on February 26, 1931.*

OTTO WALLACH, A CHEMIST, won the 1910 Nobel Prize in chemistry "in recognition of his services to organic chemistry and the chemical industry by his pioneer work in the field of alicyclic compounds." His specialty was the analysis of natural fragrant oils.

When another chemist told him that a group of volatile oils (camphene and related terpenes) could not be analyzed, Wallach took the challenge to analyze them. Such oils, fragrant substances produced by plants, are also known as ethereal oils because they tend to change form rapidly. However, Wallach was a master of experimentation. By repeatedly distilling the oils, he was able to separate the components of his complex mixtures. Then, by studying their physical properties, he distinguished the compounds. These studies of complex terpenes and, later, of alicyclic compounds, laid the foundation of the modern perfume industry.

# FORMULATION OF A THEORY OF UNIFIED WEAK AND ELECTROMAGNETIC INTERACTION

## Steven Weinberg

❧

STEVEN WEINBERG, A PHYSICIST, SHARED THE 1979 NOBEL PRIZE with Sheldon Glashow and Abdus Salam "for their contributions to the theory of the unified weak and electromagnetic interaction between elementary particles, including, inter alia, the prediction of the weak neutral current." All three scientists performed separate but related work, Glashow first, followed by Weinberg and then Salam.

Weinberg wanted to find some way to unify the fundamental forces of nature. He studied a wide variety of topics, "chosen," he said, "in many cases because I wanted to teach myself some area of physics." Building on Glashow's work, Weinberg developed a theory that explains the known facts of electromagnetic interaction and weak interaction (the "weak" force is the force that breaks apart the nucleus of an atom). His research made it possible to predict the outcome of new experiments in which elementary particles are made to impinge on one another.

Weinberg made an important step toward understanding all the forces of nature when he unified the previously separate disciplines of electrodynamics and weak interactions.

> *Steven Weinberg was born in New York City on May 3, 1933. He earned a Ph.D. at Princeton University (1957) and and served on the faculties at the University of California at Berkeley (1960–69), Harvard University (1973–83), and the University of Texas, Austin (since 1982).*

# UNDERSTANDING THE STRUCTURE OF CHLOROPHYLL

## Richard Willstätter

ↄ

*Richard Willstätter was born in Karlsruhe, Baden, Germany, on August 13, 1872. He took his doctorate at the University of Munich (1894), taught there till 1905, joined staffs in Zurich and Berlin, and worked once again in Munich (1916–25). Willstätter died in Locarno, Switzerland, on August 3, 1942.*

RICHARD WILLSTÄTTER, A CHEMIST, WON THE 1915 NOBEL PRIZE in chemistry "for his researches on plant pigments, especially chlorophyll."

Early in the twentieth century, scientists still did not fully understand the structure of chlorophyll, the green coloring matter found in nearly all flowering plants, mosses, and so on. Chlorophyll is a key component in photosynthesis, the process by which foods and oxygen are produced from carbon dioxide and water through the action of sunlight on green plants. Understanding chlorophyll, then, is important to understanding life on earth.

While separating and purifying plant pigments at Zurich, Willstätter perfected a revolutionary technique called partition chromatography. Aided by that technique, he found that the diversity of plant pigments is based on only a few chemical compounds. He separated not only chlorophyll but also carotenoids (yellow to reddish pigments) and anthocyanins (red, blue, purple pigments). He highlighted his studies by providing the first detailed structural analysis of chlorophyll.

# 7

# SOCIAL SCIENCES

ও

UNIQUE ACHIEVEMENTS BY JEWS IN THE SOCIAL SCIENCES *included some of the most celebrated and revolutionary concepts in human history. Karl Marx developed the political and sociological doctrine of Marxism. Sigmund Freud created psychoanalysis. Benedict de Spinoza produced the prototype of rationalist philosophy. Martin Buber created the I-Thou concept. Henri Bergson developed process philosophy. And Moses Mendelssohn articulated the eighteenth-century Jewish Enlightenment.*

*In the modern practical world, the social worker Lillian D. Wald introduced public health nursing, and the family counselor Ruth Westheimer became the first superstar sex therapist. Among the pioneer contributors in the field of economics were the Nobel Prize winners Kenneth J. Arrow, Milton Friedman, Lawrence Klein, Franco Modigliani, and Paul Samuelson.*

# PIONEERING CONTRIBUTIONS TO EQUILIBRIUM AND WELFARE THEORIES
## Kenneth J. Arrow

☙

*Kenneth Joseph Arrow was born in New York City on August 23, 1921. He earned his Ph.D. at Columbia University (1951) and taught at Stanford University (1949–68), Harvard University (1968–79), and Stanford again (1979–91).*

KENNETH J. ARROW, AN ECONOMIST, won the 1972 Nobel Prize in economics for his "pioneering contributions to general economic equilibrium theory and welfare theory." He shared the award with John R. Hicks, who did separate but related work.

Arrow was concerned about not only basic economic issues but also urgent social problems. He wanted to understand how a balance (equilibrium) is struck between the amounts of goods and services that some individuals want to supply and the amounts that others want to buy. His great gift was his ability to apply deep theoretical economic insights, as well as advanced mathematics, to matters of social and political relevance (such as welfare). Arrow's most striking thesis is his "impossibility theorem" (or "Arrow's theorem"), which holds that under certain conditions, it is impossible to guarantee that a ranking of societal preferences will correspond with rankings of individual preferences when more than two individuals and alternative choices are involved.

Among his major works are *Social Choice and Individual Values* (1951) and *Essays in the Theory of Risk Bearing* (1971). Arrow's important work in combining economic issues and social problems earned him his Nobel Prize.

---

### ALSO NOTEWORTHY

▲ **ADLER, ALFRED** (born February 7, 1870, in Penzing, Austria; died May 28, 1937, in Aberdeen, Aberdeenshire, Scotland). Psychiatrist who introduced the concept and treatment of inferiority feelings.

▲ **ADORNO, THEODOR W(IESENGRUND)** (originally Theodor Wiesengrund; born September 11, 1903, in Frankfurt am Main, Germany; died August 6, 1969, in Visp, Switzerland). Philosopher, sociologist, and musicologist who was the first to name and analyze the "culture industry."

**HANNAH ARENDT**

▲ **ARENDT, HANNAH** (born October 14, 1906, in Hannover, Germany; died December 4, 1975, in New York City). Philosopher and political scientist whose monumental book *Origins of Totalitarianism* (1951) relates the development of totalitarianism to nineteenth-century anti-Semitism and imperialism. *Photo credit:* American Jewish Archives, Cincinnati Campus, Hebrew Union College, Jewish Institute of Religion.

# FORMULATION OF PROCESS PHILOSOPHY
## Henri Bergson

❧

HENRI BERGSON, A PHILOSOPHER, WON THE 1927 NOBEL PRIZE in literature "in recognition of his rich and vitalizing ideas and the brilliant skill with which they are presented." He was the first to elaborate what came to be called process philosophy, which rejected static values in favor of values of motion, change, and evolution.

The crucial period in Bergon's development was the late 1880s. "I had remained up to that time," he explained, "wholly imbued with mechanistic theories....It was the analysis of the notion of time, as that enters into mechanics and physics, which overturned all my ideas. I saw, to my great astonishment, that scientific time does not *endure*."

His best-known work is *Creative Evolution* (French, 1907; English, 1911). It states that ultimate reality is a vital impulse *(élan vital)*, or spiritual force. Matter results from the decline of this vital energy. Mechanism and determinacy are opposed to intuition and liberty. Evolution is not just mechanical adaptation of organisms to the physical environment; it is a purposeful and creative process.

> *Henri-Louis Bergson was born in Paris, France, on October 18, 1859. After earning his doctorate at the University of Paris (1889), he worked as a teacher, notably at the Collège de France (1900–1914, formally retiring in 1921). In his later years, he headed diplomatic missions. He died in Paris on January 4, 1941.*

Bergson did not found a school of philosophy, but he exerted profound influences in philosophy, politics, and literature. His process philosophy affected William James, George Santayana, Alfred North Whitehead, and others.

# CREATION OF THE I–THOU CONCEPT
## Martin Buber

✑

MARTIN BUBER HELD A POSITION OF HIGH ESTEEM in both Jewish and non-Jewish communities as a religious philosopher, biblical translator and interpreter, and German literary stylist. His best-known achievement is his concept of I–Thou.

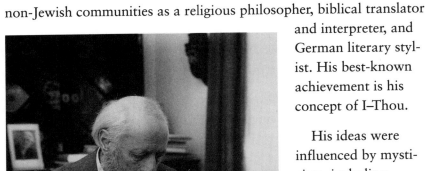

State of Israel Government Press Office

His ideas were influenced by mysticism, including Hasidism, as well as by Nietzsche and Kierkegaard. Buber's philosophy centers on the encounter, or dialogue, of the individual human with other beings, relationships that ultimately rest on and point to the relationship with God. His fullest expression of this idea is in his book *Ich und Du* (1923; as *I and Thou*, 1958).

In that book, Buber distinguishes between relationships that reflect an I–Thou attitude of personal engagement, or dialogic experience, and those that reflect an I-It attitude of detachment in which the experience is mediated by the intellect. The I–Thou experience is the more meaningful. A true relationship with God, as experienced from the human side, must be an I–Thou relationship, in which God is truly met and addressed, not merely thought of and expressed. God, the great Thou, also enables I–Thou relations between the individual human and other beings. The usual I–It relationship between humans is based on perceiving one another as mere objects of thought, with only a fraction of one's being, but the I–Thou relationship between humans is based on a personal engagement with the fullness of one's being.

Buber's I–Thou concept has proven to be one of the most distinctive and enduring ideas of the twentieth century, and it has influ-

# FOUNDING CHILD ANALYSIS
## Anna Freud

ev

ANNA FREUD WAS THE FIRST MAJOR PROPONENT of the systematic study of the emotional and mental life of the child. She was the founder of child psychoanalysis.

Her father was Sigmund Freud, the founder of psychoanalysis. She had little formal education, but she studied her father's teachings and in 1923 began to practice psychotherapy. In 1938 she and her father fled the Nazis and arrived in England. There she worked for several years as a children's analyst at a nursery, concentrating on children who had been separated from their families by World War II. In 1947 she founded the Hampstead Child Therapy Clinic and Course, where she treated mentally ill children and trained workers in child therapy.

Anna Freud viewed play as the child's adaptation to reality but not necessarily as a revelation of unconscious conflicts. She worked closely with parents and believed that analysis should have an educational influence on the child. She summarized her theories in the book *Normality and Pathology in Childhood* (1965).

Anna Freud performed a revolutionary function in the psychology of children, just as her father had in the psychology of adults.

> *Anna Freud was born in Vienna, Austria, on December 3, 1895. In her forties she immigrated to England. She died in London on October 9, 1982.*

Courtesy of *The Jewish Chronicle*

---

### ALSO NOTEWORTHY

▲ **BOAS, FRANZ** (born July 9, 1858, in Minden, Westphalia, Germany; died December 21, 1942, in New York City). The father of American anthropology.

▲ **BREUER, JOSEF** (born January 15, 1842, in Vienna, Austria; died June 20, 1925, in Vienna). Physician and physiologist whose work in treating hysteria made him, according to Sigmund Freud himself, the principal forerunner of psychoanalysis.

# FOUNDING PSYCHOANALYSIS
## Sigmund Freud

❦

*Sigmund Freud was born in Freiburg, Moravia, on May 6, 1856. His original name was Sigismund Solomon Freud; at the age of seventeen, he changed the spelling of his first name. After taking his M.D. at the University of Vienna (1881), he worked as a physician. From 1902 to 1938 he taught at the University of Vienna. In 1938 he fled the Nazis and moved to England. He died in London on September 23, 1939.*

SIGMUND FREUD WAS THE FOUNDER OF PSYCHOANALYSIS, a school of psychology embodying revolutionary and controversial views of human behavior.

Early in his career, he specialized in neurology, the study and treatment of disorders of the nervous system. The turning point in his career came in 1885, when he went to Paris to study with Jean-Martin Charcot, who treated hysterics (patients whose mental illness caused them to think they were blind or paralyzed even though they had no physical defects). Charcot introduced Freud to the possibility that mental disorders might be caused by purely psychological factors rather than by organic brain disease.

In 1886 he returned to Vienna and began to work with hysterics. Gradually he developed theories about the origin and treatment of mental illness. He coined the term *psychoanalysis* for both his theories and his treatment. By 1910 he had attained international recognition.

Freud established the theory that unconscious motives control much human behavior. He used the term *defense mechanisms* for the methods that people use to block painful childhood memories from conscious awareness. When a person ties up too much energy in defense mechanisms, the person develops an illness that Freud called a *neurosis*. He believed that sexual functioning begins at birth. If the normal development from infant sexuality to adult sexuality is interrupted, the person will become *fixated* on sex at an early, immature stage.

The mind, according to Freud, has three parts. The *id* is the mental representation of biological instincts. The *ego* mediates between the person and outside reality. The *superego* governs moral behavior.

---

### ALSO NOTEWORTHY

▲ CHOMSKY, NOAM (full name, Avram Noam Chomsky; born December 7, 1928, in Philadelphia, Pennsylvania). Linguist who was the foremost proponent of generative transformational grammar.

▲ DAWIDOWICZ, LUCY (originally Lucy Schildkret; born June 16, 1915, in New York City; died December 5, 1990, in New York City). Historian who wrote *The War against the Jews, 1933–1945* (1975), widely regarded as the most thoroughly researched book on the Holocaust. She married Szymon M. Dawidowicz in 1948.

LUCY DAWIDOWICZ

Helayne Seidman

# FOUNDING PSYCHOANALYSIS (continued)

Freud's treatment depended on a technique that he called *free association,* a patient's freely speaking about whatever comes to mind. Freud would analyze these thoughts and, if necessary, the patient's dreams, to find the earlier experiences that contributed to the patient's neurosis.

His theories affected nearly every field. In psychology and psychiatry, his ideas influenced the diagnoses and treatments of patients. Educators and child-rearing experts, influenced by his theory that neuroses are caused by repressing unpleasant memories, formulated systems that were less restrictive than previously. Even art and literature felt his influence, as in the surrealist movement, marked by the expression of dreamlike states of mind and presented without conscious control. Because of the widespread adoption of, and reaction against, his theories, Freud was one of the most influential thinkers of the twentieth century.

Austrian Press and Information Service, Washington, D.C.

---

## ALSO NOTEWORTHY

▲ **FLEXNER, ABRAHAM** (born November 13, 1866, in Louisville, Kentucky; died September 21, 1959, in Falls Church, Virginia). Educator who stimulated reforms in American secondary education, colleges and universities, and medical schools, and who founded the Institute for Advanced Study at Princeton, New Jersey (which he directed, 1930–39).

▲ **GUMPLOWICZ, LUDWIG** (in Polish, Ludwik Gumplowicz; born March 9, 1838, in Kraków, Republic of Kraków; died August 19 or 20, 1909, in Graz, Austria). Sociologist who influenced many modern social and political thinkers through his disbelief in the permanence of social progress and through his theory that the state originates in conflict rather than in cooperation or divine inspiration.

▲ **HUSSERL, EDMUND** (born April 8, 1859, in Prossnitz, Moravia; died April 1938 in Freiburg, Germany). The founder of phenomenology, a method by which philosophy attempts to gain the character of a science.

# BECOMING THE LEADING VOICE OF CONSERVATIVE ECONOMICS

## Milton Friedman

ево

*Milton Friedman was born in Brooklyn, New York, on July 31, 1912. He earned a Ph.D. at Columbia University (1946) and taught at the University of Chicago (1946–82).*

MILTON FRIEDMAN, AN ECONOMIST, won the 1976 Nobel Prize in economics for "his achievements in the fields of consumption analysis and monetary history and theory, and for his demonstration of the complexity of stabilization policy."

In the second half of the twentieth century, Friedman was one of the most important spokesmen for the old-fashioned monetarist, or "quantity," school of economics, which holds that the dominant fac-

tor in the shaping of economic events is the amount of money in circulation. This view opposes the modern philosophy that the determining factor in combating recession and inflation is a government's fiscal policy (such as taxes and spending).

One of his principal works is *Capitalism and Freedom* (with his wife, Rose D. Friedman, 1962), in which he advocates the "negative income tax," a way of using the tax system to provide a guaranteed income that would replace the existing social welfare services. Another important book is *A Monetary History of the United States, 1867–1960* (1963). Through these and other works, Friedman became the leading conservative economist of his time.

# DEVELOPMENT OF LINEAR PROGRAMMING
## Leonid Kantorovich

ↅↄ

LEONID KANTOROVICH, AN ECONOMIST, SHARED THE 1975 NOBEL PRIZE in economics with Tjalling C. Koopmans "for their contributions to the theory of optimum allocation of resources." Kantorovich was honored for pioneering the method of linear programming, later independently explored by Koopmans.

Kantorovich was eager to apply his mathematical skills for the betterment of the Soviet economy. In 1938 he was assigned the task of devising techniques for distributing raw materials more efficiently. By 1939 he had developed linear programming, a mathematical method for solving practical problems where the variables are subject to constraints. His emphasis on the decentralization of decision making and his other nondogmatic critical analyses of the Soviet economy clashed with the views of his orthodox Marxist colleagues, so that his ideas were not accepted in the Soviet Union till after 1953, when the Soviet dictator Stalin died and slightly more freedom of thought began to be allowed. But elsewhere his linear programming was widely praised and utilized.

*Leonid Vitalyevich Kantorovich was born in Saint Petersburg, Russia, on January 19, 1912. After earning a degree in mathematics from the Leningrad State University (1930), he taught there for many years (1934–60). He died in Moscow, the Soviet Union, on April 7, 1986.*

---

### ALSO NOTEWORTHY

▲ KLEIN, MELANIE (born March 30, 1882, in Vienna, Austria; died September 22, 1960, in London, England). Psychoanalyst who showed that children's play is a meaningful product of a rich fantasy life.

▲ LEWIN, KURT (born September 9, 1890, in Mogilno, Prussia, Germany; died February 12, 1947, in Newtonville, Massachusetts). Psychologist who developed the field theory of behavior, which holds that human behavior is a function of an individual's psychological environment.

▲ LOEB, SOPHIE (originally Sophie Irene Simon; born July 4, 1876, in Rovno, Russia; died January 18, 1929, in New York City). Social worker who was responsible for much of the welfare legislation passed in New York State during the early twentieth century. She helped found the Child Welfare Committee of America and was named its first president (1924).

▲ MARCUSE, HERBERT (born July 19, 1898, in Berlin, Germany; died July 29, 1979, in Starnberg, West Germany). Political philosopher whose Marxist-Freudian works greatly influenced the New Left in the 1960s.

▲ MORGENTHAU, HANS J(OACHIM) (born February 17, 1904, in Coburg, Germany; died July 19, 1980, in New York City). Political scientist and historian who was the leading analyst of modern power politics.

# CREATION OF ECONOMIC MODELS
## Lawrence Klein

cx/cs

*Lawrence Robert Klein was born in Omaha, Nebraska, on September 14, 1920. He earned a Ph.D. at the Massachusetts Institute of Technology (1944), and in 1958 he began a long association with the University of Pennsylvania.*

LAWRENCE KLEIN, AN ECONOMIST, won the 1980 Nobel Prize in economics "for the creation of economic models and their application to the analysis of economic fluctuations and economic policies."

Klein developed a series of increasingly detailed models of economic activity. His Wharton models were widely used to forecast exports, consumption, investment, and gross national product. His Link project incorporated data from a variety of countries to forecast economic fluctuations and to test the effects of proposed changes in national policies.

## ALSO NOTEWORTHY

▲ MOSKOWITZ, BELLE LINDNER ISRAELS (originally Belle Lindner; born October 5, 1877, in New York City; died January 2, 1933, in New York City). Social reformer who, especially through her friendship with Governor Alfred E. Smith of New York, became the most powerful and influential woman in the United States, promoting social welfare programs and helping to dole out political jobs. She married Charles Henry Israels in 1903 and Henry Moskowitz in 1914. *Photo credit:* American Jewish Archives, Cincinnati Campus, Hebrew Union College, Jewish Institute of Religion.

BELLE MOSKOWITZ

▲ RAND, AYN (originally Alissa [Alice] Rosenbaum; born February 2, 1905, in Saint Petersburg, Russia; died March 6, 1982, in New York City). Writer famed for her espousal of objectivism, an ethic of "rational self-interest." Best known for her novels, especially *The Fountainhead* (1943), she also wrote nonfiction and edited the journal *The Objectivist* (1962–71).

▲ RANK, OTTO (originally Otto Rosenfeld; born April 22, 1884, in Vienna, Austria; died October 31, 1939, in New York City). Psychoanalyst who broke new ground by suggesting that the basis of all neuroses is the separation of the child from the mother at birth, and by extending psychoanalytic theory to the study of myth, art, and creativity.

# BIRTH OF NATIONAL INCOME ACCOUNTING
## Simon Kuznets

ℰℐ

SIMON KUZNETS, AN ECONOMIST, won the 1971 Nobel Prize in economics for "his empirically found interpretation of economic growth, which has led to new and deepened insight into the economic and social structure and process of development." He was especially noted for creating the basic framework that led to national income accounting.

When the Great Depression began in 1929, people had a hard time understanding what was wrong; there were few facts available on the economic structure of the nation. Kuznets decided to do something that he felt was long overdue: to turn economics from an ideology into a science. He developed ways of applying statistical methods sources and uses of a nation's annual product, basing on figures going back as far as the mid-1800s, ses of population changes, technology, industrial marketing. He also described cyclical variations in now called "Kuznets cycles").

led to the process called national income accounting, h is calculated the gross national product (GNP). Kuznets has been called the Father of the GNP.

*Simon Kuznets was born in Kharkov, Ukraine, on April 30, 1901. He immigrated to the United States in 1922. His father, who had come fifteen years earlier, had changed his surname to Smith, which Simon took only as a middle name. After earning a Ph.D. at Columbia University (1926), Kuznets served on the staff at the National Bureau of Economic Research (1927–60) and taught at several institutions, including the University of Pennsylvania (1930–54) and Harvard University (1960–71). He died in Cambridge, Massachusetts, on July 8, 1985.*

---

### ALSO NOTEWORTHY

▲ ROSTOW, WALT WHITMAN (born October 7, in 1916, in New York City). Economist whose book *The Stages of Economic Growth: A Non-Communist Manifesto* (1960) provided the ideological basis for United States foreign policy toward underdeveloped nations in the 1960s. The book contained the phrase "new peaceful frontiers," which became John F. Kennedy's New Frontier campaign and presidential slogan.

▲ SAKEL, MANFRED J(OSHUA) (born June 6, 1900, in Nadvorna, Austria-Hungary; died December 2, 1957, in New York City). Psychiatrist and neurophysiologist who introduced insulin-shock therapy for schizophrenia.

# FOUNDING MARXISM
## Karl Marx

જી

*Karl Heinrich Marx was born in Trier, Rhine Province, Prussia. He earned a docorate in philosophy at the University of Jena (1841), worked as a journalist, was expelled from his homeland, and in 1849 settled in England, where he lived in poverty as a writer. He died in London, England, on March 14, 1883.*

KARL MARX WAS A POLITICAL THEORIST, SOCIOLOGIST, AND ECONOMIST. His unique achievement was to found the revolutionary political and sociological doctrine that came to be known as Marxism.

Early in his career, he was influenced in his radical leanings by his journalist colleague Moses Hess, a socialist. With Friedrich Engels, Marx wrote *The Communist Manifesto* (1848) to serve as the platform of the Communist League; it was a fiery summation of communist beliefs. Marx's major work was *Das Kapital* ("Capital"; volume 1, published 1867; volumes 2 and 3 published posthumously). In it, Marx analyzed the economics of capitalism, elaborated his labor theory of value, and predicted that capitalistic surplus value and exploitation would ultimately lead to a falling rate of profit and a collapse of capitalism.

Marxism—Marx's views and their elaboration by others—greatly influenced all the social sciences in capitalistic societies. And in Russia, China, and many Third World countries, twentieth-century revolutions set up Marxist-influenced states.

---

### ALSO NOTEWORTHY

▲ SUKENIK, ELIEZER LIPA (born August 12, 1889, in Białystok, Russian-ruled Poland; died February 28, 1953, in Jerusalem, Israel). Archeologist who identified the antiquity of the Dead Sea Scrolls.

▲ TROTSKY, LEON (originally Lev Davidovich Bronstein [or Bronshtein]; born November 7, 1879, in Yanovka, Ukraine; died August 20, 1940, in Coyoacán, near Mexico City, Mexico). Communist theorist who was a leader in Russia's October Revolution in 1917 and the head of the anti-Stalinist opposition till he was assassinated.

▲ TUCHMAN, BARBARA (originally Barbara Wertheim; born January 30, 1912, in New York City; died February 6, 1989, in Greenwich, Connecticut). One of the foremost writers of popularized historical scholarship, such as *Stilwell and the American Experiment in China, 1911–1945* (1971). Married to Lester R. Tuchman in 1940.

# SYMBOLIZING THE HASKALAH
## Moses Mendelssohn

ॐ

MOSES MENDELSSOHN, A PHILOSOPHER, GREATLY CONTRIBUTED to the emancipation and assimilation of Jews in Europe. He was the leading voice of the Haskalah (Jewish Enlightenment).

In his *Phaedo; or, On the Immortality of the Soul* (1767), Mendelssohn defended the idea of immortality against the prevalent mechanistic philosophy. In *Jerusalem; or, On Religious Power and Judaism* (1783), he asserted that there was no essential conflict between the truths of religion and reason. The essence of his philosophy was the belief in freedom of thought for all people—Jews, non-Jews, religious, nonreligious.

Through his own example, Mendelssohn showed that it was possible to combine Judaism with the rationality of the Enlightenment. He became the principal representative of the Jewish adaptation of the Enlightenment, the Haskalah, which helped bring Jews into the mainstream of European culture. Through

*Moses Mendelssohn was born in Dessau, Germany, on September 26, 1729. His father's name was Menachem Mendel Dessau; Moses took the surname Mendelssohn as the German form of the Hebrew ben Mendel ("son of Mendel"). He moved to Berlin in 1743, engaged in secular studies to balance his earlier religious education, entered the silk business, and began to write. He died in Berlin, Germany, on January 4, 1786.*

the prestige of his intellectual accomplishments, Mendelssohn did much to further the emancipation of Jews from social, cultural, political, and economic restrictions in Europe, especially Germany. One of the beneficiaries of his legacy was his grandson Felix Mendelssohn, the musician.

# BREAKTHROUGH ANALYSES IN THE ECONOMICS OF SAVERS AND FINANCIAL MARKETS
## Franco Modigliani

*Franco Modigliani was born in Rome, Italy, on June 18, 1918. In 1939 he earned a law degree at the University of Rome and immigrated to the United States. Curious about the causes and effects of the Great Depression, he turned to economics and took a doctorate in social science at the New School for Social Research (1944). Later he taught at several American institutions, notably, beginning in 1962, the Massachusetts Institute of Technology.*

FRANCO MODIGLIANI, AN ECONOMIST, won the 1985 Nobel Prize in economics "for his analysis of the behavior of household savers...and for his work on the relationship of a company's financial structure to the value placed on its stock by investors."

In his analysis of personal savings, he developed the life cycle theory, which holds that individuals build up a store of wealth in their work years for the purpose of spending in old age, not for passing on to descendants. In his research in financial markets, he found that the market value of a company's stock depended mostly on investors' expectations of what that company would earn in the future.

Modigliani's work had widespread practical applications. His analysis of savers' habits helped predict the effects of various pension plans. And the technique he developed to calculate the value of a company's expected future earnings became a basic tool in corporate decision making.

### ALSO NOTEWORTHY

▲ WECHSLER, DAVID (born January 12, 1896, in Lespedi, Romania; died May 2, 1981, in New York City). Psychologist who invented widely used intelligence tests for adults and children.

▲ WERTHEIMER, MAX (born April 15, 1880, in Prague, Bohemia; died October 12, 1943, in New Rochelle, New York). Cofounder of Gestalt psychology, which attempts to examine psychological phenomena as structural wholes, rather than by breaking them down into components.

# ESTABLISHING THE SCIENCE OF ECONOMICS
## Paul Samuelson

ᘒ

PAUL SAMUELSON, AN ECONOMIST, WON THE 1970 NOBEL PRIZE in economics "for the scientific work through which he has developed static and dynamic economic theory and actively contributed to raising the level of analysis in economic science."

Early in his career, Samuelson found the traditional language of economics painfully imprecise. His great achievement was to bring order to economic thinking by applying mathematical principles. Using mathematical formulations, he contributed to many areas of economic theory, including consumer behavior, capital and interest, international trade, public finance, welfare economics, and fiscal and monetary policy. *Foundations of Economic Analysis* (1947), his first important work, revealed many of his basic ideas, while *Economics: An Introductory Analysis* (1948) became a classic college textbook.

For his role in making the field of economics more scientific, Samuelson earned a unique place in the history of the social sciences.

*Paul Anthony Samuelson was born in Gary, Indiana, on May 15, 1915. He earned his Ph.D. at Harvard University (1941), taught at the Massachusetts Institute of Technology (1940–65), and often served as a government advisor.*

---

### ALSO NOTEWORTHY

▲ ZAMENHOF, LUDWIK LEJZER (born December 15, 1859, in Białystok, Russian-ruled Poland; died April 14, 1917, in Warsaw, Poland). Creator of the most important of the international artifical languages—Esperanto.

▲ ZUNZ, LEOPOLD (Hebrew name, Yom-Tob Lippmann; born August 10, 1794, in Detmold, Lippe; died March 18, 1886, in Berlin, Germany). Historian of Jewish literature, widely regarded as the greatest Jewish scholar of the nineteenth century. He began the movement called Science of Judaism, which focused on the analysis of Jewish literature and culture with the tools of modern scholarship.

# Symbolizing the Philosophy of Rationalism

## Benedict de Spinoza

ও

*Benedict de Spinoza was born in Amsterdam, Netherlands, on November 24, 1632. His first name is also recorded, in Hebrew, as Baruch, and, in Latin, as Bendictus; the Portuguese form of his full name is Bento de Espinosa (he was of Portuguese descent). He earned a living grinding lenses for use in optical instruments. In 1656 he was excommunicated by the Jewish authorities in Amsterdam because of his unorthodox views. He maintained, for example, that there is nothing in the Bible to support the view that God has no body, that angels exist, and that the soul is immortal. By 1663 he had settled near The Hague, Netherlands. He died in The Hague on February 21, 1677.*

BENEDICT DE SPINOZA WAS THE FOREMOST PHILOSOPHER of seventeenth-century rationalism. His greatest achievement was his *Ethics Demonstrated in the Geometrical Manner* (completed 1675, published 1677).

Spinoza, more than any other major philosopher, wrote works based not on his experiences but on his thoughts, not on his life but on the pure pursuit of truth and clarity. His writings are marked by objectivity and impersonality. As a Jew, he had few ties with his Dutch neighbors; but as an excommunicated Jew, he also had few ties with his Jewish neighbors. In 1673 he refused an offer to teach philosophy at the university in Heidelberg because he feared the position would cost him his independence and peace of mind. His philosophy was purely rational, unattached to a group of people, to a school of thought—even to himself.

In his *Theological–Political Treatise* (published 1670), he called for freedom of thought and speech. He exemplified this freedom in his own objective criticism of the Bible, summarizing that the Bible is suitable for moral guidance but not for philosophy or scientific truth.

In his *Ethics*, he investigated the nature, sources, and obstacles of a good life for a human being. The work is "geometric" in structure: it begins with axioms, postulates, and propositions and their corollaries, and then proceeds to conclusions. The good life, he maintained, consists of liberating oneself from self-absorbed passions by engaging in the intellectual life, through which one partakes of divine, eternal nature and frees oneself from the limitations of duration.

Spinoza has been called "the philosopher's philosopher" because of his rationalistic emphasis. He did not found a school of philosophy, but he has had a profound influence on the intellectual history of the Western world.

# CREATION OF PUBLIC HEALTH NURSING
## Lillian D. Wald

~

LILLIAN D. WALD CREATED THE MODERN SYSTEM of public health nursing.

In 1893 a child asked Wald to care for the child's sick mother in the poverty-stricken tenements of the Lower East Side of New York City. Wald was horrified at the unsanitary conditions and lack of nursing services in the tenements. With backing from wealthy sponsors, she and another nurse, Mary Brewster, moved into the tenements and set up the Nurses' Settlement, the first visiting nurse program in the United States not affiliated with a religious group, and the first nonsectarian public health nursing system in the world. Wald, in fact, coined the term *public health nursing*. She would visit patients at their homes and also receive patients at her own quarters.

Courtesy of the Library of Congress

*Lillian D. Wald was born to wealthy parents in Cincinnati, Ohio, on March 10, 1867. Her middle initial did not stand for a name. The early death of one of her siblings and the serious illness of another impressed on Lillian the need for good health care. In 1891 she graduated from the Bellevue School of Nursing in New York City and later became a pioneer in the field of public health care. She died in Westport, Connecticut, on September 1, 1940.*

Soon the nursing staff grew, and they moved into a house on Henry Street. The program enlarged its scope to become a full-fledged settlement house in addition to a nursing service. It became famous as the Henry Street Settlement, and Wald became the Angel of Henry Street.

In 1902 she organized in New York City the first city school nurse service in the world. She went on to initiate a wide range of other health and social services.

Wald's public health nursing system, as originally set up in New York City and as imitated in many communities around the world, has saved immeasurable suffering and countless lives.

# MASS MARKETING OF SEX COUNSELING
## Ruth Westheimer

cs

*Ruth Westheimer was born in Frankfurt am Main, Germany, on June 4, 1928. Her original name was Karola Ruth Siegel. Her parents died in the Holocaust, while she spent the war years in a Swiss school that became an orphanage. Having learned about sex from reading her father's books, she taught the other girls about menstruation. After the war, she moved to Palestine and became a kindergarten teacher. During that time, she dropped her original first name. In the early 1950s she earned a psychology degree at the Sorbonne in Paris. Later in the decade, she moved to the United States, and in 1961 she married Manfred Westheimer, a telecommunications consultant. In 1967 she became the project director of a planned parenthood clinic in Harlem. In 1970 she earned a Ph.D. in family counseling at Columbia University.*

Gideon Lewin

RUTH WESTHEIMER WAS THE FIRST TO USE MODERN MEDIA to gain a huge audience for sex counseling.

After teaching sex counseling at Lehman College and Brooklyn College, she convinced some New York City radio broadcasters of the need for sex education programming. She appeared as a guest on some shows, and in 1980 she was given her own series, *Sexually Speaking*, a fifteen-minute weekly program. Later it grew into a one-hour live phone-in show. She became the popular "Dr. Ruth."

In 1984 she began a national cable-television series, *Good Sex with Dr. Westheimer*, later called *The Dr. Ruth Show*. Another cable-television program was *Dr. Ruth's Never Too Late*. She also guests on many other TV shows and maintains a private practice as a psychologist and family counselor. "Part of my being able to talk about issues of sexuality has to do with my being so Jewish," she explains. "Because for us Jews there's never been a question of sex being a sin, but of sex being a *mitzvah* and an obligation."

Through her radio and TV appearances, Westheimer has become the world's first superstar sex therapist.

# 8

# TECHNOLOGY

*❧*

*JEWS HAVE PROFOUNDLY AFFECTED THE COURSE OF MODERN TECHNOLOGY.*
*Jewish technologists produced pioneering achievements in aviation,*
*industrial design, architectural style, and other fields.*

*Emile Berliner, for example, invented a transmitter that*
*vastly improved Alexander Graham Bell's telephone. Berliner also*
*developed the first flat-disc gramophone, a great advancement over*
*Thomas Edison's cylinder recording machine. The telephone and record*
*industries owe their present forms principally to Berliner.*

*Dennis Gabor won a Nobel Prize in physics for inventing holography,*
*the process of making a three-dimensional picture on a photographic film*
*or plate without the use of a camera. His invention has been applied*
*to the technology of many fields, including medicine.*

*Judith Resnik was an engineer who became the first Jewish astronaut.*
*She died in the 1986 Challenger space shuttle disaster.*

# FOUNDING THE MODERN TELEPHONE AND RECORD INDUSTRIES

## Emile Berliner

❧

American Jewish Archives, Cincinnati Campus, Hebrew Union College, Jewish Institute of Religion

*Emile (or Emil) Berliner was born in Hannover, Germany, on May 20, 1851. He immigrated to the United States in 1870 and took a series of odd jobs, including one as an assistant in a chemical lab, where he began to learn scientific techniques. A friend gave him a book on physics, and Berliner, fascinated by the chapters on acoustics and electricity, followed up on this interest by taking some classes at the Cooper Institute in New York City. Largely self-taught, Berliner became one of America's most important inventors. He died in Washington, D.C., on August 3, 1929.*

STRICTLY SPEAKING, EMILE BERLINER DID NOT invent the telephone or the phonograph. But his early fundamental improvements of those inventions laid the groundwork for their modern development far more profoundly than did the work of their generally recognized inventors, Alexander Graham Bell and Thomas Edison respectively.

In 1876 Bell invented his telephone. The very next year, Berliner patented an improved telephone transmitter. In 1878 Bell Telephone Company itself bought his invention, and he became an inspector for the company. During the rest of his life, he continued to invent. In 1887 he patented a gramophone that played a flat-disc record; this invention was purchased by the Victor Talking Machine Company (which later developed into RCA). In 1908 he designed the first lightweight radial engine for airplanes, later widely imitated, and from 1919 to 1926 he built some of the earliest helicopters. In 1925 he developed acoustic tiles for soundproofing.

Berliner's 1877 telephone invention was a major breakthrough. Bell's original magnetic induction technique produced a weak sound and depended on the same instrument for both talking and listening. Berliner's carbon microphone transmitter, however, carried the voice farther and more clearly, and it introduced the idea of separate parts for sending and receiving. His transmitter eventually led to the development of the modern microphone.

Berliner's 1887 gramophone completely revolutionized the way recordings were made. Edison made phonograph recordings on cylinders over which a stylus moved vertically; gravity caused distortions in the sound. Berliner's gramophone played flat discs across which the stylus moved horizontally, so that distortions were minimized. Moreover, Edison saw the instrument as merely an office tool, while Berliner envisioned its possibilities in mass entertainment and set up the first commercial recording studio (1897).

Through his microphone and his gramophone disc, the bases of the modern telephone transmitter and phonograph record, Berliner can truly be called the father of the modern telephone and record industries.

# INVENTION OF HOLOGRAPHY
## Dennis Gabor

❧

DENNIS GABOR, AN ELECTRICAL ENGINEER, won the 1971 Nobel Prize in physics "for his invention and the development of the holographic method."

Gabor had been interested in optics ever since he was a teenager, when he became fascinated by the way an image of an object could be trapped by a photographic plate. In 1947 he was trying to find a way to improve the electron microscope, which has imaging defects that limit its resolution. The answer came to him while he was watching a tennis match: "I put the problem into my own consciousness, and it came out of my unconsciousness when I was sitting on a bench in a tennis court."

His idea was to "take a bad electron picture, but one which contains the whole information, and correct it by optical means," that is, to use light to magnify and read the picture. The result would be a lensless system of three-dimensional photography. He developed the idea on a theoretical basis in 1947, but conventional light sources were inadequate to put his theory to the test. Finally, in 1965 the laser was invented, and it became the ideal light source for the purpose. He named the three-dimensional picture a *hologram* (Greek, "completely written").

Gabor's holography was probably the most important development in optical science in the twentieth century. It soon had practical applications in industry (diagnosing faults in equipment), communications (information storage), and medicine (medical imaging).

*Dennis Gabor was born in Budapest, Hungary, on June 5, 1900. His original name was Dénes Gábor. He earned a doctorate in electrical engineering at the Berlin Technical University (1927) and worked as a research engineer in Berlin till the rise of the Nazis in 1933. After being a research engineer in England during the rest of the 1930s and most of the 1940s, he moved to Canada, where he taught at the Imperial College of Science and Technology (1949–67). He died in London, England, on February 8, 1979.*

## ALSO NOTEWORTHY

▲ ADLER, DANKMAR (born July 3, 1844, in Stadtlengsfeld, Prussia; died April 16, 1900, in Chicago, Illinois). Architect and engineer who, in partnership with Louis Sullivan, created a new architectural style that found its fullest expression in the steel-framed skyscraper.

▲ DREYFUSS, HENRY (born March 2, 1904, in New York City; died October 5, 1972, in South Pasadena, California). One of the pioneer industrial designers, noted for the number and variety of his designs.

# BECOMING THE FIRST JEWISH ASTRONAUT
## Judith Resnik

e⋑

*Judith Arlene Resnik was born in Cleveland, Ohio, on April 5, 1949, and grew up in Akron, Ohio. She earned a doctorate in electrical engineering at the University of Maryland (1977) and worked as an engineer at Xerox Corporation (1977–78). In 1978 she became an astronaut. She died during a space mission on January 28, 1986.*

JUDITH RESNIK WAS THE SECOND AMERICAN WOMAN IN SPACE (the first was Sally Ride in 1983) and the first Jewish astronaut.

After finishing her education, she went to work as an engineer. But her ambition went far beyond ordinary engineering jobs. She wanted "to learn a lot about quite a number of different technologies," she said, "to be able to use them somehow, to do something that required a concerted team effort and, finally, a great individual effort."

In March 1978 she was chosen as one of six women in a group of thirty-five people selected by the National Aeronautics and Space Administration (NASA) to become astronauts. In 1984 she went into space for the first time, participating in a shuttle flight on the Discovery. Her tasks were to operate a remote-control arm and perform solar power experiments. By early 1986 she had spent over 144 hours in space. On January 28, 1986, Resnik was aboard the American space shuttle Challenger. One of her assignments was to deploy and retrieve a satellite for observing Halley's Comet. But the ship exploded moments after it lifted off at Cape Canaveral, Florida. All seven astronauts, including Resnik, were killed.

NASA

Later a crater on Venus and an asteroid were named in her honor. Resnik, the first Jewish astronaut, personified the spirit of the space program. "I want," she said, "to do everything there is to be done."

---

### ALSO NOTEWORTHY

▲ GODOWSKY, LEOPOLD, JR. (born May 27, 1900, in Chicago, Illinois). Photographic technician and musician who codeveloped (with Leopold Mannes, born of a Jewish father—the musician David Mannes—and non-Jewish mother) the Kodachrome process used in color photography (1935). Son of the musician Leopold Godowsky.

Courtesy of Arthur Kantrowitz

**ARTHUR KANTROWITZ**

▲ **KANTROWITZ, ARTHUR ROBERT** (born October 20, 1913, in New York City). Physicist who designed a missile nose cone that could withstand the intense heat of reentry from space.

▲ **KAHN, ALBERT** (born March 21, 1869, in Rhaunen, Westphalia; died December 8, 1942, in Detroit, Michigan). Pioneering industrial architect known as the father of modern factory design.

▲ **KAHN, LOUIS I(SADORE)** (born February 20, 1901, in Osel, Estonia, Russian Empire; died March 17, 1974, in New York City). Architect whose buildings, characterized by massive forms, broke with the prevailing international style of his time.

**LOUIS I. KAHN**

▲ **SCHWARZ, DAVID** (born 1845 in Kesthely, Hungary; died January 13, 1897, in Vienna, Austria). Airship inventor who, in the early 1890s, built balloon-covered aluminum-framework airships, the first rigid dirigibles.

▲ **VON KÁRMÁN, THEODORE** (originally Todor von Sköllöskislaki Kármán; born May 11, 1881, in Budapest, Hungary; died May 6, 1963, in Aachen, Germany). Research engineer known as the father of supersonic flight. He pioneered the use of applied mathematics in aeronautics and astronautics; designed aircraft, rockets, and missiles; and was the moving force behind the National Aeronautics and Space Administration (NASA) Jet Propulsion Laboratory.

# 9

# BUSINESS AND LABOR

ري

UNIQUE ACHIEVEMENTS BY JEWS *included the founding of many
important businesses, industries, and labor practices and organizations.
Jews were also responsible for breakthroughs in international relations
and in women's roles in business and labor.*

*Samuel Gompers founded the modern labor movement. As the first president
of the American Federation of Labor, he established unionism's focus
on wages and benefits.*

*Armand Hammer played a unique role in American business and
political history. He pioneered United States and Soviet Union relations
through his business connections in both countries. Besides catalyzing
business deals, he arranged peace initiatives, cultural exchanges, and
mercy missions between the two nations.*

*Helena Rubinstein created the modern cosmetics industry. She was the
world's first famous beauty expert and cosmetics manufacturer.*

*Estée Lauder made a unique contribution to the same industry. She built
the world's largest family-owned beauty company.*

# FOUNDING THE MODERN AMERICAN LABOR MOVEMENT
## Samuel Gompers

೮೨

*Samuel Gompers was born in London, England, on January 27, 1850. In 1863 he immigrated to the United States, where he became one of the country's most important labor leaders. He died in San Antonio, Texas, on December 13, 1924.*

SAMUEL GOMPERS IS KNOWN AS THE FATHER OF THE MODERN AMERICAN labor movement. His special contribution was to emphasize unionism's economic function rather than political and revolutionary objectives.

He learned about the interests and problems of laboring people from his father, a cigar maker in London. Young Gompers, too, became a cigar maker. In 1863 he and his family came to the United States, and in 1864 Gompers joined a union for cigar makers in New York City. In 1886 he became a founder and the first president of the American Federation of Labor (AFL), a position he held (except for one year, 1895) for the rest of his life.

Gompers had only limited power as president. But he built a record of tremendous accomplishments through his skill in conciliating internal differences in his organization. His great legacy was to take the labor movement away from social reformism and toward the "business" aspects of unionism, especially wages and benefits.

---

### ALSO NOTEWORTHY

▲ BERNAYS, EDWARD L. (born November 22, 1891, in Vienna, Austria; died March 9, 1995, in Cambridge, Massachusetts). Creator of public relations as a profession. He was a nephew of Sigmund Freud.

▲ BLAUSTEIN, LOUIS (born January 20, 1869, in Prussia; died July 27, 1937, in Atlantic City, New Jersey). Founder of American Oil Company (1910).

▲ BLOOMINGDALE, LYMAN GUSTAVUS (born 1841 in New York City; died 1905 in Elberon, New Jersey) and Joseph Bernard Bloomingdale (born December 22, 1842, in New York City; died November 21, 1904, in New York City). Founders of the famous Bloomingdale Brothers department store enterprise in New York City (1886).

▲ CERF, BENNETT ALFRED (born May 25, 1898, in New York City; died August 27, 1971, in Mount Kisco, New York). Cofounder of Random House publishing company (1927).

▲ DUBINSKY, DAVID (originally David Dobnievski; born February 22, 1892, in Brest Litovsk, Russian-ruled Poland; died September 17, 1982, in New York City). Labor union official who served as president (1932–66) of the International Ladies' Garment Workers' Union and raised it from near bankruptcy to $500 million in assets. He pioneered in welfare unionism that built health, cultural, and social elements into the trade-union movement.

# PIONEERING AMERICAN-SOVIET RELATIONS
## Armand Hammer

❧

ARMAND HAMMER, A WEALTHY INDUSTRIALIST AND BUSINESSMAN, was arguably the most important, influential private citizen in America during the twentieth century. More than any other individual, he early established, and long maintained, a commercial and cultural exchange between the United States and the Soviet Union.

From 1921 to 1930 he lived in the Soviet Union, where he made connections that helped him for the rest of his life. Lenin himself gave Hammer the sales concessions for leading American companies doing business in Russia. After returning to the United States, Hammer successfully engaged in various businesses. In 1956 he invested in the nearly bankrupt Occidental Petroleum Corporation; later he took over as its chief executive officer and built the company into one of America's industrial giants.

"I am first and foremost a catalyst," he said. "I bring people and situations together." Over the years, especially the 1960s through the 1980s, he traveled back and forth between the United States and the Soviet Union to catalyze business deals, peace initiatives, cultural exchanges, and mercy missions between the two superpowers. In 1973, for example, he set up a multibillion-dollar chemical fertilizer deal. In the same year, he arranged an American showing of Russian art works on personal loan to him. His efforts helped to ease the plight of Soviet Jews, and he organized American medical aid for the victims of the Chernobyl nuclear disaster.

Before the collapse of the Soviet Union, relations with that country dominated the foreign policy of the United States. And no private individual played a greater role in stablizing that relationship than Armand Hammer.

*Armand Hammer was born in New York City on May 21, 1898. His father was a medical doctor and businessman. Following in his father's footsteps, young Hammer attended medical school and simultaneously ran a pharmaceuticals business that earned him a million dollars even before he received his M.D. degree (1921). He turned to business rather than medicine and became a key figure in American business and cultural relations with the Soviet Union. He died in Los Angeles on December 10, 1990.*

### ALSO NOTEWORTHY

▲ GIMBEL, ISAAC (born April 24, 1856, in Vincennes, Indiana; died April 11, 1931, in Port Chester, New York). Cofounder and first head of the Gimbel Brothers, Inc., department store enterprise (Milwaukee, 1889; New York City, 1910). His brother Jacob (1851–1922) was the other cofounder. They were later joined by five other brothers and Jacob's adopted son. Their father, Adam Gimbel (1817–96), was also a merchant.

# FOUNDING THE WORLD'S LARGEST FAMILY-OWNED BEAUTY COMPANY
## Estée Lauder

ez

> *Estée Lauder was born in Queens, New York City, on July 1, probably in 1908. Her original name was Josephine Esther Mentzer. She got her earliest lessons in salesmanship by helping her father set up merchandise displays in his hardware store. Later she became famous for her own cosmetics business.*

ESTÉE LAUDER IS THE ACKNOWLEDGED QUEEN of the United States cosmetics industry. She early developed a reputation for producing only the highest quality products, anticipating trends, and revolutionizing marketing.

When she was a child, she saw an uncle, a chemist, make skin creams. "I recognized in my Uncle John my true path," she later said.

In 1930 she married Joseph H. Lauter, a businessman. Soon they changed the spelling of their surname to Lauder, the original Austrian form.

She refined her uncle's creams, developed other products, such as eye shadow and lipstick, and sold them to individuals and placed them in beauty salons and elsewhere. In 1946 she officially founded her company, Estée Lauder, Inc. A major breakthrough came when she succeeded in placing her products in the best department stores,

Collections of the Library of Congress

beginning with Saks Fifth Avenue in New York City. In 1953 she came out with her first fragrance.

"If you put the product into the customer's hands," she said in explaining her marketing wizardry, "it will speak for itself if it's something of quality." That thinking led her to give away vast numbers of free samples, especially in the form of a gift with each purchase. Her strategy worked: people invariably liked the new products and began buying them regularly. Her competitors copied her marketing methods.

Estée Lauder created many of the company's products herself. She also controlled marketing, while her husband watched over the financial operations till he died in 1983. In 1973 her son Leonard succeeded her as president of the company so that she could spend more time cultivating her position in society. In 1982 Leonard became chief executive officer of Estée Lauder, Inc., and her other son, Ronald, was named chairman of Lauder International. Both of her daughters-in-law have also entered the business. Lauder's empire has become the world's largest wholly family-owned beauty company.

# ESTABLISHING THE COSMETICS INDUSTRY
## Helena Rubinstein

HELENA RUBINSTEIN WAS THE WORLD'S FIRST FAMOUS BEAUTY EXPERT and cosmetics manufacturer. She developed the cosmetics business into one of the most important modern industries.

Her business began in an unusual way. When she was a young woman, she wanted to marry a medical student, but her father refused to permit the marriage. Distressed, she moved to Australia. She took with her twelve jars of a beauty cream developed by a family friend, the chemist Jacob Lykusky. Australians whose skin had been damaged by the harsh climate begged Rubinstein to share the cream. Seeing a good way to gain financial independence, she obtained a loan and opened a shop, where she sold the cream and offered personalized instruction in skin care.

American Jewish Archives, Cincinnati Campus, Hebrew Union College, Jewish Institute of Religion

> Helena Rubinstein was born in Kraków, Poland, on December 25, 1870. As a young woman, she immigrated to Australia, where she started a cosmetics business. Later she lived in England and then the United States. She died in New York City on April 1, 1965.

In 1908 she left Australia for London, where she opened the first modern beauty salon in Western Europe—before Rubinstein, women made most of their own beauty aids. In 1914 she moved to the United States. Rubinstein went on to manufacture a wide range of beauty preparations and to operate beauty salons throughout America and other countries.

She had little time for a personal life, being, she said, "confident and relaxed only in business." In fact, she did not follow a beauty routine herself because "it takes time, and time is one thing I haven't got." She spent her time making new products, establishing training programs for saleswomen, devising diet plans, organizing full beauty reconditioning programs, and creating innovative promotional techniques, such as colorful events and decorative packaging.

Her efforts succeeded in building not only a thriving personal business but also, through her imitators, a new industry.

▲ **GUGGENHEIM, MEYER** (born February 1, 1828, in Langnau, Switzerland; died March 15, 1905, in Palm Beach, Florida). Founder of worldwide mining interests that dominated the industry during the early 1900s and laid the foundation for the present United States mining industry. His seven sons assisted him. One of them, Simon Guggenheim (born December 30, 1867, in Philadelphia, Pennsylvania; died November 2, 1941, in New York City), established the John Simon Guggenheim Memorial Foundation to provide fellowships for research scholars and creative artists.

▲ **HALDEMAN-JULIUS, EMANUEL** (originally Emanuel Julius; born July 30 1889, in Philadelphia, Pennsylvania; died July 31, 1951, near Girard, Kansas). Publisher of the famed Little Blue Books. He attached his wife's surname to his own after he married.

▲ **HILLMAN, SIDNEY** (born March 23, 1887, in Zagare, Lithuania; died July 10, 1946, at Point Lookout, Long Island, New York). The first president of the Amalgamated Clothing Workers of America (1914–46); a founder of the Committee for Industrial Organization (CIO, 1935, later reorganized as the Congress of Industrial Organizations); and the first United States labor leader to take posts of executive power in the federal government.

▲ **KNOPF, ALFRED A(BRAHAM)** (born September 12, 1892, in New York City; died August 11, 1984, in Purchase, New York). Founder of the publishing house of Alfred A. Knopf (1915).

▲ **LASSALLE, FERDINAND** (originally Ferdinand Lasal or Loslauer; born April 11, 1825, in Breslau, Prussia; died August 31, 1864, near Geneva, Switzerland). One of the founders of the German labor movement and the leading spokesman for German socialism.

▲ **LEVITT, ABRAHAM** (born July 1, 1880, in Brooklyn, New York; died August 20, 1962, in Great Neck, New York) and his son William Jaird Levitt (born February 11, 1907, in Brooklyn, New York; died January 28, 1994, in Manhasset, New York). Founders, with William's younger brother, Alfred, of Levitt & Sons, which built the residential communities of Levittown in New York, Pennsylvania, and New Jersey.

▲ **LUBIN, DAVID** (born June 10, 1849, in Kłodawa, Russian-ruled Poland; died January 1, 1919, in Rome, Italy). Retail businessman who, in 1874, established the first fixed-price store in California and soon developed the largest mail-order house on the Pacific Coast. Later he grew fruit and founded the International Institute of Agriculture.

Courtesy of G.G. Michelson

**GERTRUDE G. MICHELSON**

▲ **MATZ, ISRAEL** (born January 30, 1869, in Kalvarija, Lithuania; died February 10, 1950, in Brooklyn, New York). Founder of Ex-Lax Company (1907).

▲ **MICHELSON, GERTRUDE G.** (born June 3, 1925, in Jamestown, New York). The first woman to serve on the board of directors at Macy's, the first woman on the board at General Electric, and the first woman to chair the board of trustees at an Ivy League school (Columbia University, 1989–92).

**ADOLPH SIMON OCHS**

▲ **OCHS, ADOLPH SIMON** (born March 12, 1858, in Cincinnati, Ohio; died April 8, 1935, in Chattanooga, Tennessee). Publisher who bought the declining *New York Times* and built it (1896–1935) into one of the world's greatest newspapers. Famed for his slogan "All the News That's Fit to Print."

▲ **PARNIS, MOLLIE** (born March 18, about 1905, in New York City; died July 18, 1992, in New York City). Fashion designer famous for designing clothes for American First Ladies, including Mamie Eisenhower and Betty Ford.

**MOLLY PARNIS**

*Courtesy of The Forward, New York*

▲ **REUTER, PAUL JULIUS** (originally Israel Beer Josaphat; born July 21, 1816, in Kassel, Germany; died February 25, 1899, in Nice, France). Founder, in England, of Reuters (1851), one of the world's first news agencies. He became a Christian in 1844.

▲ **ROTHSCHILD, MAYER AMSCHEL** (born February 23, 1744, in Frankfurt am Main, Germany; died September 19, 1812, in Frankfurt). Founder of the most famous European banking dynasty. He had many well-known descendants, including his son Nathan Mayer Rothschild (born September 16, 1777, in Frankfurt; died July 28, 1836, in Frankfurt), who founded the London branch of the house, and the British government officials Lionel Nathan de Rothschild and Nathaniel Mayer de Rothschild.

**MAYER AMSCHEL ROTHSCHILD**

▲ **RUBIN, SAMUEL** (born November 17, 1901, in Białystok, Russia; died December 21, 1978, in New York City). Founder of Fabergé, Inc., the famed perfume and cosmetics company.

▲ **SAMUEL, MARCUS** (first Viscount Bearsted; born November 5, 1853, in London, England; died January 17, 1927, in London). The principal founder of the Shell Transport and Trading Company (1897), which became Shell Oil.

▲ **SCHNEIDERMAN, ROSE** (originally Rachel Schneiderman; born April 6, 1882, in Saven, Russian-ruled Poland; died August 11, 1972, in New York City). President of the New York Women's Trade Union League (1918–49), president of the National Women's Trade Union League (1926–50), the only woman member of the labor advisory board of the National Recovery Administration (1933–35), and a pioneer in advancing the rights of women in the workplace and in unions.

▲ **SCHUSTER, MAX LINCOLN** (originally Max Schuster; born March 2, 1897, in Kalusz, Austria; died December 20, 1970, in New York City). Cofounder, with Richard Leo Simon, of the publishing firm Simon and Schuster (1924). He took the middle name Lincoln because of his admiration for Abraham Lincoln.

▲ SIMON, NORTON WINFRED (born February 5, 1907, in Portland, Oregon; died June 2, 1993, in Los Angeles). Entrepreneur who developed Hunt Foods, Inc., into a giant food-processing company in the 1940s; later diversified it into the corporate conglomerate Hunt Foods and Industries, Inc.; and then merged it with other companies to form Norton Simon, Inc. He also established the Norton Simon Museum of Art in Pasadena, California, built from his own collection.

▲ SIMON, RICHARD LEO (born March 6, 1899, in New York City; died July 29, 1960, in North Stamford, Connecticut). Cofounder, with Max Lincoln Schuster, of the publishing firm Simon and Schuster (1924).

▲ STERN, MAX (born October 27, 1898, in Fulda, Germany; died May 20, 1982, in New York City). Founder of Hartz Mountain, the pet-products business built into a giant by Max's son Leonard Norman Stern (born March 28, 1938, in New York City).

▲ STRAUS, ISIDOR (born February 6, 1845, in Otterberg, Rhenish Bavaria; died April 15, 1912, at sea on the S.S. *Titanic*) and his brother Nathan Straus (born January 31, 1848, in Otterberg; died January 11, 1931, in New York City). Merchants who acquired a partnership in R.H. Macy and Company in 1888; became its sole owners in 1896; and later built it into the biggest department store in the world. Brothers of the government figure Oscar Straus.

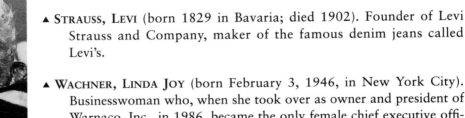

LINDA WACHNER

▲ STRAUSS, LEVI (born 1829 in Bavaria; died 1902). Founder of Levi Strauss and Company, maker of the famous denim jeans called Levi's.

▲ WACHNER, LINDA JOY (born February 3, 1946, in New York City). Businesswoman who, when she took over as owner and president of Warnaco, Inc., in 1986, became the only female chief executive officer of a *Fortune* 500 industrial company and the only woman to head a public company that she had neither founded nor inherited.

# 10
# LITERATURE
∽

JEWISH WRITERS WHOSE UNIQUE ACHIEVEMENTS EARNED THEM NOBEL PRIZES
*in literature included S.Y. Agnon, for his sophisticated Hebrew
folklore-based fiction; Saul Bellow, for creating a major new style
in American prose fiction; Nadine Gordimer, for her antiapartheid writings;
Boris Pasternak, for his celebration of life in the midst of death in the early
Soviet Union, especially in the novel* Doctor Zhivago; *Nelly Sachs, for her poetry
on the Holocaust; Isaac Bashevis Singer, for producing probably the last
great Yiddish works; and Elie Wiesel, for being the most eloquent spokesman
for the victims and survivors of the Holocaust.*

*Among the other Jewish writers of singular accomplishment were
Edna Ferber, the supreme writer of American regional growth;
Anne Frank, whose touching diary raised her to a symbol of all Holocaust
victims; Franz Kafka, who initiated the literature of disorientation and anxiety
in the modern world; Arthur Miller, the last great American writer of plays
dealing with social and ethical concerns; and Marcel Proust, who created
new literary techniques in his novel* Remembrance of Things Past.

# CREATION OF SOPHISTICATED HEBREW FOLKLORE FICTION

## S.Y. Agnon

☙

*S.Y. Agnon was born in Buczacz, Galicia, on July 17, 1888. His original name was Shmuel Yosef Halevi Czaczkes. In 1908 he issued his first published story, "Agunot" ("Deserted Wives"), and he took his pen name from that title; agnon is Hebrew for "cut off," implying loss and yearning, qualities pivotal in all of his work. In 1924 he moved permanently to Palestine. He died in Rehovot, Israel, on February 17, 1970.*

IN 1966 S.Y. AGNON SHARED THE NOBEL PRIZE FOR LITERATURE with Nelly Sachs. Agnon was honored "for his profoundly distinctive narrative art with motifs from the life of the Jewish people." His unique contribution was his use of traditional folk sources to create a sophisticated kind of Hebrew-language fiction.

Agnon derived his subject matter, themes, and style from the Jewish milieu of his childhood and youth. The subject matter is typically a blend of folklore and fantasy with actual Jewish life in his native Galicia. His main theme is that modern society has had a disintegrat-

State of Israel Government Press Office

ing effect on the sacred traditions of eastern European Jewry. His style synthesizes old Hebrew forms—biblical narrative, postbiblical homily, Hasidic folktale—and blurs the boundary between the real and the imaginary. His novel *The Bridal Canopy* (Hebrew, 1931; English, 1937) is based on a Hebrew folk epic and relates the adventures of a poor Hasid as he searches for husbands and dowries for his three daughters. In his novel *A Guest for the Night* (Hebrew, 1939; English, 1968), a Jew revisits his eastern European hometown, where he finds social and cultural disintegration.

Through these and other mystical, introspective works, Agnon became the world's foremost writer of folk-based literature in the Hebrew language.

### ALSO NOTEWORTHY

▲ **ALEICHEM, SHALOM** (or Sholom/Sholem Aleichem; originally Sholem [or Solomon] Yakov Rabinowitz; born 1859 in Pereyaslav, Russia; died May 13, 1916, in New York City). Popular Yiddish author, known in the United States as the Yiddish Mark Twain, who wrote the first Yiddish stories for children, the works that helped to establish the Yiddish Art Theater in New York City, and the stories that formed the libretto for the musical *Fiddler on the Roof*.

# BECOMING THE FIRST MAJOR JEWISH NOVELIST IN AMERICA
## Saul Bellow

❧

SAUL BELLOW WON THE NOBEL PRIZE FOR LITERATURE IN 1976 "for the human understanding and subtle analysis of contemporary culture that are combined in his works." He created the first major new style in American prose fiction since Hemingway and Faulkner.

Bellow's novels spring from his idea that fiction moves back and forth between the world of appearances and another world, one that "moves us to believe that the good we hang onto so tenaciously—in the face of evil, so obstinately—is no illusion." His works are marked by an impassioned, learned, idiomatic first-person voice that can articulate the mood of an entire people through the revelation of the individual character.

*Saul Bellow was born in Lachine, Quebec, Canada, on June 10, 1915. He moved to Chicago in 1924, attended the University of Chicago (1933–35), graduated from Northwestern University with a major in anthropology (1937), became a college teacher, and started writing.*

*The Adventures of Augie March* (1953) is a coming-of-age novel. *Seize the Day* (1956) shows a lost soul struggling to redeem himself. In *Herzog* (1964) an academic comes to terms with his alienation from himself and society. *Humboldt's Gift* (1975) explores the conflict between the materialistic values of society and the spiritual values of art and high culture. *The Dean's December* (1982) attacks the negative social forces that challenge human dignity.

*The Jewish Week, New York*

During a time when the concept of individualism was degenerating, Bellow, in his novels, stood out as the principal spokesman for the realization of individual selfhood. In the process, he became the most original literary voice of his time and the first American Jewish writer to transcend the boundaries of "Jewish-American literature" and establish himself as a major American novelist.

# BREAKING THE SOVIET MOLD IN POETRY
## Joseph Brodsky

&

*Joseph Brodsky was born in Leningrad, the Soviet Union, on May 24, 1940. His original name was Josip (or Iosip/Iosif) Alexandrovich Brodsky. In his early thirties he immigrated to the United States, where he was associated with various universities and served as the nation's official poet laureate (1991–92). He died in New York City on January 28, 1996.*

JOSEPH BRODSKY WON THE 1987 NOBEL PRIZE in literature for his important lyric and elegiac poetry.

Much of the feeling in his poetry came from his early life experiences. He left school at the age of fifteen and held a series of brief, minor jobs while he began his writing. Because of his independent spirit and his lack of a steady job, Soviet authorites labeled him a "social parasite," and in 1964 he was sentenced to five years of hard labor. In 1965 the sentence was commuted, but in 1972 he was expelled from his homeland. He settled in the United States.

Contrary to the Soviet ideal of social themes, Brodsky's poetry explores personal matters. His works are meditative on life, death, and the meaning of existence. Many of his early Russian-language poems were translated into English and published in *Selected Poems* (1973). Representative Russian and English poetry is in his *History of the Twentieth Century* (1986).

Brodsky, rejected by Soviet authorities as a "social parasite" but later accepted by the rest of the world as a Nobel Prize winner, perfectly exemplified why the Soviet system failed.

### ALSO NOTEWORTHY

▲ ANSKY, S. (or S[hloime] An-Ski; originally Solomon Zanvel [or Seinwil] RAPPOPORT; born 1863 in Chashnik, Russia; died November 8, 1920, in Warsaw, Poland). Yiddish author of *The Dybbuk* (1926).

▲ ASIMOV, ISAAC (born January 2, 1920, in Petrovichi, the Soviet Union; died April 16, 1992, in New York City). America's most prolific writer of science fiction and popular science nonfiction.

▲ BLUME, JUDY (born February 12, 1938, in Elizabeth, New Jersey). Author who revolutionized children's literature with her books that dealt frankly with sexual and other sensitive matters and that lacked traditional moralizing and authoritarian pronouncements. Her works included *Are You There, God? It's Me, Margaret* (1970) and *Forever...* (1975).

▲ CAHN, SAMMY (originally Samuel Cohen; born June 18, 1913, in New York City; died January 15, 1993, in Los Angeles). Lyricist of many well-known songs, including "I'll Walk Alone" (1944), "Three Coins in the Fountain" (1954), "Love and Marriage" (1955), "High Hopes" (1959), and "Call Me Irresponsible" (1963).

# EXAMINING MASS BEHAVIOR
## Elias Canetti

❧

ELIAS CANETTI WON THE 1981 NOBEL PRIZE in literature "for writings marked by a broad outlook, a wealth of ideas, and artistic power." His works explore the emotions of crowds and the position of the individual at odds with society.

His interest in crowds developed when he witnessed street rioting over inflation in Frankfurt, Germany, during the 1920s. He explored crowd mentality in *Die Blendung* (1935), a novel that was published in the United States as *The Tower of Babel* (1947) but is best known as *Auto-da-Fé* ("Act of Faith," 1964). The horrifying story of the destruction of a scholar's life in a corrupt society, the book was among the earliest works to dissect fascism.

Canetti's masterwork is *Crowds and Power* (German, 1960; English, 1962). It is a nonfiction book that draws on folklore, myth, literature, and history in its analysis of mass movements. Its genesis was Canetti's witnessing the July 15, 1927, burning of the Palace of Justice in Vienna by a group of protesting workers.

*Auto-da-Fé* stands as one of the most powerful novels of the twentieth century. And *Crowds and Power* performed a seminal role in its examination of mass behavior and the allure of dictatorship.

> *Elias Canetti was born in Ruse (in Turkish, Ruschuk or Rustchuk), Bulgaria, on July 25, 1905. He earned a doctorate in chemistry at the University of Vienna (1929) but soon turned to literature. His first two languages were Spanish and English, but he always wrote in his third language, German. "The language of my intellect," he explained, "will remain German—because I am Jewish. But I bring along a human legacy." He died in Zurich, Switzerland, on August 13, 1994.*

---

### ALSO NOTEWORTHY

▲ **CHAYEFSKY, PADDY** (originally Sidney Chayefsky; born January 29, 1923, in New York City; died August 1, 1981, in New York City). Playwright known for his realistic dramas about the joys and sorrows of ordinary people, including the television play "Marty" (1953) on the *Philco Television Playhouse,* later made into a popular movie (1955).

▲ **DANNAY, FREDERIC** (originally Daniel Nathan; born October 20, 1905, in Brooklyn, New York; died September 3, 1982, in White Plains, New York). Joint creator and author of the Ellery Queen mysteries, along with Manfred B. Lee, his cousin.

▲ **DA PONTE, LORENZO** (originally Emanuele Conegliano; born March 10, 1749, in Céneda, near Treviso, Veneto, Italy; died August 17, 1838, in New York City). Poet who wrote the librettos for Mozart's operas *Le nozze di Figaro* (1786), *Don Giovanni* (1787), and *Così fan tutte,* 1790).

▲ **GERSHWIN, IRA** (originally Israel Gershvin; born December 6, 1896, in New York City; died August 17, 1983, in Beverly Hills, California). Lyricist of many songs with music by his brother George Gershwin, including "Fascinating Rhythm" (1924), "The Man I Love" (1924), "'S Wonderful" (1927), "I Got Rhythm" (1930), and songs from the folk opera *Porgy and Bess* (1935).

▲ **GINSBERG, ALLEN** (born June 3, 1926, in Newark, New Jersey). Poet of the Beat Generation in the 1950s, noted for his poem "Howl" (1955).

# PORTRAYING AMERICAN REGIONAL GROWTH
## Edna Ferber

cx/cs

> Edna Ferber was born in Kalamazoo, Michigan, on August 15, 1887. She began her career as a journalist but found the work exhausting. Turning to fiction, she won fame as a short-story writer and then became a best-selling novelist. She died in New York City on April 16, 1968.

EDNA FERBER'S NOVELS CELEBRATE THE AMERICAN SCENE. More than any other writer of her era, she portrayed the growth and vitality of the people, sometimes several generations of people, in various regions in the United States.

Ferber's characters and themes evolved from her own experiences. Her characters were ordinary Americans struggling against odds to make their way in life. She identified with such people. "Being a Jew makes it tough to get on," she explained, "and I like that." Her ruggedness was reinforced when she worked as the first woman news reporter in her midwestern locality; often frightened and offended, she fought and succeeded anyway.

American Jewish Archives, Cincinnati Campus, Hebrew Union College, Jewish Institute of Religion

Her work as a journalist also influenced her fictional themes, which center on the way people respond to large historical events in real-life situations in various parts of America. *So Big* (1924), for example, is about a sensitive woman's need for strength on the harsh Illinois frontier. *Show Boat* (1926) examines a theatrical family on the Mississippi River. *Cimarron* (1930) covers the Oklahoma land rush. *Giant* (1952) explores developments in modern Texas, and *Ice Palace* (1958) does the same for Alaska.

Through these works and more, Ferber became America's greatest woman novelist of her time and the most important writer on the development of American regions.

# Symbolizing the Holocaust Victims
## Anne Frank

❧

EVEN THOUGH SHE WROTE ONLY ONE WORK and lived only fifteen years, Anne Frank earned a special place for herself in history. While death and destruction surrounded her, and fear of capture haunted her every day of her hiding from the Nazis during World War II, she still managed to create in her diary a monument to the courage and strength of the human spirit. Because of the remarkable skill, insight, and humor in her diary and because of the way her young life ended, she has come to represent all of the lives and hopes that were lost during the Holocaust.

In July 1942 the four members of her family, along with four other persons, went into hiding in an annex to her father's place of business in Amsterdam. During the next two years, she wrote in her diary about such topics as daily events, family relationships, what it felt like to hide, the efforts of others to protect them from the Nazis, and the passage from puberty and adolescence to young womanhood. In August 1944 Anne and her companions were captured by the Nazis. In March 1945, three months short of her sixteenth birthday, she died of typhus at the Bergen-Belsen concentration camp.

*Anne Frank was born in Frankfurt am Main, Germany, on June 12, 1929. In 1939 she went with her family to Amsterdam, Netherlands, where, in 1942, she went into hiding from the Nazis. In 1944 she was captured. She died in the concentration camp at Bergen-Belsen, Germany, in March 1945.*

*The Jewish Week, New York*

Her father, who survived Auschwitz, in 1947 published her diary, in Dutch, as *Het achterhuis* ("The Secret Annex"). In 1952 it was translated into English as *Anne Frank: The Diary of a Young Girl*. Her story became a Broadway play in 1955 and a film in 1959. The diary has also been translated into dozens of other languages and sold many millions of copies all over the world. Anne Frank is now a symbol of all Holocaust victims, especially the children.

# CREATING THE WORLD'S MOST PROMINENT ANTIAPARTHEID LITERATURE

## Nadine Gordimer

Nadine Gordimer was born in Springs, Transvaal, South Africa, on November 20, 1923. She began to write at the age of nine and achieved her first published story at fifteen. Later she became the world's most important writer against the system of apartheid (racial segregation and discrimination) in her homeland.

NADINE GORDIMER'S WRITINGS EXPLORE THE EFFECTS of South Africa's apartheid system on both the ruling whites and the oppressed blacks. For her literary contribution to this topic, she was awarded the 1991 Nobel Prize in literature.

In spite of the political and social problems in South Africa, she decided to stay there and use her writing talent to fight apartheid. "I lived with and among a variety of colors and kinds of people," she said. "This discovery was a joyous personal one, not a political one, at first; but, of course, as time has gone by, it has hardened into a sense of political opposition to abusive white power."

Courtesy of South African Embassy in Israel

But her works are not simply propaganda; they have great literary merit and deal with issues from a variety of angles and through well-rounded characters. "Books make South Africans, black and white, see themselves, as they cannot from inside themselves," she explained. "They get a kind of mirror image with which to compare their own feelings and motives. I think fiction raises their consciousness in this way."

Among her novels are *A Guest of Honour* (1970), *The Conservationist* (1974), and *A Sport of Nature* (1987). Through these and many other works, Gordimer became the world's most prominent antiapartheid writer.

# PIONEERING THE MODERN LITERATURE OF DISORIENTATION AND ANXIETY
## Franz Kafka

ço

FRANZ KAFKA WAS ONE OF THE FOUNDERS OF MODERN LITERATURE. His fiction was the first to focus on the disorientation and anxiety of the modern world, on a nightmarish vision of reality, and on the artist as an individual, not as Everyman.

Kafka's fiction sprang from the milieu in which he was raised. Linguistically and culturally, he was a minority within a minority—a German-speaking Jew in a Czech-speaking Christian city. And within the Jewish community, there were Zionists and anti-Zionist socialists. Members of these groups formed various alliances with other groups in a crisscrossing fashion that tended to make roles and relationships ambiguous. In addition to contending with these forces, Kafka had an uneasy relationship with his philistine father, felt isolated from others because of his illness, and suffered from the mental conflict between his literary goals and his daily tasks as a civil servant.

*Franz Kafka was born in Prague, Bohemia, on July 3, 1883. Under pressure from his father, he earned a law degree at the University of Prague (1907). He then worked as a civil servant (1908–17) till tuberculosis forced him to resign. He died in a sanatorium near Vienna, Austria, on June 3, 1924.*

Not surprisingly, loneliness, ambivalence, and alienation are basic themes in his writings, which he called his "dreamlike inner life." He wrote three unfinished novels and many stories. His best-known work is the story "The Metamorphosis" (written 1912, published 1915), in which a young man turns into an insect; the story explores the young man's sense of isolation and existential guilt.

Austrian Press and Information Service, Washington, D.C.

Kafka's work was so seminal and distinctive that his name has spawned the word *Kafkaesque,* an adjective meaning "pertaining to a world that has its own rules, not amenable to human will."

# WRITING PLAYS OF
# SOCIAL AND ETHICAL CONCERNS
## Arthur Miller

೦౭

*Arthur Miller was born in New York City on October 17, 1915. His family was financially devastated by the Depression, and he had to work in a warehouse for two years to earn tuition money for the University of Michigan, where he studied dramatic arts and graduated in 1938. In the early 1940s he worked as a radio scriptwriter, and in 1944 he began to write stage plays. He is now universally regarded as the dean of American playwrights.*

ARTHUR MILLER IS THE LAST GREAT AMERICAN PLAYWRIGHT whose themes deal primarily with social and ethical concerns. His masterpiece is *Death of a Salesman*.

From the beginning of his career, he focused on working-class people, their personal values, and their relationship to the ethics of other forces in the world. Among his best plays are *All My Sons* (1947), *The Crucible* (1953), *A View from the Bridge* (1955), *Incident at Vichy* (1964), and *The American Clock* (1980). At the age of nearly eighty, he was still producing powerful work in this tradition when he wrote his play *Broken Glass* (1994), an examination of ethnic separation and the resurgence of anti-Semitism.

His most highly regarded work is *Death of a Salesman* (1949). The play shows the gradual disillusionment, ending in suicide, of the salesman Willy Loman, a tragic figure who has lost his abilty to sell himself as well as his product. Besides being an indictment of commercialism and false values, the work expresses the longing of everyone for self-identity; Loman wants, Miller says, "to win out over anonymity and meaninglessness, to love and be loved, and above all, perhaps, to *count*." The work reflects, Miller says, the confusion of values between the individual and social forces, "the unbroken tissue that was man and society, a single unit rather than two." The play has entered the world repertory; even in China, people have produced and been profoundly affected by it.

## ALSO NOTEWORTHY

▲ GLUECKEL OF HAMELN (or Glückel of Hameln; originally Glückel Pinkerle; born 1646 in Hamburg, Germany; died 1724 in Metz, France). Writer whose memoirs are famous for at least three reasons: they are the only accessible full-length memoir by a Jewish woman before the nineteenth century; they provide important information about central European Jewish life in her time; and they are a key source for linguistic study because they were written in Judeo-German, the precursor of Yiddish.

*Courtesy of Moshe and Alice Shalvi*

**GLUECKEL OF HAMELN**

▲ GOLDFADEN, ABRAHAM (originally Abraham Goldenfoden; in Yiddish, Avron Goldfadn; born July 24, 1840, in Starokonstantinov, Russia; died January 9, 1908, in New York City). Hebrew and Yiddish poet and playwright who founded the modern Yiddish theater, in Iasi, Romania, in 1876.

# MAINTAINING HUMANISTIC LITERATURE UNDER THE SOVIET REGIME
## Boris Pasternak

ೞ

BORIS PASTERNAK WON THE NOBEL PRIZE IN LITERATURE in 1958 for his "contemporary lyrical poetry" and for his fiction in "the great Russian epic tradition." His masterpiece is the novel *Doctor Zhivago*.

His early grounding in religion and humanism affected his writing, and the Soviet authorities censured him for his focus on personal rather than political themes. When he was notified of his Nobel Prize, he immediately accepted the honor with pleasure. But within days, the Soviets, who presumed that the award was offered because of Pasternak's non-Soviet work, publicly vilified him and expelled him from the writers' union. Consequently he had to refuse the actual presentation of the Nobel Prize.

That conflict with the authorities was a fitting epilogue to his greatest work, *Doctor Zhivago*. He completed the novel in 1955 but was unable to publish it in the Soviet Union. It was first issued in Italy in 1957 (English translation, 1958). The Soviets found nothing to like about the book. The hero, Zhivago, is reflective, artistic, and philosophical, in contrast to the Marxist-Leninist revolutionary hero favored by the Soviet authorities. The work is an epic narrative of events that Pasternak himself lived through, including the Russian revolutions of 1905 and 1917, and the long aftermath of violence and destruction. But despite those events, the hero displays a humanistic outlook and a faith in life itself; *zhivago*, in Russian, means "life."

*Doctor Zhivago*, with its universal heroic values and poetic insight, is one of the world's great novels.

> *Boris Leonidovich Pasternak was born in Moscow, Russia, on February 10, 1890. His parents—his father was a painter, his mother a pianist—influenced his love of the arts and humanities, and in his youth Pasternak studied music, philosophy, and religion (he converted to Christianity). Later he became one of the greatest Russian writers. He died in Peredelkino, near Moscow, on May 30, 1960.*

## ALSO NOTEWORTHY

▲ **HARBURG, E.Y.** (originally Isidore Hochberg, anglicized as Edgar Harburg, later nicknamed Yipsel ["Squirrel"], making the full name Edgar Yipsel Harburg; born April 8, 1898, in New York City; died March 5, 1981, in Los Angeles). Lyricist whose songs included "Brother, Can You Spare a Dime?" (1932), "Over the Rainbow" and other songs in the film *The Wizard of Oz* (1939), "Happiness Is a Thing Called Joe" (1943), and "How Are Things in Glocca Morra?" (1947).

# CREATING THE NOVEL OF INNER ODYSSEY
## Marcel Proust

*೧*

*Marcel Proust was born of a Catholic father and Jewish mother in Auteuil, near Paris, France, on July 10, 1871. His family was wealthy, and he spent much of his life associating in high society. Most people thought he was just a snob and a social climber. It was not till after his death in Paris on November 18, 1922, that the full scope of his literary achievement was recognized.*

WITH ONLY A SINGLE IMPORTANT WORK TO HIS CREDIT, Marcel Proust broke the literary mold of his day, created valuable new techniques, and earned a permanent position in the history of literature. The work was the huge seven-part novel *Remembrance of Things Past* (1913–27).

Proust was among the first in fiction to emphasize the importance of everyday events as catalysts in the formation of a person's sense of reality; he saw selective memory as the key to inner truth. For example, Proust himself said that the smells and tastes of tea and toast evoked within him a recollection of his youthful days in his grandfather's garden. The outer self participated, he believed, "in our habits, in society, in our vices. If we want to understand that self, it is only by trying to re-create it deep within ourselves that we can succeed." *Remembrance of Things Past*, then, replaces traditional plot and dramatic action with the inner odyssey of the first-person narrator; the outer events of French society life serve merely to spark "remembrances of things past" as the narrator discovers his true self.

This was a new kind of novel and is now regarded as one of the major literary works of the twentieth century.

### ALSO NOTEWORTHY

▲ HART, LORENZ MILTON (born May 2, 1895, in New York City; died November 22, 1943, in New York City). Lyricist noted for his use of the techniques and subtleties of serious poetry in his commercial song lyrics. He wrote the lyrics, and Richard Rodgers the music, for the Broadway musicals *Spring Is Here* (1929), including "With a Song in My Heart"; *Jumbo* (1935), with "The Most Beautiful Girl in the World"; *Babes in Arms* (1937), with "The Lady Is a Tramp"; *The Boys from Syracuse* (1938), with "Falling in Love with Love"; and *Pal Joey* (1940), with "Bewitched, Bothered, and Bewildered." For the film *Love Me Tonight* (1932), they produced "Isn't It Romantic?" "Lover," and "Mimi." One of their most memorable works was the independent song "Blue Moon" (1934, originally as "Prayer" and then "The Bad in Every Man," both 1934). Through his mother, he was a descendent of the German poet Heinrich Heine.

▲ HART, MOSS (born October 24, 1904, in New York City; died December 20, 1961, in Palm Springs, California). Playwright who coauthored, with George S. Kaufman, the comedies *You Can't Take It with You* (1936) and *The Man Who Came to Dinner* (1939).

# EARNING THE TITLE OF POETESS OF THE HOLOCAUST
## Nelly Sachs

⌘

NELLY SACHS SHARED THE 1966 NOBEL PRIZE IN LITERATURE with the Israeli novelist and story writer S.Y. Agnon. Sachs was honored for "her outstanding lyrical and dramatic writing, which interprets Israel's destiny with touching strength." "Agnon represents the state of Israel," Sachs said. "I represent the tragedy of the Jewish people."

The Holocaust transformed Sachs from a minor German poet into a major literary figure. Her entire family, except her mother, was killed in concentration camps. Writing now became her "mute outcry" against the horrors of the era; "I only wrote because I had to free myself," she explained. She wrote about contemporary Jewish experiences but linked them to traditional Jewish mystical ideas from the *Zohar* (a mystical interpretation of the Torah). Her style was marked by unrhymed free verse and by startling imagery. For example, in her best-known poem, "O the Chimneys," the smoke from the chimneys in the Nazi extermination camps symbolizes the body of Israel.

Sachs came to be known as the Poetess of the Holocaust.

Photo Reprtragebild, Stockholm

*Nelly Sachs was born in Berlin, Germany, on December 10, 1891. In her youth, she was known as Leonie. By the age of seventeen, she was writing traditional poems in the German language. In 1940 she fled the Nazis and immigrated to Sweden, where she earned a living translating Swedish poetry into German. Later she became an important German-language poet. She died in Stockholm, Sweden, on May 12, 1970.*

## ALSO NOTEWORTHY

▲ HECHT, BEN (born February 28, 1894, in New York City; died April 18, 1964, in New York City). Coauthor, with Charles MacArthur, of the play *The Front Page* (1928), which greatly influenced the public's perception of the newspaper world. As a journalist in the 1920s, he perfected a widely imitated type of human-interest sketch. His other works included the screenplay for *Gunga Din* (with MacArthur, 1939) and the Zionist play *A Flag Is Born* (1946).

▲ HEINE, HEINRICH (originally Harry Heine; born December 13, 1797, in Düsseldorf, Germany; died February 17, 1856, in Paris, France). Writer best known for his early lyrics (such as "The Lorelei"), which have probably been set to music more often than those of any other poet. He changed his first name when he converted to Protestantism.

# BECOMING BROADWAY'S MOST SUCCESSFUL COMEDY WRITER

## Neil Simon

✑

Neil Simon was born in the Bronx section of New York City on July 4, 1927. His full name was Marvin Neil Simon. He wrote for television comedians, including Sid Caesar and Phil Silvers, before turning to the stage and becoming the most successful Broadway comedy writer of his time.

NEIL SIMON'S PLAYS CENTER ON THE COMIC INCONGRUITIES of everyday life, typically by showing a conflict, often with serious undertones, between two opposing personalities. His play *The Odd Couple* has become an American classic.

Simon's first Broadway play was the hit *Come Blow Your Horn* (1961), followed by many more outstanding comedies, such as *Barefoot in the Park* (1963), *Plaza Suite* (1968), *The Prisoner of Second Avenue* (1971), *The Sunshine Boys* (1972), *Biloxi Blues* (1985), *Lost in Yonkers* (1991), and *Laughter on the 23rd Floor* (1993). His original screenplays include *Murder by Death* (1976) and *The Goodbye Girl* (1977).

His best-known work is *The Odd Couple* (1965). As usual, Simon threw together two characters with radically different personalities: Oscar, who is sloppy, carefree, and lowbrow; and Felix, who is compulsively neat, intense, and highbrow. Both coming off failed marriages, they try to room together, but their arrangement fails for the same reason that their marriages failed—each has a huge ego that he refuses to change to accommodate others. The audience clearly sees the characters' incompatibility, but Oscar and Felix do not; the resulting underlying sense of comic doom is what Simon had in mind when he called the play a "black comedy." *The Odd Couple* is a superb example of incongruity (in this case, the illogical juxtaposition of the two characters) in Simon's works; he deliberately focuses on that quality because he sees it as a primary feature in human reality. Even with its steady stream of sidesplitting laughs, *The Odd Couple* brilliantly conveys its theme of the dangers of self-love.

### ALSO NOTEWORTHY

▲ HELLER, JOSEPH (born May 1, 1923, in Brooklyn, New York). Author of the novel *Catch-22* (1961), one of the most important works of protest literature to appear after World War II.

▲ HELLMAN, LILLIAN FLORENCE (born June 20, 1905, in New Orleans, Louisiana; died June 30, 1984, on Martha's Vineyard, Massachusetts). The most highly regarded woman playwright of her time. Her plays included *The Children's Hour* (1934), *The Little Foxes* (1939), *Watch on the Rhine* (1941), and *Toys in the Attic* (1960).

*Photo credit:* American Jewish Archives, Cincinnati Campus, Hebrew Union College, Jewish Institute of Religion.

LILLIAN HELLMAN

# PRESERVING YIDDISH IN GREAT TWENTIETH-CENTURY LITERATURE
## Isaac Bashevis Singer

ISAAC BASHEVIS SINGER WON THE 1978 NOBEL PRIZE in literature for his "impressive narrative art, which, with roots in a Polish-Jewish cultural tradition, brings universal human conditions to life." In a deliberate attempt to preserve Yiddish, he wrote in that disappearing language and then translated his works into English.

"Yiddish has not yet said its last word," according to Singer. "It was the tongue of martyrs and saints, of dreamers and cabalists." He believed that "in a figurative way, Yiddish is the wise and humble language of us all, the idiom of the frightened and hopeful humanity." For those reasons, he chose Yiddish for his fiction, which he felt "has no other purpose than to give enjoyment to a reader."

State of Israel Government Press Office

*Isaac Bashevis Singer was born in Leoncin, Poland, in 1904. The Polish form of his name was Icek-Hersz Zynger. In 1923 he abandoned his religious studies at a rabbinical seminary and took a job with a Yiddish periodical in Warsaw. In 1935 he immigrated to the United States, where he worked as a journalist and pursued his fiction writing. He died in Surfside, near Miami, Florida, on July 24, 1991.*

Yet while entertaining his readers, Singer also profoundly articulated the tensions between orthodox and secular values. His works often center on the history and culture of the Polish-Jewish village (or *shtetl*), show an interest in the irrational and supernatural, and emphasize themes involving faith, doubt, and corruption. Among his books are the novel *Satan in Goray* (1935), the collection *Gimpel the Fool and Other Stories* (1957), and the novel *The Magician of Lublin* (1960).

Singer was the foremost Yiddish writer of the twentieth century and probably the last in the line of great Yiddish authors.

# SPEAKING FOR THE HOLOCAUST
# VICTIMS AND SURVIVORS
## Elie Wiesel

ဢ

*Eliezer Wiesel was born in Sighet, Romania, on September 30, 1928. During 1944–45 he was interned in the Nazi concentration camps at Auschwitz and Buchenwald. After the war, he worked as a Paris journalist and then, in 1956, moved to the United States, where he became a university teacher and seriously pursued his writing.*

ELIE WIESEL IS A SPOKESMAN FOR THE VICTIMS AND SURVIVORS of the Holocaust. Most of his fiction, essays, and commentaries evoke the memory of that period, even when the topic is not overtly present.

Three of his novels are representative of his output. *Night* (Yiddish, 1956; French, 1958; English, 1960) relates a boy's experiences at a death camp. In *The Accident* (French, 1961; English, 1962) the protagonist meditates on his guilt for having survived the Holocaust. *The Gates of the Forest* (French, 1964; English 1966) explores

Courtesy of Elie Wiesel

mankind's relationship with God during the Holocaust. Other books include *The Oath* (French, 1973; English 1973), *The Testament* (French, 1980; English, 1981), and *The Fifth Son* (French, 1983; English, 1985).

For his special contribution to world thought, Wiesel was awarded the 1986 Nobel Peace Prize. "Wiesel is a messenger to mankind," the Nobel spokesperson said. "His message is one of peace, atonement, and human dignity. His belief that the forces fighting evil in the world can be victorious is a hard-won belief."

### ALSO NOTEWORTHY

▲ HEYSE, PAUL JOHANN LUDWIG VON (born March 15, 1830, in Berlin, Germany; died April 2, 1914, in Munich, Germany). Winner of the Nobel Prize for literature in 1910, known especially for his novellas.

▲ IONESCO, EUGÈNE (originally Eugen Ionescu; born November 26, 1909, in Slatina, Romania; died March 28, 1994, in Paris, France). Playwright whose one-act "antiplay" *The Bald Soprano* (1949) initiated a revolution in dramatic techniques and helped to inaugurate the theater of the absurd. His most popular play was *Rhinoceros* (1959).

▲ **KAUFMAN, GEORGE S(IMON)** (born November 16, 1899, in Pittsburgh, Pennsylvania; died June 2, 1961, in New York City). The most successful American playwright between the two world wars. His comedies included *Beggar on Horseback* (1924), in collaboration with Marc Connelly; *Dinner at Eight* (1932), with Edna Ferber; and *You Can't Take It with You* (1936) and *The Man Who Came to Dinner* (1939), both coauthored by Moss Hart.

▲ **KOESTLER, ARTHUR** (born September 5, 1905, in Budapest, Hungary; died March 3, 1983, in London, England). Writer noted for his works on political ethics, notably the novel *Darkness at Noon* (1940).

▲ **LAZARUS, EMMA** (born July 22, 1849, in New York City; died November 19, 1887, in New York City). Writer whose poem "The New Colossus" (1883)—including the lines "Give me your tired, your poor,/Your huddled masses yearning to breathe free"—was inscribed on the Statue of Liberty in 1886.

**EMMA LAZARUS**

Schwadron Collection,
Hebrew University, Jerusalem

▲ **LEE, MANFRED B(ENNINGTON)** (originally Manford Lepofsky; born January 11, 1905, in Brooklyn, New York; died April 3, 1971, in Waterbury, Connecticut). Joint creator and author of the Ellery Queen mysteries, along with Frederic Dannay, his cousin.

▲ **LERNER, ALAN JAY** (born August 31, 1918, in New York City; died June 14, 1986, in New York City). Lyricist of the Broadway musicals *Brigadoon* (1947); *Paint Your Wagon* (1951); *My Fair Lady* (1956), with "I Could Have Danced All Night"; *Camelot* (1960), with "If Ever I Would Leave You"; and *On a Clear Day You Can See Forever* (1965), with the title song.

▲ **MAILER, NORMAN KINGSLEY** (Hebrew name, Nachum Malech Mailer; born January 31, 1923, in Long Branch, New Jersey). Author of the classic war novel *The Naked and the Dead* (1948).

▲ **MALAMUD, BERNARD** (born April 26, 1914, in Brooklyn, New York; died March 18, 1986, in New York City). Novelist and short-story writer noted for his symbolic works dealing with the Jewish milieu, including the novels *The Assistant* (1957) and *The Fixer* (1966).

▲ **MAMET, DAVID ALAN** (born November 30, 1947, in Chicago, Illinois). Playwright who revitalized the American theater with his language-oriented plays, in which he showed a genius for turning the vernacular into poetry. *Glengarry Glen Ross* (1984) is one of his best-known plays.

▲ **MANKIEWICZ, HERMAN J(ACOB)** (born November 7, 1897, in New York City; died March 5, 1953, in Los Angeles). Screenwriter who was the principal author of the script for the great film *Citizen Kane* (1941). Brother of the film director Joseph L. Mankiewicz.

▲ **MOÏSE, PENINA** (born April 23, 1797, in Charleston, South Carolina; died September 13, 1880, in Charleston). Author of the first American Jewish hymnal, *Hymns Written for the Use of Hebrew Congregations* (1856).

▲ **ODETS, CLIFFORD** (born July 18, 1906, in Philadelphia, Pennsylvania; died August 14, 1963, in Los Angeles). Playwright known for his Depression-era proletarian plays, especially *Awake and Sing!* (1935), *Waiting for Lefty* (1935), and *Golden Boy* (1937).

▲ **PERELMAN, S(IDNEY) J(OSEPH)** (born February 1, 1904, in Brooklyn, New York; died October 17, 1979, in New York City). Humorist and writer whose wit and wordplay greatly influenced trends in American humor. He wrote short pieces for the *New Yorker,* collaborated with the Marx Brothers on the scripts for their films *Monkey Business* (1931) and *Horse Feathers* (1932), and coauthored (with Ogden Nash) the musical play *One Touch of Venus* (1943).

▲ **PINTER, HAROLD** (born October 10, 1930, in London, England). Playwright known for his complex, layered plays that sometimes completely do away with physical activity on the stage. They include *The Caretaker* (1960), *The Homecoming* (1965), *Silence* (1969), and *Betrayal* (1978).

▲ **RICE, ELMER** (originally Elmer Leopold Reizenstein; born September 28, 1892, in New York City; died May 8, 1967, in Southhampton, Hampshire, England). Playwright known for his innovative and polemical works, such as the plays *The Adding Machine* (1923), *Street Scene* (1929), and *We, the People* (1933).

▲ **ROSTEN, LEO CALVIN** (also known as Leonard Q. Ross; born April 11, 1908, in Lodz, Poland). Author of *The Education of H\*Y\*M\*A\*N K\*A\*P\*L\*A\*N* (1937) and *The Joys of Yiddish* (1968).

▲ **ROTH, PHILIP MILTON** (born March 19, 1933, in Newark, New Jersey). Author of the novels *Goodbye, Columbus* (1960) and *Portnoy's Complaint* (1969).

▲ **SALTEN, FELIX** (also known as Martin Finder; originally Siegmund Salzmann; born September 6, 1869, in Budapest, Hungary; died October 8, 1945, in Zurich, Switzerland). Author of *Bambi* (German, 1926; English, 1928).

▲ **SCHULBERG, BUDD WILSON** (born March 27, 1914, in New York City). Writer of tough, realistic fiction, including the novel *The Harder They Fall* (1947) and the screenplay for *On the Waterfront* (1954). Son of the movie producer B.P. Schulberg.

▲ **SENESH, HANNAH** (or Hannah Szenes; born July 17, 1921, in Budapest, Hungary; died November 7, 1944, in Budapest). Poet, diarist, and heroine of World War II, during which she left Palestine, returned to Hungary to operate behind enemy lines, and was captured and executed by the Nazis. Her writings evoked the Jewish spirit of the era.

▲ **SIEGEL, JERRY** (or Jerome Siegel; originally Jacob Siegel; born October 17, 1914, in Cleveland, Ohio; died January 28, 1996, in Los Angeles). Writer who, with artist Joe Shuster, created the comic-strip character Superman in the 1930s.

GERTRUDE STEIN

▲ **STEIN, GERTRUDE** (born February 3, 1874, in Allegheny, Pennsylvania; died July 27, 1946, in Neuilly-sur-Seine, near Paris, France). Writer who coined the term *lost generation* for young Americans after World War I; rejected traditional syntax and created a style with slow-moving, repetitive images; and wrote the opera libretto *Four Saints in Three Acts* (1929). *Photo credit:* American Jewish Archives, Cincinnati Campus, Hebrew Union College, Jewish Institute of Religion.

▲ **STONE, IRVING** (originally Irving Tennenbaum; born July 14, 1903, in San Francisco, California; died August 26, 1989, in Los Angeles). Pioneering writer of the modern biographical novel, including *Lust for Life* (about Vincent van Gogh, 1934) and *The Agony and the Ecstasy* (about Michelangelo, 1961).

▲ **TRILLING, LIONEL** (born July 4, 1905, in New York City; died November 5, 1975, in New York City). Literary critic who was the foremost proponent of his time of literature as a part of cultural history. He used psychological, sociological, and philosophical methods in his literary criticism.

▲ **URIS, LEON MARCUS** (born August 3, 1924, in Baltimore, Maryland). Novelist whose works interweave actual events and people with fictional plots and characters. He is best known for *Exodus* (1958).

▲ **VELIKOVSKY, IMMANUEL** (born June 10, 1895, in Vitebsk, Russia; died November 17, 1979, in Princeton, New Jersey). Writer, trained as a physician and psychologist, who propounded controversial theories of cosmogony and history, as in his book *Worlds in Collision* (1950).

▲ **WASSERSTEIN, WENDY** (born October 18, 1950, in Brooklyn, New York). The most prominent American playwright dealing with the subject of feminism, notably in *The Heidi Chronicles* (1988).

**WENDY WASSERSTEIN**

James Hamilton

▲ **WERFEL, FRANZ** (born September 10, 1890, in Prague, Bohemia; died August 26, 1945, in Beverly Hills, California). In his early poetry, one of the founders of the expressionist movement in German literature; in his later prose fiction, a popular novelist, known especially for *The Song of Bernadette* (German, 1941; English, 1942).

▲ **WOUK, HERMAN** (born May 27, 1915, in New York City). Novelist who wrote *The Caine Mutiny* (1951).

▲ **YEZIERSKA, ANZIA** (born about 1880 in Plinsk, Russian-ruled Poland; died November 21, 1970, in Ontario, California). Novelist and short-story writer known as the Queen of the Ghetto because her literary works so well document the struggles of poor immigrant Jews on the Lower East Side of New York City.

**HERMAN WOUK**

David Hume Kennedy

▲ **ZANGWILL, ISRAEL** (born February 14, 1864, in London, England; died August 1, 1926, in Midhurst, West Sussex, England). Novelist and playwright whose play *The Melting Pot* (1908) named and explored the image of America as a crucible in which the European nationalities would be transformed into a new race.

# 11
# JOURNALISM

*ৎ৯*

JEWISH JOURNALISTS HAVE CONTRIBUTED PATHBREAKING ACHIEVEMENTS
*in both print and broadcasting media.*

*Alfred Fried won a Nobel Peace Prize for his unique work as a literary pacifist. Ann Landers became the most widely read columnist in the world, and Sylvia Porter the most read economic reporter. Walter Winchell created the gossip column.*

*Morley Safer and Mike Wallace developed an original, much-imitated kind of investigative television journalism on 60 Minutes. And Barbara Walters raised the television interview to an art form.*

# LEADING LITERARY PACIFISM
# IN THE EARLY TWENTIETH CENTURY
## Alfred Fried

❧

*Alfred Hermann Fried was born in Vienna, Austria, on November 11, 1864. Self-educated, he worked as a bookseller before becoming a journalist and publisher. He died in Vienna on May 5, 1921.*

ALFRED FRIED WON THE 1911 NOBEL PEACE PRIZE for being "the most industrious literary pacifist in the past twenty years." He shared the award with Tobias Asser, who worked separately.

Fried, whose surname means "peace," was influenced by Bertha von Suttner's antiwar novel *Lay Down Your Arms!* (1889). In 1891 he founded the pacifist periodical *Lay Down Your Arms!*, later called *The Peacekeeper*. In 1892 he founded the German Peace Society, which became the center of the German pacifist movement before World War I. He advocated "fundamental pacifism" and believed that "international anarchy" should be met by both legislative measures and spiritual regeneration. In addition to his work as a journalist, he produced about seventy books and pamphlets, notably his *Handbook of the Peace Movement* (two volumes, 1911–13).

### ALSO NOTEWORTHY

▲ BERNSTEIN, CARL (born February 14, 1944, in Washington, D.C.). Journalist who, with Bob Woodward, was largely responsible for revealing the Watergate cover-up through investigative reports published in the *Washington Post* (1972–74). Woodstein, as the two reporters were collectively known, summarized their findings in the book *All the President's Men* (1974).

▲ BLOWITZ, HENRI (full name, Henri Georges Stephane Adolphe Opper de Blowitz; originally Adolf Opper; born December 28, 1825, in Blowitz, Pilsen, Bohemia; died January 18, 1903, in Paris, France). Journalist who originated the technique of interviewing celebrities, including Bismarck and Pope Leo XIII.

▲ BUCHWALD, ART(HUR) (born October 20, 1925, in Mount Vernon, New York). The most prominent newspaper columnist of his time in the field of social and political satire.

▲ HERSH, SEYMOUR MYRON (born April 8, 1937, in Chicago, Illinois). Investigative reporter known as the master of the governmental exposé. His stories exposed the My Lai massacres and Central Intelligence Agency (CIA) domestic spying.

# WRITING THE MOST WIDELY READ COLUMN IN THE WORLD

## Ann Landers

ℰℐ

Courtesy of Ann Landers

"ANN LANDERS" ATTRACTS MORE readers than any other newspaper column in the world. By the early 1990s, over ninety million people read the personal-advice column regularly.

"I really care about what happens to people," Ann Landers has said about her job, "and when I first began to read those letters, it was an eye-opener. I came from a very solid Midwestern Jewish home. You see, I led a very sheltered life. I had never seen a man hit his wife. I had never seen any drunkenness. I had never seen any poverty. I knew these things were happening, but they never happened to me. The mail grew me up in a hurry."

Her advice was basically common sense and usually conservative, though in later years she relaxed her views on sex and divorce. Her Jewish background influenced her because, she said, "I am inclined to support the underdog."

Shortly after the new Ann Landers began her column in 1955, her twin sister, Mrs. Pauline E. Phillips (née Friedman), took the name Abigail Van Buren and began her own advice column, "Dear Abby," in the *San Francisco Chronicle*. The two feuded for several years but eventually made up.

In 1975 Ann Landers faced the trauma of divorce. But she rebounded and continued to give the same reasonable advice while her readership grew to the largest in the world.

*Ann Landers was born in Sioux City, Iowa, on July 4, 1918. Her original name was Esther Pauline Friedman. As a young woman, she spent many happily married years as Mrs. Esther P. Lederer. Then, in 1955, the first Ann Landers, whose real name was Ruth Crowley, died, and the* Chicago Sun Times *ran a contest to replace her as the writer of a personal-advice column. Mrs. Lederer won the contest and became the new Ann Landers.*

# BECOMING AMERICA'S MOST WIDELY READ ECONOMIC REPORTER

## Sylvia Porter

❧

*Sylvia Porter was born in Patchogue, Long Island, New York, on June 18, 1913. Her original name was Sylvia Feldman. In 1931 she married Reed R. Porter, a bank employee. Sylvia Porter became a famous financial journalist. She died in Pound Ridge, New York, on June 5, 1991.*

A FAMILY MISFORTUNE CHANGED SYLVIA PORTER'S CAREER from writing to economics. But when she combined the two disciplines, she struck gold, becoming America's most widely read economic reporter.

She entered Hunter College with the intention of majoring in English literature and becoming a writer. But when her mother lost a small fortune in the 1929 stock market crash, Sylvia switched to economics so that she could understand what had happened to her mother and so many others.

After graduating from Hunter in 1932, she started working as an investment counselor and writing articles for financial journals. In

Courtesy of the Library of Congress

1935 she began writing an occasional, and soon a daily, financial column for the *New York Post* newspaper. In 1947 the column was nationally syndicated. Later she moved to the *New York Daily News,* and eventually the column was syndicated out of the *Los Angeles Times.* She also wrote over twenty books.

Porter had a genius for phrasing complicated economic jargon in readable prose. She educated people about the stock market, pointed out rackets and injustices, showed how to save money on various services and products, and, in general, served as the nation's first consumer advocate.

Porter's column was published in over four hundred newspapers around the world, with an estimated readership of forty million people.

# HOSTING A REVOLUTIONARY TELEVISION FORMAT
## Morley Safer

எ

THE CBS NEWSMAGAZINE *60 MINUTES* has become an institution on American television. The show brought a new kind of program format (in-depth investigative reports, often openly critical, on a small number of news topics) to the medium, one that has been widely imitated by both serious and tabloid television journalists. Since 1970 one of the principal cohosts (or coeditors) has been Morley Safer.

In late 1970 he replaced Harry Reasoner as one of the two hosts on *60 Minutes*. The other host, Mike Wallace, had an abrasive, hard-hitting style, while the gentler Safer became known for his witty essays. "I don't like to walk into those closets and shake the skeletons," he admitted. However, Safer, too, dug into meaty topics. He covered Vietnam, investigated organized crime and business frauds, and elicited revealing comments from innumerable interviewees, including Betty Ford and the infamous Tokyo Rose.

Safer strives to put together "the observed kind of story," he says, as opposed to the story that is merely told. His technique has served him well on one of American television's most respected and popular shows since the 1960s.

> *Morley Safer was born in Toronto, Ontario, Canada, on November 8, 1931. After graduating from the University of Western Ontario (1952), he worked for the Canadian Broadcasting Corporation before coming to the United States in 1964. He joined the CBS television network as a news correspondent.*

---

### ALSO NOTEWORTHY

▲ LIPPMANN, WALTER (born September 23, 1889, in New York City; died December 14, 1974, in New York City). Journalist and political philosopher who influenced policy makers for over fifty years and in his late years was widely regarded as the dean of American newspapermen.

▲ SCHORR, DANIEL LOUIS (born August 31, 1916, in New York City). Controversial CBS Washington correspondent (1966–76) whose application of the solid techniques of old-fashioned print journalism made him the most effective reporter, with a long list of scoops, in American broadcasting.

WALTER LIPPMAN

▲ SWOPE, HERBERT BAYARD (born January 5, 1882, in Saint Louis, Missouri; died June 20, 1958, in Sands Point, New York). The first winner of the Pulitzer Prize in journalism (1917), for his World War I war correspondence from Germany.

# HOSTING A REVOLUTIONARY TELEVISION FORMAT
## Mike Wallace

☙

*Mike Wallace was born in Brookline, Massachusetts, on May 9, 1918. His original name was Myron Leon Wallace. While attending the University of Michigan, he gained some experience on the campus radio station and became hooked on broadcasting. After graduating from the university (1939), he worked in radio as a news and entertainment writer-announcer. In the early 1950s he appeared on television talk, quiz, and game shows. In 1956 he reported news on television, in the late 1950s hosted* The Mike Wallace Interview, *and in 1963 was given the* CBS Morning News with Mike Wallace. *In 1968 he began to work on the* 60 Minutes *program.*

MIKE WALLACE HAS BEEN A COHOST (or coeditor) of the pathbreaking CBS television newsmagazine *60 Minutes* since its inception in 1968. The show brought a new kind of program format (in-depth investigative reports, often openly critical, on a small number of topics) to the medium, one that has been widely imitated by both serious and tabloid television journalists.

In 1968 Wallace and Harry Reasoner (replaced in 1970 by Morley Safer) became the first hosts of *60 Minutes*. Wallace created a new kind of television journalistic style with his newsmaking interviews and his aggressive investigative reports. One of his earliest interviews was with two of the American soldiers who had participated in the My Lai massacres in Vietnam. He also interviewed world leaders, including Menachem Begin and Ayatollah Khomeini, as well as such artists as Vladimir Horowitz and Leonard Bernstein. His reports often take the form of exposés of government or business abuses. His methods have been called "ambush journalism," in which he and his film crew pursue and surprise someone who is filmed giving an awkward verbal response or exploding in defensive behavior that suggests wrongdoing.

Wallace sees each story as a drama "built around a value conflict." His technique propelled him to the highest echelon of investigative reporters on one of American television's most respected and popular shows since the 1960s.

### ALSO NOTEWORTHY

▲ VAN BUREN, ABIGAIL (originally Pauline Esther Friedman; born July 4, 1918, in Sioux City, Iowa). Writer of the "Dear Abby" syndicated advice column. Twin sister of Ann Landers.

▲ WHITE, THEODORE HAROLD (born May 6, 1915, in Boston, Massachusetts; died May 15, 1986, in New York City). Political journalist who changed the shape of his field through his detailed chronicles of the American presidential campaigns of 1960–72.

# RAISING THE TELEVISION INTERVIEW TO AN ART FORM

## Barbara Walters

ೞ

BARBARA WALTERS WAS THE FIRST WOMAN NEWS ANCHOR on network television. But her greatest contribution to television history was her raising of the television interview to an art form.

Her career as an interviewer sprang from early influences in her life. When she was a child, her father owned several nightclubs, so she became accustomed to meeting celebrities. Another influence was her mentally retarded sister. "I had tremendous guilt and sadness about her," Walters later confessed. "Maybe that's what interested me so much about people. My heroes are those who work with the handicapped."

*Courtesy of The Jewish Week, New York*

In 1961 she joined NBC's *Today* show as a writer and occasional reporter. She soon gained a reputation for her probing interviews with celebrities. "I'm good at drawing people out," she explained. "There's a thin line between asking critical questions well and making someone mad." She was always well prepared for each individual. "I don't like to wing it. And you have to listen and be ready to ask a follow-up question. It's good to start by asking people about their childhood. It relaxes them."

Walters stayed with the *Today* show for many years, as a regular panel member (1964–74) and as a cohost (1974–76). In 1976 she switched to ABC so that she could become the first female news anchor on network television, serving with Harry Reasoner as coanchor of the network's evening news. In the same year she began her long and continuing series of special interviews. In 1978 she left her evening news job, and in 1979 she began as a correspondent with the popular newsmagazine *20/20,* serving as cohost, with Hugh Downs, since 1984.

Walters has staged many coups as an interviewer. In 1977, for example, she set up a joint interview with Egyptian President Anwar Sadat and Israeli Prime Minister Menachem Begin. In early 1995 her interview with Olympic diving champion Greg Luganis broke the story of his homosexuality and contraction of AIDS. Among her other interviewees were countless movie stars and heads of state. Barbara Walters has turned the television interview into a new kind of entertainment art form, of which she is the acknowledged master.

> *Barbara Jill Walters was born in Boston, Massachusetts, on September 25, 1931. After graduating from Sarah Lawrence College in the early 1950s, she worked as a writer and producer on various New York City television stations. Later she joined network television and became well known for her skills as an interviewer.*

# ORIGINATING THE GOSSIP COLUMN
## Walter Winchell

᭐

THE GOSSIP COLUMN had a tremendous influence on American life and public affairs in the twentieth century. The originator of this type of journalism was Walter Winchell.

As a youngster, he entered vaudeville, where his inquisitiveness led him to acquire gossip and eventually a job as a correspondent with the *Vaudeville News*. In 1924 he began writing his "On Broadway" gossip column for the *New York Evening Graphic*. In 1929 he switched to the *New York Daily Mirror,* which syndicated his column till 1963. He also broadcast a weekly radio program from 1932 till the early 1950s.

American Jewish Archives, Cincinnati Campus, Hebrew Union College, Jewish Institute of Religion

Winchell dug into the lives of political and show-business figures, less interested in pure truth than in a good story. But sometimes he got hold of historically important scoops, as when, in 1940, he broke the news of Franklin Delano Roosevelt's decision to seek an unprecedented third term as president of the United States. His most identifiable characteristic was his language, based in the show-biz idiom with a liberal sprinkling of his own coinages, such as *cupiding* ("in love"), *middle-aisled* ("married"), *Reno-vated* ("divorced"), *shafts* ("legs"), and *storked* ("pregnant").

Winchell's brash, opinionated style and his exploitation of the public interest in the private affairs of the famous had a tremendous impact on contemporary journalism.

# 12
# MUSIC

❧

JEWISH COMPOSERS WHO MADE UNIQUE CONTRIBUTIONS TO MUSIC *included Harold Arlen, who scored* The Wizard of Oz; *Irving Berlin, who wrote innumerable classic popular songs; Ernest Bloch, the first great composer of modern Jewish national music; Aaron Copland, the first internationally renowned composer of American-flavored concert music; Bob Dylan, who led the urban folk-music revival; George Gershwin, who fused popular and classical music; Philip Glass, who developed minimalist music; Jerome Kern, the father of modern American theater music; Gustav Mahler, who both summed up the nineteenth century and foreshadowed the twentieth; Jacques Offenbach, who established operetta as an art form; and Arnold Schoenberg, inventor of the twelve-tone technique of composition.*

*Among those Jewish performers who created unique niches for themselves in the history of music were Benny Goodman, "the King of Swing"; Yascha Heifetz, "the King of Violinists"; Vladimir Horowitz, "the King of Piano Virtuosos"; Arthur Rubinstein, the supreme Chopin interpreter; Dinah Shore, "the Queen of Jukeboxes"; Isaac Stern, the first violin virtuoso wholly a product of American training; Barbra Streisand, who created a new manner of singing songs by "acting" them; and Rosalyn Tureck, "the High Priestess of Bach." Felix Mendelssohn profoundly affected the music world as a conductor through his concert innovations, and as a composer through his fusion of classical and romantic styles. Leonard Bernstein, a composer and performer, was the first great American-trained musician.*

# COMPOSING THE MUSIC FOR THE MOST BELOVED FILM FANTASY

## Harold Arlen

&

HAROLD ARLEN WAS ONE OF AMERICA'S MOST VERSATILE and historically important songwriters. His best-known achievement was his memorable score to the world's most beloved film fantasy, *The Wizard of Oz* (1939).

He composed the music for a wide range of songs for films and the stage. They included "It's Only a Paper Moon" (1933, originally "If You Believe in Me," 1932), an unsurpassed reflection of the national mood during the Great Depression; the comically risqué "Lydia, the Tattooed Lady" (1939); the hypnotic "That Old Black Magic" (1942); and the torch song "The Man That Got Away" (1954).

He was America's foremost composer of tunes that fused Anglo-American and Afro-American elements. Among such songs were "Stormy Weather" (1933) and "Blues in the Night" (1941).

His score for *The Wizard of Oz* played a unique role in film history. It was one of the earliest movie musicals to attempt to integrate songs into the development of plot and character, and it was the first movie of wide popularity and influence to so integrate the songs.

Arlen and his lyricist, E.Y. Harburg, provided the story's principal character, the young girl Dorothy, with the early song "Over the Rainbow," which, in both its words and its music, expresses the girl's longing to live in an ideal place and thus lays the groundwork for her later dream trip to the land of Oz. The little Munchkins sing "Ding-Dong! The Witch Is Dead," which, by focusing on the wickedness of the dead witch, prepares the audience for the even greater wickedness of her sister throughout the rest of the story. The

*Harold Arlen was born in Buffalo, New York, on February 15, 1905. His original name was Hyman Arluck. He learned the art of singing from his father, who was a cantor, and from recordings of cantorial and opera music. By 1928 the young man had changed his surname to Arlen, a blend of the first syllable of his orignal name, Arluck, and the sound of the second syllable of his mother's maiden name, Orlin. Arlen became one of the most successful popular-song composers in the United States. He died in New York City on April 23, 1986.*

## ALSO NOTEWORTHY

▲ ADLER, LARRY (originally Lawrence Cecil Adler; born February 10, 1914, in Baltimore, Maryland). The world's greatest harmonica player and the first to raise the instrument to concert status.

# MUSIC FOR THE MOST BELOVED FILM FANTASY *(continued)*

Munchkins also sing "Follow the Yellow Brick Road," which sets Dorothy on course for her trip to the Emerald City in Oz.

The Scarecrow, the Tin Man, and the Cowardly Lion sing, respectively and successively, "If I Only Had a Brain," "If I Only Had a Heart," and "If I Only Had the Nerve," each to the same melody, thus unifying the characters into a trio and tying together a long stretch of the plot, but also differentiating their personalities through their different needs. The same three and Dorothy sing "We're Off to See the Wizard" every time they start up again toward the Emerald City.

The residents of the Emerald City sing "The Merry Old Land of Oz" to welcome the four visitors and to explain the customs of the country. Arlen and Harburg wrote a special number, "If I Were King of the Forest," to further explain the Cowardly Lion's character and to take advantage of the special talent for comic bravura by the actor playing the part, Bert Lahr.

Through *The Wizard of Oz*, which debuted on television in 1956 and has been broadcast annually since 1959, Arlen's music has come to be cherished by generations of fans.

---

## ALSO NOTEWORTHY

▲ **APEL, WILLI** (born October 10, 1893, in Konitz, Germany; died March 14, 1988, in Bloomington, Indiana). Musicologist whose *Harvard Dictionary of Music* (1944, revised 1969) was profoundly influential as the first American general reference book to give as much attention to early and non-Western music as to the more familiar repertory.

▲ **AUER, LEOPOLD** (born June 7, 1845, in Veszprém, Hungary; died July 15, 1930, in Loschwitz, near Dresden, Germany). Violinist who was the principal early propagator of the Russian bow grip (which consists of pressing the bow stick with the center joint of the index finger, resulting in a rich tone) and arguably the world's greatest violin teacher, producing such masters as Mischa Elman, Jascha Heifetz, Nathan Milstein, and Efrem Zimbalist.

▲ **BEAUX ARTS TRIO,** consisting of pianist Menahem Pressler (born December 16, 1923, in Magdeburg, Germany), violinist Isidore Cohen (born December 16, 1922, in New York City), and cellist Bernard Greenhouse (born January 3, 1916, in Newark, New Jersey). Piano trio formed in 1955, the first permanent ensemble to raise the status of the piano trio to the level of that of the string quartet.

▲ **BERNSTEIN, ELMER** (born April 4, 1922, in New York City). Composer of many memorable film scores, including those for *The Man with the Golden Arm* (1955), *The Ten Commandments* (1956), *The Magnificient Seven* (1960), *To Kill a Mockingbird* (1962), *The Great Escape* (1963), and *Roommates* (1995).

▲ **BLITZSTEIN, MARC** (born March 2, 1905, in Philadelphia, Pennsylvania; died January 22, 1964, in Fort-de-France, Martinique). Composer who created a new American musical-theater idiom, based in contemporary musical language, vernacular speech style, and sociological awareness. His best-known work is *The Cradle Will Rock* (1937).

▲ **BOCK, JERRY** (originally Jerrold Lewis Bock; born November 23, 1928, in New Haven, Connecticut). Composer of the musical *Fiddler on the Roof* (1964), with "If I Were a Rich Man," "Sunrise, Sunset," and "Tradition."

# COMPOSING AMERICA'S MOST
# SOPHISTICATED POPULAR MUSIC
## Burt Bacharach

༄

*Burt Bacharach was born in Kansas City, Missouri, on May 12, 1928. He studied classical music at several institutions, including the New School for Social Research in New York City; one of his teachers was the world-renowned composer Darius Milhaud. But classical composers generally earned very little money, so Bacharach switched to popular music and became the most gifted songwriter of his generation.*

BURT BACHARACH IS PROBABLY THE MOST SOPHISTICATED CRAFTSMAN among American popular-song composers of his time. Since the beginning of the rock-music era, none of his peers has produced such an individual sound.

After some years as a piano accompanist for pop singers, such as Vic Damone, Bacharach met the lyricist Hal David, with whom he scored a quick success with the song "Magic Moments" (1957). In 1960 he met the singer Dionne Warwick. "What emotion I could get away with!" he said of composing for her. During the 1960s the team of Bacharach-David-Warwick dominated American popular music. Bacharach's songs included "Close to You" (1963), "What the World Needs Now Is Love" (1965), "Alfie" (1966), "I'll Never Fall in Love Again" (1968), and "Raindrops Keep Fallin' on My Head" (1969). Later he worked with other lyricists, notably Carole Bayer Sager, whom he married and with whom he wrote "That's What Friends Are For" (1982).

Bacharach borrowed elements from bop, rock, soul, progressive jazz, Tin Pan Alley, Latin American music, and other sources but synthesized them into a distinctive Bacharach sound. His music is characterized by complex rhythms and unusual accents, boldly original harmonic progressions, and unconventional but memorable melodic patterns that often leap about with a naturalness that only an exceptionally gifted melodist can achieve. Probably more than any other pop-song composer, he was responsible for the development of flexible phrasing, that is, phrase lengths that often vary from the traditional four or eight measures. These features have been widely imitated since Bacharach popularized them, but no one has been able to compete in style and sophistication with the original Bacharach sound.

# CREATING THE LONGEST LIST OF CLASSIC POPULAR SONGS

## Irving Berlin

ಐ

IRVING BERLIN WAS AMERICA'S MOST SUCCESSFUL SONGWRITER. Love songs, comic songs, show-business songs, holiday songs, patriotic songs—in all these categories and more, Berlin wrote classics.

Berlin's first classic was "Alexander's Ragtime Band" (1911), which changed American popular music forever with its swing and energy. In 1912 his wife, Dorothy Goetz, died while they were on their honeymoon. He remembered her in "When I Lost You" (1912), his first true ballad.

During World War I, he wrote the army revue *Yip Yip, Yaphank* (1918), with "Oh, How I Hate to Get Up in the Morning." For the 1919 *Ziegfeld Follies* on Broadway, he contributed "A Pretty Girl Is like a Melody," which became the theme song for future editions of the show, as well as the classic comic song "You'd Be Surprised."

For Broadway's *The Cocoanuts* (1925), he wrote "Always," which was rejected for the show but later became a standard love song. For the Broadway musical *Annie Get Your Gun* (1946), he created "Anything You Can Do I Can Do Better" and "There's No Business like Show Business." For various stage shows and films he provided other classics, such as "What'll I Do?" (1923), "Puttin' On the Ritz" (1930), "Let's Have Another Cup of Coffee" (1932), and "Cheek to Cheek" (1935).

Berlin is probably best remembered for his holiday and patriotic songs. No Easter is complete without his "Easter Parade" (1933, a flop in 1917 as "Smile and Show Your Dimple") or Christmas without his "White Christmas" (1942). For *Yip, Yip, Yaphank* he wrote one song that he himself rejected and filed away for twenty years. When, in 1938, the singer Kate Smith asked him for a patriotic song, he pulled the old reject out of the drawer, revised it a little, and gave her "God Bless America," which soon became the nation's second national anthem.

No songwriter has bequeathed America a longer list of classic popular songs.

*Irving Berlin was born in Temun, Russia, on May 11, 1888. His original name was Israel Baline. After learning to sing from his father, a cantor, he worked as a street singer, a saloon singer, a songplugger, and a singing waiter before turning to songwriting. Berlin never learned to read music, so he hummed and improvised pieces on the piano while associates wrote down his tunes. He wrote his own lyrics. Berlin died in New York City on September 22, 1989, at the age of 101.*

# BECOMING THE FIRST GREAT
# AMERICAN-TRAINED MUSICIAN
## Leonard Bernstein

❧

Leonard Bernstein was born in Lawrence, Massachusetts, on August 25, 1918. He was the most versatile musician of his time. He died in New York City on October 14, 1990.

LEONARD BERNSTEIN PLAYED A UNIQUE DUAL ROLE in American music. He was simultaneously a respected leader among art-music connoisseurs and a cultlike figure with the general public. A gifted conductor, a skilled composer of both art and popular music, an excellent pianist, an articulate writer, an inspirational teacher and television commentator, Bernstein—Lenny, as he was affectionately known to friends and admirers—dominated the world's music scene from the 1950s through the 1980s. What made his achievements even more historically noteworthy was the fact that he was the first internationally renowned musician wholly a product of American schooling. He studied piano with a succession of New England teachers, majored in music at Harvard University (graduating in 1939), attended the Curtis Institute of Music in Philadelphia (1939–41), and studied conducting under Serge Koussevitzky at the Berkshire Music Center in Massachusetts during the summers of 1940 and 1941.

At that time, most important classical-music posts in America went to Europeans or to Americans with European training. But Bernstein's skills were so evident that he was given an assistant conductorship with the New York Philharmonic in August 1943. That November he made a spectacular debut as a last-minute substitute for an ailing guest conductor. From 1945 to 1948, he served as head conductor of the New York City Symphony Orchestra; and from 1958 to 1969, he was the first American-born music director and chief conductor of the New York Philharmonic. From the mid-1940s on, Bernstein guest-conducted most of the major orchestras in the world. He often appeared as pianist-conductor in performances of piano concertos. In 1953 he became the first American-born musician to conduct at La Scala in Milan, Italy, during the regular opera season. In 1967 he became the first conductor to release recordings

### ALSO NOTEWORTHY

▲ BRODSKY, ADOLPH (originally Adolf Brodsky; born April 2, 1851, in Taganrog, Russia; died January 22, 1929, in Manchester, England). Violinist who gave the world premiere of Tchaikovsky's famous *Violin Concerto* (1881).

▲ CARLEBACH, SHLOMO (born 1925 in Berlin, Germany; died October 20, 1994, in New York City). Rabbi who was the foremost songwriter in contemporary Judaism, his songs being heard at virtually every Jewish wedding and bar mitzvah.

of all nine Mahler symphonies as a single unit. He also led the world premieres of many works, especially by American composers, such as Charles Ives and Aaron Copland.

Bernstein composed classical works that synthesized a wide variety of influences, including Jewish cantillation, as in his *First Symphony: Jeremiah* (1942), and jazz, as in his *Second Symphony: The Age of Anxiety* (1949). His popular-music works were headed by the Broadway musical *West Side Story* (1957).

Bernstein taught at the Berkshire Music Center (1948–55, later serving as an advisor) and at Brandeis University (1951–56). He was the first major musician to make an impact on television, explaining music to a general audience on *Omnibus* (1954–58) and serving as conductor-commentator of the televised New York Philharmonic Young People's Concerts (1958–72) and the eleven-part series *Bernstein, Beethoven* (1981–82) with the Vienna Philharmonic. Most of his books grew out of his other activities; *The Joy of Music* (1959), for example, came from his television scripts, and *The Unanswered Question: Six Talks at Harvard* (1976) was a publication of his Harvard lectures of 1972–73.

The Carson Office

By achieving so much success without a European background, Bernstein opened new doors of opportunity for countless other American-trained musicians who followed him.

---

## ALSO NOTEWORTHY

▲ **DAVID, FERDINAND** (born probably June 19 [sometimes listed as January 19], 1810, in Hamburg, Germany; died July 18, 1873, near Klosters, Switzerland). Violinist who gave the world premiere of Mendelssohn's famous *Violin Concerto* (1845).

▲ **DEUTSCH, OTTO ERICH** (born September 5, 1883, in Vienna, Austria; died November 23, 1967, in Vienna). Music scholar who raised the documentary biography to a new level of importance and who published a thematic catalog of Schubert's works, which are now universally identified by the numbers attached to them by Deutsch.

▲ **DIAMOND, NEIL LESLIE** (born January 24, 1941, in New York City). Singer and songwriter whose recordings include "Cherry, Cherry" (1966) and "Heartlight" (1982).

▲ **DUKAS, PAUL** (born October 1, 1865, in Paris, France; died May 17, 1935, in Paris). Composer famous for his orchestral tone poem *L'apprenti sorcier* ("The Sorcerer's Apprentice," 1897).

# COMPOSING THE FIRST GREAT MODERN JEWISH NATIONAL MUSIC
## Ernest Bloch

&

*Ernest Bloch was born in Geneva, Switzerland, on July 24, 1880. He studied violin and composition in Belgium and Germany, worked a few years in his father's clock shop, and taught at the Geneva Conservatory (1911–15). In 1916 he moved to the United States, where he taught at the Mannes School of Music in New York City (1917–20) and then directed the Cleveland Institute of Music (1920–25) and the San Francisco Conservatory (1925–30). In 1930 a grant from a music lover enabled him to devote himself to composition. He died in Portland, Oregon, on July 15, 1959.*

ERNEST BLOCH WAS THE FIRST GREAT COMPOSER of modern Jewish national music. "I am a Jew," he said. "I aspire to write Jewish music...because it is the only way in which I can produce music of vitality."

Bloch composed in various styles at different times in his life. His first works, up to the early 1910s, reflected the influence of German postromanticism and French impressionism. The 1920s were marked by neoclassicism. And his late works, in the 1940s and 1950s, summarized the various styles in his career.

During the 1910s and early 1920s, Bloch composed what has been described as his Jewish Cycle, works that draw from the rhapsodic manner and intervallic and rhythmic patterns characteristic of Jewish liturgical and secular music. In the 1930s he returned for a time to this manner.

"It is the Jewish soul that interests me," he explained, "the complex, glowing, agitated soul that I feel vibrating throughout the Bible" and "that I strive to hear in myself and to translate in my music." His Jewish Cycle included *Three Jewish Poems* for orchestra (1913), *Israel Symphony* for voices and orchestra (1916), *Schelomo* for cello and orchestra (1916), and *From Jewish Life* for cello and piano (1924). His 1930s Jewish works were highlighted by *Avodath hakodesh* ("Sacred Service," 1933). Late in life he composed *Hebraic Suite* for viola and orchestra (1951).

Bloch proved that important concert music could be composed in the spirit of Jewish music without resorting to simple quotations of folk and liturgical melodies.

### ALSO NOTEWORTHY

▲ **EDWARDS, GUS** (originally Gustave Edward Simon; born August 18, 1879, in Inowrazlaw, Poland; died November 7, 1945, in Los Angeles). Composer of the popular songs "If a Girl like You Loved a Boy like Me" (1905), "School Days" (1907), and "By the Light of the Silvery Moon" (1909). Also a vaudeville singer who discovered, and put into his act, many future celebrities, including Eddie Cantor, George Jessel, and Groucho Marx.

# SYMBOLIZING AMERICAN ART MUSIC
## Aaron Copland

❧

AARON COPLAND WAS THE FIRST INTERNATIONALLY RENOWNED composer of art music with an American accent. He utilized jazz, folk music, and his own personal qualities to create sounds that could have originated nowhere but the United States.

He began by infusing his works with jazz elements, especially a fresh rhythmic vigor. With the jazz features, he combined a modern approach to dissonance and his personal mannerisms with respect to harmonic spacing and other techniques. His *Piano Concerto* (1926) highlighted this early phase in his career.

His orchestral *Symphonic Ode* (1929) ushered in a more abstract version of his first style. Some listeners heard a "Jewish," or "prophetic," quality in the work because of its profound, dramatic, speechlike musical utterances cast in a mold of tragic grandeur.

Boston Symphony Orchestra

*Aaron Copland was born in New York City on November 14, 1900. He studied music privately in New York City and then, under Nadia Boulanger, in France (1921–24). Boulanger encouraged him to study contemporary music, especially that of Stravinsky, but to follow his own instincts. Copland did both. He was excited by Stravinsky's powerful new music. But Stravinsky had European and Russian instincts, while Copland had American. Copland returned to the United States determined to compose music that was both modern and American. He died in North Tarrytown, New York, on December 2, 1990.*

The same quality is evident in many Copland works throughout his career. This abstract phase also produced the *Piano Variations* (1930).

The Great Depression and World War II induced in Copland, as in so many other artists, an egalitarianism. To reach a larger audience, he decided to express his ideas "in the simplest possible terms." He borrowed folksongs, created original themes in the spirit of such tunes, and in general simplified his style. The result was a series of American-flavored works that brought Copland his greatest fame. They included the ballets *Billy the Kid* (1938), *Rodeo* (1942), and *Appalachian Spring* (1944); the film scores *Our Town* (1940) and *The Red Pony* (1949); *Fanfare for the Common Man* for brass and percussion (1942); and the orchestral pieces *A Lincoln Portrait* (1942), *Third Symphony* (1946), and *Clarinet Concerto* (1948).

Copland was widely imitated by other American composers who were grateful to him for breaking Europe's long stranglehold on American music practices.

# LEADING THE FOLK-MUSIC REVIVAL
## Bob Dylan

❦

*Bob Dylan was born in Duluth, Minnesota, on May 24, 1941. His original name was Robert Allen Zimmerman. He took his stage name from the poet Dylan Thomas. As a youth, Bob Dylan had two idols: the country singer Hank Williams and the actor James Dean. Williams gave Dylan a sound to strive for; Dean gave an image. Both died young, giving a poignancy to much of what Dylan later expressed in his songs. He was self-taught as a musician, though he learned a great deal by listening to the folksingers Woody Guthrie and Pete Seeger.*

BOB DYLAN WAS THE MOST INFLUENTIAL FIGURE in the urban folk-music revival of the 1960s and 1970s. As a singer and songwriter, he led several movements in the changing folk-music scene.

He began his career playing an acoustic guitar and singing traditional folk material, as in his first album, *Bob Dylan* (1962). Soon he had to write his own songs so that he could express his own thoughts and feelings. At first, his works were individual confessions, but later they grew into social protests against racism, nuclear weapons, and other curses of the time. More than any other popular songwriter of that era, Dylan caught the mood of American youth, especially in his song "Blowin' in the Wind," on his album *The Freewheelin' Bob Dylan* (1963). He became the undisputed leader of urban folk music.

Courtesy of Bob Dylan

In 1965 he picked up an electric guitar, accompanied himself with a rock band, and led the folk-rock fusion of the mid-1960s. An album exemplifying that style was his *Highway 61 Revisited* (1965), with "Like a Rolling Stone."

After recuperating from a serious 1966 motorcycle accident, Dylan mellowed. He led a country-rock fusion characterized by lyrics that were tranquil and personal, as opposed to the earlier social messages. *Nashville Skyline* (1969) was in the country-rock style.

In later years Dylan merged folk, country, and rock. He displayed this style in albums such as *Desire* (1975) and *Infidels* (1983).

Dylan's influence lay in his music, his lyrics, and his performance style. His music integrated black and white folk elements into a personal sound. His lyrics were elusive and abstract, leading to endless quests to interpret them. His performances were marked by an unpolished voice, a conversational delivery, and spontaneous phrasing. All of these traits have been widely imitated since Dylan's rise to leadership in the urban folk-music revival.

# FUSING POPULAR AND CLASSICAL MUSIC
## George Gershwin

✍

GEORGE GERSHWIN WAS THE FIRST COMPOSER to bring widespread attention to the possibility of merging twentieth-century American popular music with classical traditions to produce memorable symphonic works. His success encouraged many other composers to attempt a similar fusion.

In 1919 he composed his first score for a Broadway musical, and in the 1930s he wrote for films. His work in those fields produced such well-known songs as "Swanee" (1919), "The Man I Love" (1924), "I Got Rhythm" (1930), and "Love Walked In" (1938).

Though grounded in the popular commercial world of Tin Pan Alley and Broadway, his style also showed the influence of jazz in some of its rhythmic, melodic, and harmonic characteristics. In 1923 the bandleader Paul Whiteman asked him to compose an extended piece to display jazz as a serious art form. Gershwin responded with his *Rhapsody in Blue* (1924). His motivation was to show people that jazz was not limited in its technical and expressive possibilities. "The rhapsody...began as a purpose," he explained, "not a plan." He went on to compose many more works that blended elements from jazz, Tin Pan Alley, Broadway, and classical music. They included the *Concerto in F* for piano and orchestra (1925), the *Preludes for Piano* (1926), the orchestral piece *An American in Paris* (1928), and the opera *Porgy and Bess* (1935). These pieces were written in much the same style as his songs, but with more working out of ideas.

Gershwin's fusion of popular and classical music influenced the works of many composers, as in Aaron Copland's use of jazz in the 1920s, the quasi-symphonic music in films of the 1930s and 1940s, innumerable light orchestral pieces by Ferde Grofé and others, and the third-stream music (modern jazz plus contemporary art music) since the 1950s.

*George Gershwin was born in Brooklyn, New York, on September 26, 1898. His original name was Jacob Gershvin (misspelled "Gershwine" on his birth certificate), but his family always called him George. He had some formal lessons in piano and theory, but throughout his career his technical knowledge of music remained rudimentary. At the age of fifteen, he left school to become a Tin Pan Alley songplugger and a piano accompanist. Soon he rose to fame as a popular-song composer. He died in Los Angeles on July 11, 1937.*

Courtesy of the Academy of Motion Picture Arts and Sciences

◀ George *(left)* and Ira Gershwin.

# LEADING THE MINIMALIST
# MOVEMENT IN MUSIC
## Philip Glass

☙

*Philip Glass was born in Baltimore, Maryland, on January 31, 1937. After earning a B.A. at the University of Chicago (1956) and an M.S. at the Juilliard School of Music (1962), he studied under Nadia Boulanger in Paris. He then studied Eastern music, established his own ensemble, and created a wholly new style of musical composition.*

MINIMALISM IS AN ARTISTIC MOVEMENT, developed in the 1960s, that attempts to achieve maximum effects with minimum means. The best-known and most influential musician in this movement is Philip Glass.

Jack Mitchell

In his early works, Glass composed in various Western modernist idioms, but he tired of them. "I found twelve-tone music ugly and didactic," he later explained, "and I didn't care for French or German or any other kind of 'school.'" He wanted to write music that had "a sense of community," that is, music that captured the spirit of the times for a general audience—a quality lacking in the main currents of modern Western art music. Yet he did not want to shift completely over to commercial popular music.

During the winter of 1965–66 in Paris, he met the Indian sitarist Ravi Shankar. Glass soon began to study Indian and other Eastern music by traveling in the Middle East and Asia. Returning to the United States, he formed the Philip Glass Ensemble (1968), consisting of players on a variety of electronic devices and electrically amplified keyboards and wind instruments. Completely rejecting the extravagance and self-serving complexity of Western modernist music, Glass adopted the philosophy of minimalism. His new music was characterized by unique sonorities, melodic repetition, harmonic stasis, Eastern-based rhythmic phrases that constantly repeated with subtle and ingenious contractions or extensions, and mystic-consciousness-inducing length.

His early works included *Music in Similar Motion* (1969) and *Another Look at Harmony* (1974). Later, especially after he turned to the composition of large-scale dramatic works, his music became increasingly expressive and rich in harmony and incident. Those qualities are evident in his film score *Koyaanisqatsi* ("Life out of Balance," 1982) and in his operas *Einstein on the Beach* (1976), *Satyagraha* ("Truth and Firmness," 1980), *Akhnaten* (1984), and *The Voyage* (1992). Through these and similar works, Glass has given minimalism its widest music audience.

# BECOMING THE KING OF SWING
## Benny Goodman

☙

BENNY GOODMAN, CLARINETIST AND BANDLEADER, made jazz history for many achievements. He had a peerless jazz technique, setting the standard for his instrument. He was the first white bandleader successfully to adopt a genuine jazz style, as distinct from the simplified versions of jazz in earlier white groups. He was the first major white bandleader to integrate his groups with black performers. He was the first great jazz musician to succeed in classical music. But he is still best remembered as the leader of the swing era in jazz.

In 1934 Goodman formed a large dance band. "I wanted to create a tight, small-band quality," he later explained, "and I wanted every one of my boys to be a soloist." Under his direction, his arrangers produced works that moved away from the unlimited individual expression of early jazz and toward a technical brilliance in well-organized ensemble playing. "I didn't just ask for good musicianship; I insisted on it. Nothing less than perfection would do." Into these sophisticated big-band arrangements, soloists, including Goodman himself, interpolated improvisations. The band's performance in August 1935 at the Palomar Ballroom in Los Angeles is often cited as the beginning of the swing era, which flourished into the 1940s.

*International Musician*

Goodman was acknowledged as the King of Swing.

*Benjamin Goodman was born in Chicago, Illinois, on May 30, 1909. He started the clarinet at age ten; took lessons from Franz Schoepp, a member of the Chicago Symphony Orchestra, from age twelve to age fourteen; and left school at fourteen to play in a succession of jazz groups. Goodman later formed many bands of his own for varying periods of time. In 1938, at the peak of his jazz fame, he began to play classical music with great success. He appeared in recitals and as soloist in concerts with major symphony orchestras, playing music of Mozart, Brahms, Copland, and other masters. In his later years, his performances often consisted of jazz in the first half of the program and classical music in the second half. He died in New York City on June 13, 1986.*

---

### ALSO NOTEWORTHY

▲ ELMAN, MISCHA (born January 20, 1891, in Talnoye, near Kiev, Ukraine; died April 5, 1967, in New York City). One of the two (with Jascha Heifetz) greatest violinists of his time, and the creator of the legendary "Elman tone," a rich, sensuous, expressive sound.

▲ ENGEL, JOEL (originally Yuly [or Julius] Engel; born April 16, 1868, in Berdyansk, Ukraine; died February 11, 1927, in Tel Aviv, Palestine). Composer now regarded as the earliest pioneer of modern Jewish music.

# EARNING THE TITLE OF KING OF VIOLINISTS
## Yascha Heifetz

ﾐ

*Yascha Heifetz was born in Vilnius, Lithuania, on February 2, 1901. At the age of three, he began to take lessons from his father, a violinist in the local orchestra. At four he entered the Royal School of Music in Vilnius, and by six he could play Mendelssohn's difficult* Violin Concerto. *At nine he entered the Saint Petersburg Conservatory and studied under Leopold Auer. At ten he made his official debut, in Saint Petersburg, and soon he was touring Russia and Europe. He settled in the United States and became the preeminent violinist of his time. He died in Los Angeles on December 10, 1987.*

THE NAME YASCHA HEIFETZ IS SYNONYMOUS WITH VIOLINISTIC perfection. By his early teens, he had developed a technical mastery so complete that he could devote himself to honing interpretative skills unbelievable in one so young. For the following fifty years, he reigned as the undisputed master of his instrument in both solo and chamber performances. His last public performance came in 1972.

"Don't imagine everything came to me out of a clear sky," Heifetz reminded observers. He worked hard to perfect his technique, and he was so successful that his playing seemed effortless. Unlike many earlier concert artists, he avoided exhibitionism, preferring to let his music speak for itself. He had a powerful tone with an intense (but not sentimental) vibrato, a transparent texture, and well-balanced phrasing. Heifetz sought to give a single, ideal approach to a given piece at each performance. He played with an incredible concentration, boldness, and musical understanding.

Heifetz's performances became the standard by which every other violinist's technique was measured. He was universally known as the King of Violinists.

## ALSO NOTEWORTHY

▲ EWEN, DAVID (born November 26, 1907, in Lemberg, Galicia; died December 28, 1985, in Miami, Florida). The world's most prolific writer of general-audience music books.

▲ FELDMAN, MORTON (born January 12, 1926, in New York City; died September 3, 1987, in Buffalo, New York). Composer who invented a kind of graph notation in which pitches and rhythms are notated only in very general terms.

▲ FEUERMANN, EMANUEL (born November 22, 1902, in Kolomea, Galicia; died May 25, 1942, in New York City). Regarded by some musicians as the best cellist of the twentieth century.

▲ FIEDLER, ARTHUR (born December 17, 1894, in Boston, Massachusetts; died July 10, 1979, in Boston). The first American to be chief conductor of the Boston Pops Orchestra (1930–79).

▲ FRIED, MIRIAM (born September 9, 1946, in Satu-Mare, Romania). Violinist who became the first woman to win the Queen Elisabeth International Competition in Brussels (1971).

# Earning the Title of King of Piano Virtuosos
## Vladimir Horowitz

❧

VLADIMIR HOROWITZ WAS POSSIBLY THE GREATEST TECHNICIAN in piano history. Certainly in the twentieth century, no pianist earned more acclaim for his sheer virtuosity.

Photofest

His early dream was to become a composer, but when the Bolshevik takeover of Kiev left his family destitute, he turned his attention to the piano as a way of making money. He began touring Russia and then Europe. In 1928 he made his American debut, and eventually he settled in the United States. Except for three famous "retirements" (1936–38, the early 1960s, and 1969–74), Horowitz continued to perform well into his eighties. In 1986 he made a highly publicized visit to Russia (his first return there since he left in 1925), giving a Moscow performance that was televised in the United States.

Horowitz played in the Russian grand manner, having received that style from Blumenfeld, who in turn was taught by the legendary Anton Rubinstein. Like his mentors, Horowitz, in his early years, emphasized bravura and sonority. He was unrivaled in his speed, force, and control of articulation and dynamics. In his later years, he grew from a pure virtuoso into a more complete artist in his subtle, shaded interpretations. The romantic works of Liszt and Rachmaninoff were his special forte.

Horowitz was universally known as the King of Piano Virtuosos.

> Vladimir Horowitz was born in Berdichev, Ukraine, on October 1, 1904. His original name was Vladimir Gorovitz. At the age of six, he began to take lessons from his mother. In 1912 he entered the Kiev Conservatory, where he studied piano under Felix Blumenfeld. Horowitz immigrated to the United States and became a world-famous pianist. He died in New York City on November 5, 1989.

### ALSO NOTEWORTHY

▲ GETZ, STAN(LEY) (born February 2, 1927, in Philadelphia, Pennsylvania; died June 6, 1991, in Malibu, California). Jazz tenor saxophonist who helped pave the way for the "cool" jazz of the 1950s, was the first American musician closely identified with the bossa nova movement in the early 1960s, was one of the greatest melodic improvisers in modern jazz, and set new standards of virtuosity on his instrument.

# FOUNDING MODERN AMERICAN THEATER MUSIC

## Jerome Kern

છ⁀ઝ

*Jerome Kern was born in New York City on January 27, 1885. His mother gave him early piano lessons, and on his tenth birthday she took him to see a Broadway musical. He was immediately hooked on the theater. After brief periods of study in Germany (1902) and at the New York College of Music (1902), he began to compose songs for Broadway. He died in New York City on November 11, 1945.*

JEROME KERN COMPOSED SOME OF AMERICA'S BEST-LOVED SONGS, including "Look for the Silver Lining" (1920), "Smoke Gets in Your Eyes" (1933), "The Way You Look Tonight" (1936), and "The Last Time I Saw Paris" (1941). But his greatest achievement was to father modern American theater music. In both the character of individual songs and the structure of entire shows, he established the models for American theater composers right up to the present day.

He began his stage work by composing music for songs to be interpolated into the stage works of other composers. His most important such song was "They Didn't Believe Me," interpolated into the New York City version of the British musical *The Girl from Utah* (1914). The song established the basic character of all modern American musical-theater songs. It was more musically sophisticated than earlier American theater tunes, yet it also avoided the typical European flavor in the music of American operetta composers, such as Victor Herbert.

Kern also revolutionized the musical structure of entire shows. He was invited to compose the score for a musical to be produced at the Princess Theater in New York City. Because of the small size of the theater and the limited cast and sets, the production had to be in a more intimate style than was typical of musicals at that time. Kern molded his songs to fit individual characters and to help tell the story. This integration of music, character, and story was not typical of the operettas and musicals of that time, which often stopped the story, if any, to perform irrelevant numbers. This first Princess Theater musical was *Nobody Home* (1915). It was followed by others at the same venue, including *Oh, Boy!* (1917), with "Till the Clouds Roll By."

## ALSO NOTEWORTHY

▲ GODOWSKY, LEOPOLD (born February 13, 1870, in Soshly, near Vilnius, Lithuania; died November 21, 1938, in New York City). Pianist who developed the playing method of "weight and relaxation," in which the pianist's power comes not from muscular force but from the relaxed use of arm weight. Father of the photo technician Leopold Godowsky, Jr.

▲ GOLD, ERNEST (originally Ernest Goldner; born July 13, 1921, in Vienna, Austria). The first film composer to have a star on Hollywood's Walk of Fame. His best-known score is *Exodus* (1960).

# MODERN AMERICAN THEATER MUSIC *(continued)*

The culmination of this development was *Show Boat* (1927), often cited as the first serious modern American musical play. The songs, including "Ol' Man River," were integral to the plot, atmosphere, and characterizations. Even the background music was important. Throughout the score, themes referring to specific characters and concepts were quoted and developed in an almost operatic fashion.

Kern became the acknowledged originator and master of a new kind of theater music, one that was imitated by virtually all of the great theater composers who followed him.

Robert W. Coburn

---

### ALSO NOTEWORTHY

▲ **GRAFFMAN, GARY** (born October 14, 1928, in New York City). Pianist who was the first established concert artist to refuse to play before a segregated audience (1964, Jackson, Mississippi).

▲ **HANSLICK, EDUARD** (born September 11, 1825, in Prague, Bohemia; died August 6, 1904, in Baden, near Vienna, Austria). The first great professional music critic.

▲ **HERRMANN, BERNARD** (born June 19, 1911, in New York City; died December 24, 1975, in Los Angeles). Composer of many great film scores, including *Psycho* (1960).

▲ **HESS, MYRA** (full name, Julia Myra Hess; born February 25, 1890, in Hampstead, near London, England; died November 25, 1965, in London). Pianist who kept music alive in England during World War II, even through the Nazi air raids, by initiating the National Gallery Concerts in London and by concertizing all over the country.

▲ **HUBERMAN, BRONISLAW** (born December 19, 1882, in Czestochowa, Poland; died June 15, 1947, in Corsier-sur-Vevey, Switzerland). Violinist who, in 1936, organized the Palestine Orchestra (since 1948 called the Israel Philharmonic Orchestra).

▲ **IDELSOHN, ABRAHAM ZVI** (born July 13, 1882, in Filzburg, near Libava, Latvia; died August 14, 1938, in Johannesburg, South Africa). The founder of modern Jewish musicology.

▲ **JOACHIM, JOSEPH** (born June 28, 1831, in Kitsee, near Pressburg, Slovakia; died August 15, 1907, in Berlin, Germany). Violinist who, through his willingness to submerge his own personality into the works and intentions of composers, helped to create the modern art of interpretative playing. He gave the world premiere of Brahms's great *Violin Concerto* (1879).

▲ **KIPNIS, ALEXANDER** (born February 13, 1891, in Zhitomir, Ukraine; died May 14, 1978, in Westport, Connecticut). Arguably the greatest bass of his time, especially in German opera. Father of Igor Kipnis.

▲ **KIPNIS, IGOR** (born September 27, 1930, in Berlin, Germany). The preeminent harpsichordist of his time. Son of Alexander Kipnis.

# LINKING THE MUSIC OF THE NINETEENTH AND TWENTIETH CENTURIES
## Gustav Mahler

ॐ

IN HIS LIFETIME, GUSTAV MAHLER WAS BEST KNOWN AS AN IMPORTANT and unconventional conductor. Today, however, he is remembered as the composer who linked the nineteenth and the twentieth centuries: the last great Austro-German symphonist and among the first to anticipate modernist techniques.

As a composer, Mahler reflected the duality of his time. Still imbued with the great Western music tradition, he nevertheless sensed its coming breakdown. In his music he simultaneously embraced the tradition and sadly acknowledged its disintegration. Mahler's music is a mosaic of diverse romantic elements, such as long lyric melodic lines, rich harmony, colorful orchestration, folk tunes, popular dance rhythms, nature painting (birdcalls, for example), funeral marches, and passages described as spooky or mysterious. Simultaneously, the breakdown is reflected by taking basic technical features of the tradition—such as upbeats, accents, dynamics, tempo fluctuations, and four-measure phrasing—and exaggerating them to their limits in intensity, repetition, and length. At peak moments these grotesque images are suddenly juxtaposed with passages of supreme simplicity and serenity, as if longing for the innocence and purity of an earlier time. The growth of these traits can be heard in his first eight symphonies (1888–1906), *Des Knaben Wunderhorn* ("The Youth's Magic Horn," 1898), and *Kindertotenlieder* ("Songs on the Death of Children," 1904). In his last two completed works, *Das Lied von der Erde* ("The Song of the Earth," 1909) and the *Ninth Symphony* (1909), he pointed toward the future with his leaner textures, contrapuntal style, and weakened tonality.

Clearly, while emotionally trying to preserve the tradition, Mahler was artistically compelled to pull away from it. He felt the same rootlessness in his personal life: "I am thrice homeless. As a Bohemian born in Austria. As an Austrian among Germans. And as a Jew throughout the world."

> *Gustav Mahler was born in Austrian-ruled Kalischt, Bohemia, on July 7, 1860. After attending the Vienna Conservatory (1875–78), he held a series of European conducting posts, culminating in his tenure as director of the Vienna Opera (1897–1907). To obtain that position, he had himself baptized a Catholic, but as an adult he practiced no religion, inclining rather toward a pantheistic mysticism. He ended his career as conductor of the Metropolitan Opera (1908–1909) and the New York Philharmonic (1909–1911). Mahler's conducting was marked by precision and faithfulness to the spirit of the score, but also by unusual tempos and body movements. His greatest contribution as a conductor was to raise the public's taste from light works to classics by the masters. He died in Vienna, Austria, on May 18, 1911.*

---

### ALSO NOTEWORTHY

▲ **KLEMPERER, OTTO** (born May 14, 1885, in Breslau, Silesia; died July 6, 1973, in Zurich, Switzerland). Conductor who, in his late years, became the world's most authoritative interpreter of the Austro-German repertory from Haydn to Mahler.

# ESTABLISHING CONCERT INNOVATIONS AND COMPOSING CLASSICAL-ROMANTIC FUSIONS
## Felix Mendelssohn

ↄ

FELIX MENDELSSOHN HOLDS A DUAL PLACE IN MUSIC HISTORY. He laid the groundwork for modern symphony organizations and concerts, and he composed a rich body of music in a personal blend of romantic and classical elements.

From 1835 to 1847, Mendelssohn led the Gewandhaus Concerts in Leipzig as conductor and music organizer. As conductor, he revolutionized orchestral playing by abandoning the previous time-beater approach; instead, he trained his orchestra into a precision unit and became the first true "interpreter" of orchestral music. His role as organizer was just as revolutionary. He raised audience tastes from minor works to pieces by Bach (he was largely responsible for the rediscovery of this composer), Mozart, Beethoven, Schumann, and other masters. He recruited the finest soloists, including Franz Liszt. He did away with the customary variety programs and began to organize concerts in the modern fashion: typically an overture, a large-scale work, a concerto, and a shorter piece. And he refused to go along with the tradition of separating the movements of a symphony by inserting lighter forms of music.

As a composer, Mendelssohn created a recognizably individual style that bridged eighteenth-century classicism and nineteenth-century romanticism. A child of his time, he adopted the romantics' use of literature and other extramusical stimuli to inspire his compositions. But under the influence of his grandfather's rationalist philosophy, his father's conservatism, his friend Goethe's classicism, and his own inclinations, Mendelssohn composed music that, despite its romantic extramusical references, displays the techniques, forms, clarity, elegance, and grace of classical and preclassical music. In 1825 he composed his *String Octet* and in 1826 his concert overture *A Midsummer Night's Dream*. No one in the history of music, not even Mozart, has written such gloriously inspired and finished music at the tender ages of sixteen and seventeen. Among his other works that are still frequently played are the concert overture *Calm Sea and Prosperous Voyage* (1828), the *Reformation Symphony* (1832), the *Italian Symphony* (1833), the *Violin Concerto* (1844), and the *Songs without Words* for piano (1830–45).

As both organizer and composer, Mendelssohn played a key role in music history.

*Jakob Ludwig Felix Mendelssohn was born in Hamburg, Germany, on February 3, 1809. His paternal grandfather was Moses Mendelssohn, an Enlightenment philosopher and a leader in the movement for Jewish freedom. To attain civil equality for his children, Felix's father had his family baptized into the Lutheran church. In 1822 the family took the dual surname Mendelssohn Bartholdy (without a hyphen); for the rest of his life, Felix sometimes used the single surname and sometimes the dual. The family was wealthy, and Felix received most of his music education at home from a succession of teachers. He became skilled on several instruments, principally the piano. In his brief life, Mendelssohn won fame as both a conductor and a composer. He died in Leipzig, Germany, on November 4, 1847.*

# USING MUSIC FOR HUMANITARIAN GOALS
## Yehudi Menuhin

ॐ

*Yehudi Menuhin was born in New York City on April 22, 1916. At the age of two he moved with his parents to San Francisco, where at four he began to study the violin. He also studied in Europe. A genuine child prodigy, he was a world celebrity by the age of eleven. Later he became an acknowledged master musician, not only as a soloist but also as a chamber-music player and a conductor. His violin playing is noted for its purity of style and its depth of interpretative power.*

YEHUDI MENUHIN IS ONE OF THE MOST GIFTED VIOLINISTS of his time. Perhaps more importantly, no musician of his time has so effectively used music for humanitarian ends.

Since early in his career, Menuhin has used his position in the concert community to help inspire people in distress and bring together people who are in conflict. During World War II, he played over five hundred concerts for Allied troops. In July 1945 in Germany, he performed for displaced people and survivors of death camps. In November 1945 he became the first American artist to perform in the Soviet Union after the war. In 1947 he became the first Jewish artist to play with the postwar Berlin Philharmonic Orchestra under the baton of Wilhelm Furtwängler, who had held his position under the Nazi regime.

In 1950 he made the first of many musical visits to Israel. In 1951 he made one of the earliest postwar concert tours of Japan by an American. In 1952 he made his first visit to India, soon bringing Indian musicians to the United States for cultural exchange. In 1955 his efforts helped bring about a cultural exchange between the Soviet Union and the United States. In 1967 he gave concerts in Arab-speaking countries for the benefit of Arab refugees. In addition, he actively supports over two hundred nonmusical organizations around the globe, including the America–Israel Society, the Fellowship of Reconciliation, and the League of Non-Violence. Through these and many other activities, Menuhin has become the world's preeminent humanitarian musician.

Columbia Artists Management

# CONDUCTING THE MOST FAMOUS PREMIERE OF THE TWENTIETH CENTURY
## Pierre Monteux

PIERRE MONTEUX CONDUCTED A WIDE RANGE OF WORKS with many orchestras. But he is best remembered for conducting the most famous world premiere of the twentieth century.

He led the world premieres of many compositions, including works by Ernest Bloch, Charles T. Griffes, and Roger Sessions. During his years with the Ballets Russes, he premiered Igor Stravinsky's *Petrushka* (1911), Maurice Ravel's *Daphnis et Chloé* ("Daphnis and Chloé," 1912), Claude Debussy's *Jeux* ("Games," 1913), and Stravinsky's *Le Rossignol* ("The Nightingale," 1914).

His premiere of Stravinsky's ballet *Le sacre du printemps* ("The Rite of Spring," 1913), at the Théâtre des Champs-Elysées in Paris, was one of the most violent events in music history. The score was revolutionary, not only in its rhythms and harmonies but also in its paganistic subject matter. Pro- and anti-Stravinsky factions fought it out in the theater while Monteux conducted. People hissed, hooted, shouted, whistled, and even struck each other. The dancers could barely hear the music, yet Monteux courageously conducted to the final curtain. Stravinsky later said that he admired Monteux for being "as nerveless as a crocodile" during the ordeal.

Boston Symphony Orchestra

*Pierre Monteux was born in Paris, France, on April 4, 1875. The Monteux family did not practice the Jewish religion, and Pierre eventually converted to Roman Catholicism. After graduating from the Paris Conservatory (1896), he played the viola and gradually took more and more conducting jobs. Monteux conducted the Ballets Russes (1911–14, 1916, and 1924), the Boston Symphony Orchestra (1919–24), the Symphonic Orchestra of Paris (1929–38), the San Francisco Symphony Orchestra (1936–52), and the London Symphony Orchestra (1961–64). Monteux also frequently guest-conducted. He died in Hancock, Maine, on July 1, 1964.*

In 1963 Monteux celebrated the fiftieth anniversary of his famous world premiere by conducting the work in London—this time to enthusiastic applause.

### ALSO NOTEWORTHY

▲ KOLISCH, RUDOLF (born July 20, 1896, in Klamm am Semmering, Austria; died August 1, 1978, in Watertown, Massachusetts). Violinist who, in 1922, formed the Kolisch String Quartet, the first string quartet to play the standard repertory from memory.

▲ KORNGOLD, ERICH WOLFGANG (born May 29, 1897, in Brünn, Moravia; died November 29, 1957, in Los Angeles). The first great composer of film scores, including *Anthony Adverse* (1936), *The Adventures of Robin Hood* (1938), and *Kings Row* (1942).

# EARNING THE TITLE OF KING OF OPERETTA
## Jacques Offenbach

⌒

*Jacques Offenbach was born in Cologne, Germany, on June 20, 1819. His original name was Jacob Offenbach (his father, Isaac Juda Eberst, changed his surname to Offenbach after settling in Offenbach, Germany). Jacob changed his first name to Jacques after moving to Paris to study. In 1844 he was baptized so that he could marry a Catholic. He conducted at the Théâtre-Français in Paris (1850–55), and in the same city he ran his own musical theater, the Bouffes-Parisiens (1855–62), for which he composed after leaving its management. He died in Paris on October 5, 1880.*

Fritz Luckhardt, Vienna

AN OPERETTA IS A "LITTLE OPERA," usually a comic-romantic story with light music often interrupted by dialogue. The composer who established operetta as an international genre was Jacques Offenbach.

Offenbach's operettas are noted for their lilting melodies and their steady stream of humor. His favorite method of creating a comic effect was to insert an incongruous element, such as a cancan for the gods in *Orphée aux enfers* ("Orpheus in the Underworld," 1858). His other operettas included *La belle Hélène* ("The Beautiful Helen," 1864), *La vie parisienne* ("The Parisian Life," 1866), and *La Grande-Duchesse de Gérolstein* ("The Grand Duchess of Gerolstein," 1867). He devoted his last years to his most ambitious work, *Les contes d'Hoffmann* ("The Tales of Hoffmann," first performed posthumously in 1881), with the famous "Barcarolle." Offenbach's success encouraged composers in other countries to explore the operetta genre, notably Johann Strauss II in Austria, Arthur Sullivan in England, and Victor Herbert in the United States. Eventually the operetta evolved into the familiar twentieth-century musical.

---

### ALSO NOTEWORTHY

▲ KOSTELANETZ, ANDRE (born December 22, 1901, in Saint Petersburg, Russia; died January 13, 1980, in Port-au-Prince, Haiti). Conductor who pioneered the use of radio in making classical music available to millions of new listeners.

▲ KOUSSEVITZKY, SERGE (born July 26, 1874, in Vyshni Volochek, near Tver, Russia; died June 4, 1951, in Boston, Massachusetts). Probably the most influential conductor of new symphonic music in the twentieth century.

# BECOMING THE DEAN OF AMERICAN MUSICAL-THEATER COMPOSERS
## Richard Rodgers

☙

RICHARD RODGERS MAINTAINED A HIGHER DEGREE OF CONSISTENT EXCELLENCE than any other composer in the history of Broadway. Through his theatrical experiments and innovations, he helped to develop the simple musical comedy into the complex indigenous American art form of the musical play.

Rodgers and his first principal lyricist, Lorenz Hart, began with traditional song-and-dance fare but soon moved toward the modern musical play, in which songs are an integral part of the storytelling and character-revealing process, notably in *Chee-Chee* (1928). In the early 1930s, Rodgers and Hart applied the same integration technique to films, as in *Love Me Tonight* (1932), with "Lover," "Isn't It Romantic?" and "Mimi." Returning to Broadway, they created *Jumbo* (1935), with "The Most Beautiful Girl in the World." There followed several works that were traditional in structure but had outstanding individual elements, such as *On Your Toes* (1936), with the first ballet ("Slaughter on Tenth Avenue") ever treated as an integral part of the story line in a musical; *Babes in Arms* (1937), with an unusually wide variety of songs, including "The Lady Is a Tramp"; and *Pal Joey* (1940), with "Bewitched, Bothered, and Bewildered."

With a new lyricist, Oscar Hammerstein II, Rodgers rose to even greater heights. *Oklahoma!* (1943), with "Oh, What a Beautiful Mornin'," continued to develop the integration technique. *Carousel* (1945) opened not with the traditional medley overture but with a single instrumental piece, "Carousel Waltz," which set the mood for the entire play; songs included "If I Loved You" and "You'll Never Walk Alone," a rare theatrical hymn. The popular *South Pacific*

> *Richard Rodgers was born in Hammels Station, Long Island, New York, on June 28, 1902. He derived his love of the musical theater from his parents. After studying at Columbia University (1919–21) and the Institute of Musical Art (now called the Juilliard School of Music, 1921–23), he began composing for Broadway. He died in New York City on December 30, 1979.*

---

### ALSO NOTEWORTHY

▲ LANDOWSKA, WANDA (born July 5, 1879, in Warsaw, Poland; died August 16, 1959, in Lakeville, Connecticut). Leader of the twentieth-century revival of the harpsichord. Her parents were Jews who converted to Catholicism.

▲ LAREDO, RUTH (originally Ruth Meckler; born November 20, 1937, in Detroit, Michigan). The first American woman pianist to win international recognition. She married the violinist Jaime Laredo.

WANDA LANDOWSKA

(1949) had several hit songs, notably "Some Enchanted Evening."

*International Musician*

Rodgers and Hammerstein capped their work together with *The King and I* (1951) and *The Sound of Music* (1959), both of which furthered the integration of music and story, and both of which still stand as perhaps the summits of artistic achievement in American popular musical theater. *The King and I* included the songs "Getting to Know You," "Hello, Young Lovers," "I Whistle a Happy Tune," and "Shall We Dance?" as well as the instrumental "March of the Royal Siamese Children" and the stunning narrated ballet "The Small House of Uncle Thomas." *The Sound of Music* opened with the "Preludium," a skillfully composed vocal substitute for a conventional overture. Rodgers evoked the Austrian atmosphere in "The Lonely Goatherd," with its yodeling; "Laendler," an instrumental folklike dance; and "Edelweiss," a folklike song. He developed "Do-Re-Mi," initially an elementary music lesson, into a brilliant contrapuntal piece. Other songs included "Climb Ev'ry Mountain," "My Favorite Things," and "The Sound of Music."

Because of the overwhelming cumulative effect of his achievements—integrating music and story, experimenting with dance and instrumental innovations, and producing an unrivaled body of memorable songs—Rodgers became the acknowledged dean of American musical-theater composers.

### ALSO NOTEWORTHY

▲ LAVRY, MARC (born December 22, 1903, in Riga, Latvia; died March 1967 in Haifa, Israel). Composer whose folk opera *Dan ha-shomer* ("Dan the Guard," 1945) was the first Palestinian opera in Hebrew to receive a stage performance.

▲ LEVI, HERMANN (born November 7, 1839, in Giessen, Germany; died May 13, 1900, in Munich, Germany). Conductor who led the world premiere of Wagner's *Parsifal* (1882).

▲ LEVINE, JAMES LAWRENCE (born June 23, 1943, in Cincinnati, Ohio). Principal conductor (since 1973) and music director (since 1976) of the Metropolitan Opera in New York City, wielding more artistic control, by contract, than any previous director of the company.

▲ LOESSER, FRANK (born June 29, 1910, in New York City; died July 28, 1969, in New York City). The most important young American songwriter to emerge during World War II. His songs (lyrics and music) included "Praise the Lord and Pass the Ammunition" (1942); "Luck Be a Lady," from the Broadway musical *Guys and Dolls* (1950); "Thumbelina," from the film *Hans Christian Andersen* (1952); "Somebody, Somewhere" and "Standing on the Corner," from the Broadway show *The Most Happy Fella* (1956); and "I Believe in You," from the Broadway musical *How to Succeed in Business without Really Trying* (1961).

# CREATING THE IDEAL CHOPIN INTERPRETATION
## Arthur Rubinstein

ARTHUR RUBINSTEIN EXCELLED AS A PERFORMER of the whole range of nineteenth-century romantic piano music. But his special niche in music history was as the preeminent Chopin interpreter of his time.

As a young pianist, Rubinstein played modern composers, such as Debussy and Prokofiev. Later he concentrated on nineteenth-century romantics, especially Brahms and Chopin. He was the romantic pianist par excellence, retaining the poetic exuberance of the romantic tradition but rejecting the distortions and exaggerations. Rubinstein's unique style was like the man himself: witty, intelligent, urbane.

His approach was best heard in his interpretations of Chopin. As a child he had heard Chopin, Rubinstein's own countryman, played

with gross sentimentality. When, as a teenager, he began to play Chopin without traditional affectation, people accused him of being "dry" or "severe." Only much later did his approach come to be generally appreciated as the ideal standard of Chopin interpretation: an outgoing lyricism and a rich tone color, presented in a spirit of aristocratic, yet passionately eloquent, poetry.

When Rubinstein died in 1982, the world lost one of its most beloved musicians and certainly its most renowned Chopin interpreter.

*Arthur Rubinstein was born in Lodz, Poland, on January 28, 1887. His given name was originally Artur, but in later years he signed himself "Arthur," "Artur" or "Arturo" depending on his location. He began playing the piano by ear at the age of three, and at seven he made his debut. After a period of study in Berlin (1897–1903), he began touring Europe and the New World as a concert pianist. Rubinstein himself later admitted that up to 1932 he was a lazy performer, seldom practicing. But in that year he got married and thereafter took his playing more seriously. In fact, his energy became legendary. In his late years he gave over one hundred concerts a year, and even in his seventies and eighties, he would often play both Brahms concertos or three by Beethoven in one evening. In the mid-1970s his eyesight began to fail him, and in 1976 he gave a series of farewell concerts. He died in Geneva, Switzerland, on December 20, 1982.*

# Development of the Twelve-Tone Compositional Technique
## Arnold Schoenberg

❧

*Arnold Schoenberg was born in Vienna, Austria, on September 13, 1874. His surname was originally spelled Schönberg. He studied cello and composition privately and then embarked on a career as a serious composer while earning a living as a conductor, arranger, and teacher. In 1933 he fled the Nazis and settled in the United States, where he Americanized the spelling of his surname and taught at the University of Califor He died in the Brentwood section of Los Angeles on July 13, 1951.*

ARNOLD SCHOENBERG WAS A SEMINAL FIGURE in twentieth-century culture. His twelve-tone technique profoundly affected the course of modern music.

Schoenberg composed his early works under the influence of Wagnerian chromaticism and Mahlerian postromanticism, as in the symphonic cantata *Gurre-Lieder* ("Songs of Gurre," composed 1901, orchestrated 1911). That chromaticism evolved into a style called atonal music, in which a sense of key is deliberately avoided, as in the song cycle *Pierrot lunaire* ("Pierrot in the Moonlight," 1912). Schoenberg, however, felt that he had created chaos in his freely atonal works, and he sought organizing principles to replace the traditional ones (associated with tonality) that he had abandoned.

His solution was the twelve-tone technique (also known as dodecaphony), in which composition is based on a series, or row, of all twelve tones of the chromatic scale, arranged in any order the composer chooses; the series is then permutated and combined in various ways to form a sort of continuous variation throughout the work. He began to experiment with the system in 1920. His first completed work using the twelve-tone technique was the last of his *Five Piano Pieces* (1923), the other four in the set using different serial procedures. His *Piano Sonata* (1923) was the first work built entirely on a twelve-tone series. There followed such important works as the *Variations for Orchestra* (1928), the unfinished opera *Moses und Aron* ("Moses and Aaron," 1932), the *Violin Concerto* (1936), and the choral piece *A Survivor from Warsaw* (1947), which recounts the true story of Polish Jews who, while being prepared for the gas chamber during the Holocaust, asserted their human dignity by singing the ancient Hebrew song "Shema Yisrael" ("Hear, O Israel").

Schoenberg's twelve-tone technique was adopted and varied by innumerable composers, including Anton von Webern and his many followers. Even Schoenberg's archrival Igor Stravinsky, long an opponent of dodecaphony, adopted a personalized version of the system in his late years. Though the technique has faded in popularity among avant-garde composers since the 1960s, it has settled into a permanent place as one of many technical resources available to, and used by, contemporary musicians.

# EARNING THE TITLE OF QUEEN OF THE JUKEBOXES
## Dinah Shore

❦

DURING THE 1940S AND 1950S, the most popular female singer in the United States was Dinah Shore. She was the undisputed queen of the jukeboxes.

While attending Vanderbilt University, Shore had a job on a local radio show whose theme song was "Dinah," which she sang not in the usual fast tempo but in a slow, personal manner. After graduating from Vanderbilt with a sociology major (1938), she won a job with a New York City radio station by auditioning with "Dinah." She then took the name Dinah Shore (the change was legalized in 1944). Immediately popular, she appeared on many radio programs and issued a long string of hit recordings. From the 1950s on, she hosted television variety and talk shows.

Shore attributed much of her singing success to the childhood influence of her nursemaid, Yah-Yah. Through Yah-Yah, young Shore heard black congregations singing spirituals and learned to imitate such singers as Ethel Waters and Ella Fitzgerald. Shore developed a unique throaty, dramatic way of singing in which each word was made meaningful to the listener. Especially early in her career, she was particularly associated with the blues, as in her recordings of "Dinah's Blues" (1940), "Memphis Blues" (1940), and "Blues in the Night" (1942). Among her other hits were "Yes, My Darling Daughter" (1940), "Jim" (1941), "Body and Soul" (1941), "Shoofly Pie and Apple Pan Dowdy" (1946), "Buttons and Bows" (1948), "Whatever Lola Wants" (1955), "Love and Marriage" (1955), "Chantez-Chantez" (1957), and "Fascination" (1957).

Her style was sometimes called "sentimental" or even "gushy," but her phenomenal success in the 1940s and 1950s proved that her approach resonated in some significant way deep within the American psyche.

*Dinah Shore was born in Winchester, Tennessee, on March 1, 1917. Her original name was Frances Rose Shore. At the age of eighteen months, she was stricken with poliomyelitis, which caused paralysis in her right leg and foot. She went through six years of rigid physical therapy. That experience left her shy but ambitious to prove her worth despite her infirmity. She developed the habit of singing, dancing, and showing off everywhere she went. Even before she could talk plainly, she was singing for the customers in her father's department store. Her mother, an aspiring opera singer, also encouraged the girl's musical interest. Shore became a popular singer, film star, and radio and television personality. She died in Beverly Hills, California, on February 24, 1994.*

# BECOMING THE FIRST AMERICAN VIOLIN VIRTUOSO

## Isaac Stern

❧

*Isaac Stern was born in Kremenets, the Soviet Union, on July 21, 1920. The following year he moved with his parents to the United States and settled in San Francisco. In the mid-1930s he made his San Francisco and New York City debuts. His Carnegie Hall debut came in 1943, followed by his debut with the New York Philharmonic in 1944 (he subsequently appeared with this orchestra more times than any other violinist in its history). His European career began in 1948, and later he added Australia, Japan, South America, and the Soviet Union to his tours. Stern has a special relationship with Israel, whose cultural growth he, more than any other artist, has aided by giving performances, by advising young Israeli musicians (including Itzhak Perlman), and by leading the America-Israel Cultural Foundation.*

THE FIRST MAJOR VIOLINIST TO BE WHOLLY A PRODUCT OF AMERICAN training, Isaac Stern received his entire musical education in California, mainly at the San Francisco Conservatory, where he completed his studies in 1937. His principal teacher was Naoum Blinder, concertmaster of the San Francisco Symphony Orchestra.

Stern's playing reflects his vibrant personality. Subordinating technique to the musical comcept, he performs with a total emotional involvement and predicates his approach on a desire for intense communication with his audience. He has the rare ability to mold each musical passage into an inevitable whole.

Stern's repertory is vast. He has recorded nearly every piece in the standard violin literature. Twentieth-century music is heavily represented in his performances, including works by Bloch, Copland, and Stravinsky. Among his world premieres were works by Schuman, Bernstein, and Penderecki.

Stern has used his musical gifts to further human rights causes. In 1967, for example, he became the first American artist to sever relations with the Soviet Union over its  restrictions on Soviet artists. In 1975 he was presented with the first Albert Schweitzer Music Award for "a life dedicated to music and devoted to humanity." Also a cultural activist, he led, in 1960, the Save Carnegie Hall campaign; and he founded, during President Kennedy's administration, the National Council on the Arts, the precursor of the National Endowment for the Arts.

On both the music stage and the world stage, Stern proved by example that American training was more than sufficient to prepare a violinist for the highest achievements.

# SINGING SONGS BY "ACTING" THEM
## Barbra Streisand

ᜃ

BARBRA STREISAND CREATED a unique singing style in which she not only *sings* songs but also *acts* them. In her performances, she displays remarkable vocal resources and extremely original song interpretations, each song clearly being conceived as a deeply felt personal experience.

Courtesy of Barbra Streisand

Because her first love was acting, Streisand, when she turned to singing in the early 1960s, conceived of a musical performance as a *form* of acting. She selected unusual or seldom-heard songs and performed them with unique interpretations that displayed an incredible range of emotion. For example, she transformed the playful ditty "Who's Afraid of the Big Bad Wolf?" into a surrealistic yet childlike lament. Her first album, *The Barbra Streisand Album* (1963), created a cult of Streisand followers because of its revolutionary treatment of popular songs as vehicles for serious expression; for example, she performed "Happy Days Are Here Again" as a hysterical lament.

During the 1960s, she succeeded Judy Garland as the queen of theatrical and torch songs. Streisand was most closely identified with "People," from the Broadway musical *Funny Girl,* and in general she performed show tunes, standards, and special material in a nonrock ballad style. In the 1970s, however, she added rock and soft-rock arrangements to her repertoire, as in the albums *Stoney End* (1971) and *Streisand Superman* (1977). The album *The Way We Were* (1974) contained both her earlier and her rock styles. In *The Broadway Album* (1985) and *Back to Broadway* (1993), Streisand reasserted her position as America's premiere performer of the artistically rich and musically sophisticated genre of theatrical songs, with which she can most dramatically display her unique talent as a singing actress.

*Barbara Joan Streisand was born in New York City on April 24, 1942. She dropped the middle a in her first name after she began her career. Her father's death when she was a toddler made her feel deprived yet special: "It's like someone being blind; they hear better. With me, I felt more, I sensed more—I wanted more." To escape her loneliness, she frequented movie theaters and dreamed of becoming an actress. After graduating from high school in 1959, she took acting lessons. But acting jobs were slow in coming, so she began to take jobs as a nightclub singer. That work led to parts in the Broadway musicals* I Can Get It for You Wholesale *(1962) and* Funny Girl *(1964), followed by a distinguished film career in musical pictures, such as* Funny Girl *(1968) and* A Star Is Born *(1976), and in nonmusicals in which she occasionally sang, including* The Way We Were *(1973). Streisand became the first woman to coscript, produce, direct, and star in a major motion picture, the musical* Yentl *(1983). In 1994 she made her first concert tour in nearly thirty years.*

# Becoming the High Priestess of Bach

## Rosalyn Tureck

❧

*Rosalyn Tureck was born in Chicago, Illinois, on December 14, 1914. She took private piano lessons from several teachers, including the concert pianist Jan Chiapusso, who introduced her to the serious study of Bach. At the age of fifteen, she began to give all-Bach recitals in Chicago. At the Juilliard School of Music (1931–35), she studied under Olga Samaroff. Later Tureck became a world-famous concert performer.*

ROSALYN TURECK IS THE WORLD'S PREEMINENT EXPERT on the music of Johann Sebastian Bach. The press has dubbed her the High Priestess of Bach.

The defining incident in Tureck's life occurred in early December 1931, before her seventeenth birthday. She was practicing Bach's "Prelude and Fugue in A Minor" from the first book of the *Well-tempered Clavier* when she suddenly lost consciousness. Tureck awoke to a sort of epiphany—a sense of having an immediate and intuitive insight into the structure, psychology, and form of Bach's music.

It was a new concept of Bach and required an entirely new technique for playing his music. Previously, Bach had been taught and played from the same perspective that guided classical and romantic music. Tureck, however, grasped the structure and forms of Bach's music as emphasizing counterpoint, not harmony, which is uppermost in classical and romantic music. She changed her fingering apparatus, particularly by making each finger as independent as possible. And she abandoned the modern piano ideals of lush sonorities and virtuoso display; instead, her Bach performances came to be  characterized by a fidelity to Bach's own scores. "I do what Bach tells me to do," she explained. "I never tell the music what to do."

In 1937 Tureck gave a highly praised series of six all-Bach recitals at Town Hall in New York City. Since then, she has toured many parts of the world, playing standard classical and romantic music but emphasizing Bach. In December 1958 she became the first woman to conduct the New York Philharmonic when she led it as conductor and soloist in two Bach concertos. She organized the Tureck Bach Players (mid-1950s); the International Bach Society (1966, since 1981 known as the Tureck Bach Society); the Institute for Bach Studies (1968); and many Bach festivals in various cities. Tureck has recorded all of Bach's major keyboard works, performed and talked about Bach on television and on film, and written extensively about Bach, as in the book *An Introduction to the Performance of Bach* (1960).

No one has done more to promote a true understanding of this musical giant than Rosalyn Tureck, the High Priestess of Bach.

▲ LOEWE, FREDERICK ("Fritz") (originally Frederick Löwe; born June 10, 1901, in Berlin, Germany; died February 14, 1988, in Palm Springs, California). Composer of the Broadway musicals *Brigadoon* (1947), with "Almost like Being in Love"; *Paint Your Wagon* (1951), with "They Call the Wind Maria"; *My Fair Lady* (1956), with "I Could Have Danced All Night," "I've Grown Accustomed to Her Face," "On the Street Where You Live," and "The Rain in Spain"; and *Camelot* (1960), with "If Ever I Would Leave You."

▲ MANILOW, BARRY (born June 17, 1946, in New York City). Singer and songwriter whose recordings include "Mandy" (1974) and "Somewhere down the Road" (1982).

▲ MANNES, DAVID (born February 16, 1866, in New York City; died April 25, 1959, in New York City). Violinist who founded the David Mannes School of Music (1916, renamed the Mannes College of Music in 1953).

▲ MARX, ADOLF BERNHARD (born 1795 in Halle, Germany; died May 17, 1866, in Berlin, Germany). Apparently the first theorist to use the term *Sonatenform* ("sonata form") to describe a type of one-movement structure.

▲ MASSARY, FRITZI (originally Friederike Massaryk; born March 21, 1882, in Vienna, Austria; died January 30, 1969, in Los Angeles). Soprano who reigned as the greatest operetta diva of her time and raised the art of operetta singing to a new artistic level.

▲ MERRILL, ROBERT (originally Moishe [anglicized as Morris] Miller; born June 4, 1919, in New York City). The preeminent baritone of his generation at the Metropolitan Opera and the first American to sing five hundred performances with the company.

▲ MEYERBEER, GIACOMO (originally Jakob Liebmann Beer; born September 5, 1791, in Vogelsdorf, near Berlin, Germany; died May 2, 1864, in Paris, France). Composer of the earliest grand operas. Half brother of the astronomer Wilhelm Beer.

▲ MILHAUD, DARIUS (born September 4, 1892, in Aix-en-Provence, France; died June 22, 1974, in Geneva, Switzerland). The first composer consistently to exploit polytonality (the use of two or more tonalities, or keys, simultaneously).

▲ MILLER, MITCH (full name, Mitchell William Miller; born July 4, 1911, in Rochester, New York). Arguably America's finest classical oboist; the most innovative artists-and-repertory man in popular-music history (introducing important new singers, including Tony Bennett and Johnny Mathis, as well as new musical styles and recording techniques); and, through his specialty, the sing-along, the best-selling recording artist of his time.

▲ MILSTEIN, NATHAN MIRONOVICH (born December 31, 1904, in Odessa, Ukraine; died December 21, 1992, in London, England). Violinist known not only for his virtuosity and musicianship but also for his longevity. In his eighties, he still publicly performed with no discernible loss in his skills.

▲ ORMANDY, EUGENE (originally Jenö Blau; born November 18, 1899, in Budapest, Hungary; died March 12, 1985, in Philadelphia, Pennsylvania). Conductor who built the Philadelphia Orchestra into the world's preeminent virtuoso orchestra, gave it the mellow but voluptuous "Philadelphia sound," and led it in the first televised broadcast by a major symphony orchestra (on CBS, March 20, 1948).

▲ **PERLMAN, ITZHAK** (born August 31, 1945, in Tel Aviv, Palestine). Arguably the most gifted violinist of his generation.

▲ **PETERS, ROBERTA** (born May 4, 1930, in New York City). Soprano who was on the roster of the Metropolitan Opera in New York City for over thirty-five years, the longest career of any coloratura in the history of the Met.

ROBERTA PETERS

Courtesy of ICM Artists, Ltd.

▲ **PIATIGORSKY, GREGOR** (born April 17, 1903, in Ekaterinoslav, Ukraine; died August 6, 1976, in Los Angeles). Cellist who was known as the Russian Casals and was a member of the Million Dollar Trio with the pianist Arthur Rubinstein and the violinist Jascha Heifetz.

▲ **PREVIN, ANDRÉ GEORGE** (originally Andreas Ludwig Priwin; born April 6, 1929, in Berlin, Germany). Next only to Leonard Bernstein, perhaps the most multitalented musician of his time. He won four Academy Awards for arranging film musicals, such as *My Fair Lady* (1964). He composed dramatic background scores for movies, including *Elmer Gantry* (1960). He composed serious piano, chamber, and orchestra music. He issued piano jazz recordings in the 1950s. He performed as a concert pianist during the 1950s and 1960s. And he is one of the world's best conductors. He was the first American to serve as the principal conductor of a major British orchestra, the London Symphony Orchestra (1968–79).

Courtesy of *The Jewish Week*, New York

SHULAMIT RAN

▲ **RAN, SHULAMIT** (born October 21, 1949, in Tel Aviv, Israel). The first woman to become composer-in-residence of a major American orchestra, the Chicago Symphony (1991).

▲ **REICH, STEVE** (full name, Stephen Michael Reich; October 3, 1936, in New York City). Composer of the most important minimalist work of Jewish character, *Tehillim* ("Psalms," 1981).

▲ **REINER, FRITZ** (born December 19, 1888, in Budapest, Hungary; died November 15, 1963, in New York City). Conductor widely regarded as the greatest baton technician of his time.

▲ **ROCHBERG, GEORGE** (born July 5, 1918, in Paterson, New Jersey). Composer who is the leading spokesman for, and exponent of, postmodernism in music (a movement in reaction against the philosophy and practices of modern music).

▲ **RODZINSKI, ARTUR** (born January 1, 1892, in Spalato, Dalmatia; died November 27, 1958, in Boston, Massachusetts). The greatest builder of orchestras of his time. He molded the Cleveland Orchestra (1933–43) into the outstanding ensemble it still is, built and trained the NBC Symphony Orchestra (1937) for Arturo Toscanini, and restored the New York Philharmonic (1943–47) and the Chicago Symphony (1947–48).

▲ **ROSEN, NATHANIEL KENT** (born June 9, 1948, in Altadena, California). The first cellist to win the Naumburg Competition (1977) and the first American cellist to win the Tchaikovsky Competition (1978).

▲ ROSENBLATT, JOSEF (born May 9, 1882, in Belaya Tserkov, near Kiev, Ukraine; died June 19, 1933, in Jerusalem, Palestine). Singer known to Jews and non-Jews alike as the King of Cantors. He was the first to reveal to the outside world, through concerts and recordings, the beauties of traditional synagogal music. Rosenblatt recorded the nonliturgical Jewish music in *The Jazz Singer* (1927), the first successful motion picture with sound.

▲ ROSENTHAL, MORITZ (born December 18, 1862, in Lemberg, Galicia; died September 3, 1946, in New York City). The famed Little Giant of the Piano, the last of the great pianists trained by the legendary Franz Liszt.

▲ ROSSI, SALAMONE (or Salomone [or Salamon de' or Shlomo] Rossi; born probably August 19, 1570, probably in Mantua, Italy; died about 1630, probably in Mantua). Composer who was an important pioneer in the baroque period, helping to develop the vocal duet, the trio sonata, and the idiomatic use of the violin.

▲ RUBINSTEIN, ANTON (born November 28, 1829, in Vikhvatinetz, Russia; died November 20, 1894, in Peterhof, Russia). One of the two (with Franz Liszt) most lionized pianists of his time; the first director of the Saint Petersburg Conservatory (1862); and composer of the most popular orchestral piece of the second half of the nineteenth century in Europe, the *Ocean Symphony* (1851, revised 1863 and 1880). Brother of Nikolay Rubinstein. Their parents converted the family to the Russian Orthodox church.

▲ RUBINSTEIN, NIKOLAY (born June 14, 1835, in Moscow, Russia; died March 23, 1881, in Paris, France). Pianist, conductor, and founder of the Moscow Conservatory (1866). Brother of Anton Rubinstein. Their parents converted the family to the Russian Orthodox church.

▲ RUSSELL, HENRY (born December 24, 1812, in Sheerness, England; died December 8, 1900, in London, England). The most influential songwriter in the United States (when he visited the New World in the 1830s and 1840s) before Stephen Foster, and the most popular in Great Britain during the first half of the nineteenth century. His American songs included "Woodman, Spare That Tree" (1837); "The Indian Hunter" (1837), which was the first American popular song to demand equal justice for the Indian; and "The Old Arm Chair" (1840), which initiated America's "mammy" songs. His best-known English ballad was "Cheer! Boys, Cheer!" (about 1850), while "A Life on the Ocean Wave" (1838) was adopted as the official march of the British Royal Marines in 1889.

▲ SADIE, STANLEY JOHN (born October 30, 1930, in London, England). Musicologist and editor of *The New Grove Dictionary of Music and Musicians* (1980), by far the most important music reference book in the English language.

▲ SCHNABEL, ARTUR (born April 17, 1882, in Lipnik, Moravia; died August 15, 1951, in Axenstein, Switzerland). Pianist who was the greatest Beethoven interpreter of his time and who recorded the first complete set of Beethoven piano sonatas.

▲ **SCHUMAN, WILLIAM HOWARD** (born August 4, 1910, in New York City; died February 15, 1992, in New York City). President of the Juilliard School of Music (1945–62), where he created a new approach to music education, and founder and first president of the Lincoln Center for the Performing Arts (1962–69), where he championed new American music. He composed the first music commissioned directly by the United States government, the orchestra work *Credendum: Article of Faith* (1955), written for the United Nations Educational, Scientific, and Cultural Organization (UNESCO). His most popular piece is the *New England Triptych* for orchestra (1956).

▲ **SHAW, ARTIE** (originally Abraham Isaac Arshawsky, later Arthur Jacob Arshawsky; born May 23, 1910, in New York City). Outstanding jazz clarinetist who rose to fame with his *Clarinet Concerto* (1939); headed one of the most popular and unusual (because of its emphasis on string instruments) swing bands of the big-band era (peaking in the 1940s); and founded the Gramercy Five (1940), a highly regarded chamber ensemble.

Courtesy of Naomi Shemer

**NAOMI SHEMER**

▲ **SHEMER, NAOMI** (originally Naomi Sapir; born July 13, 1930, in Kibbutz Kinneret, Palestine). Israel's most famous songwriter. Her best-known song is "Jerusalem of Gold" (1967).

▲ **SILLS, BEVERLY** ("Bubbles") (originally Belle Miriam Silverman; born May 25, 1929, in New York City). Soprano who was arguably the most popular American opera singer of her time. She was praised not only for her voice but also for her intelligence and musical knowledge, qualities rarely noted among opera divas. She retired from singing in 1980. During the 1980s, as general director of the New York City Opera, she restored the company to financial stability.

Courtesy of *The Jewish Week*, New York

**BEVERLY SILLS**

▲ **SIMON, PAUL** (born October 13, 1941, in Newark, New Jersey) and Art(hur) Garfunkel (born November 5, 1941, in New York City). Singing duo in the forefront of the folk-rock fusion of the 1960s and 1970s. Their performances often featured the songs of Simon and the tenor voice of Garfunkel. Among their recordings were "The Sounds of Silence" (1965), "Mrs. Robinson" (1968, originally for the 1967 movie *The Graduate)*, and "Bridge over Troubled Water" (1970). In his solo career, Simon pioneered the use of Third World elements in American popular music, as in *Graceland* (1986), which combines American and black South African music heritages.

▲ **SIROTA, GERSHON** (born 1874 in the Russian province of Podolia; died 1943 in Warsaw, Poland). The first cantor to make recordings (1903).

▲ **SOLTI, GEORG** (originally György Solti; born October 21, 1912, in Budapest, Hungary). Conductor who pioneered the use of stereo techniques in recordings to simulate the theatrical dimensions of opera performances.

▲ SONDHEIM, STEPHEN JOSHUA (born March 22, 1930, in New York City). Composer and lyricist who became the undisputed leader of American musical theater through such works as *A Funny Thing Happened on the Way to the Forum* (1962); *A Little Night Music* (1973), with "Send in the Clowns"; *Sweeney Todd* (1979); *Sunday in the Park with George* (1984); and *Into the Woods* (1987).

▲ STEINBERG, WILLIAM (originally Hans Wilhelm Steinberg; born August 1, 1899, in Cologne, Germany; died May 16, 1978, in New York City). Conductor who, in 1936, at the invitation of Bronislaw Huberman, trained the new Palestine Symphony Orchestra (since 1948 called the Israel Philharmonic Orchestra) for performance, and, after the inaugural concerts led by Arturo Toscanini, served as the ensemble's first principal conductor. Steinberg later conducted in the United States and became famous during his years with the Pittsburgh Symphony Orchestra (1952–76).

▲ STOLLER, MIKE (born March 13, 1933, in New York City). Composer of some of rock and roll's earliest classics, such as "Hound Dog" (1956) and "Jailhouse Rock" (1957), both made famous though recordings by Elvis Presley.

▲ STRAUS, OSCAR (born March 6, 1870, in Vienna, Austria; died January 11, 1954, in Ischl, Austria). Composer of internationally famous operettas, including *A Waltz Dream* (1907) and *The Chocolate Soldier* (1908), each of which had an artistic unity (sometimes achieved through the use of leitmotivs) unique in the operettas of his time.

▲ STYNE, JULE (originally Julius Stein; born December 31, 1905, in London, England; died September 20, 1994, in New York City). Composer of many memorable popular songs. His film songs included "I'll Walk Alone" *(Follow the Boys,* 1944) and "Three Coins in the Fountain" *(Three Coins in the Fountain,* 1954). His Broadway musicals included *Gentlemen Prefer Blondes* (1949), with "Diamonds Are a Girl's Best Friend"; *Two on the Aisle* (1951), with "Give a Little, Get a Little"; *Bells Are Ringing* (1956), with "The Party's Over"; *Gypsy* (1959), with "Let Me Entertain You"; and *Funny Girl* (1964), with "People."

▲ SULZER, SALOMON (originally Salomon Loewy [or Levy]; born March 30, 1804, in Hohenems, Austria; died January 17, 1890, in Vienna, Austria). Chief cantor in Vienna for fifty-five years (1826–81) and composer whose *Song of Zion* (volume 1, 1838–40; volume 2, 1865–66) was the first complete and thoroughly organized repertory in Hebrew arranged for a cantor and a four-part male choir. In 1809 his parents changed their surname from Loewy to Sulzer, after the Austrian village of Sülz.

▲ TERTIS, LIONEL (born December 29, 1876, in West Hartlepool, England; died February 22, 1975, in London, England). The world's foremost violist and the one who was most responsible for the public's acceptance of the viola as a solo instrument.

▲ THOMAS, MICHAEL TILSON (born December 21, 1944, in Hollywood, California). Conductor who was the youngest ever to be appointed assistant conductor of the Boston Symphony Orchestra (1969), succeeded Leonard Bernstein as conductor-commentator of the nationally televised New York Philharmonic Young People's Concerts (1971–76), became one of the few American-born conductors with an international following, and developed one of the widest-ranging repertories of any contemporary conductor. Grandson of actor Boris Thomashefsky.

▲ TIOMKIN, DIMITRI (born May 10, 1894, in Poltava, Ukraine; died November 11, 1979, in London, England). Composer of film scores, including *Lost Horizon* (1937), *Cyrano de Bergerac* (1950), *The High and the Mighty* (1954), and *Giant* (1956). His title song for *High Noon* (1952) initiated the modern practice of linking a commercially successful song with a nonmusical picture.

▲ VON TILZER, ALBERT (originally Albert Gumm; born March 29, 1878, in Indianapolis, Indiana; died October 1, 1956, in Los Angeles). Composer of the classic popular songs "Take Me Out to the Ball Game" (1908), "Put Your Arms around Me, Honey" (1910), and "I'll Be with You in Apple Blossom Time" (1920). Brother of Harry Von Tilzer, whose pseudonym Albert adopted.

▲ VON TILZER, HARRY (originally Harry Gumm; born July 8, 1872, in Detroit, Michigan; died January 10, 1946, in New York City). Composer of the classic popular songs "A Bird in a Gilded Cage" (1900), "Wait 'Til the Sun Shines, Nellie" (1905), and "I Want a Girl Just like the Girl That Married Dear Old Dad" (1911). Brother of Albert Von Tilzer. Harry adopted his mother's maiden name, Tilzer, and added Von to it for distinction.

▲ WALDTEUFEL, EMILE (originally Charles Emile Lévy; born December 9, 1837, in Strasbourg, France; died February 12, 1915, in Paris, France). The world's most popular waltz composer next to the Strauss family. His works included *Les patineurs* ("The Skaters," 1882), *Estudiantina* ("Students," 1883), and *España* ("Spain," 1886).

▲ WALTER, BRUNO (originally Bruno Schlesinger; born September 15, 1876, in Berlin, Germany; died February 17, 1962, in Beverly Hills, California). Conductor who led the world premieres of Mahler's *Das Lied von der Erde* ("The Song of the Earth," 1911) and *Ninth Symphony* (1912).

▲ WAXMAN, FRANZ (originally Franz Wachsmann; born December 24, 1906, in Königshütte, Upper Silesia; died February 24, 1967, in Los Angeles). Composer of film scores, including *Bride of Frankenstein* (1935), *Rebecca* (1940), and *Sunset Boulevard* (1950).

▲ WEINER, LAZAR (born October 24, 1897, in Cherkassy, near Kiev, Ukraine; died January 10, 1982, in New York City). The most important composer produced by the Yiddish milieu in the United States, known especially for his Yiddish art songs.

▲ WOLPE, STEFAN (born August 25, 1902, in Berlin, Germany; died April 4, 1972, in New York City). Composer who developed a profoundly original system of atonal composition based on a sort of continuous variation in which focal pitches and small groups of other pitches are combined to form motives (arranged so that all twelve tones are used in close juxtaposition), which are then varied to create lines and harmonies. One of his finest works was the cantata *Yigdal* ("May He Be Magnified," 1945).

▲ ZUKERMAN, PINCHAS (born July 16, 1948, in Tel Aviv, Israel). The finest combination violinist-violist-conductor of his time.

# 13

# ART

⌘

Jews have produced innovations *in painting, sculpture, photography, cartooning, book illustration, set and costume design, and other fine arts.*

*Marc Chagall, for example, created a wide range of art works—including paintings, set designs, ceramics, and stained-glass windows—that were unified by his distinct "poetic" style. While other major twentieth-century artists emphasized formal elements in their works, Chagall stood virtually alone in reviving art as a symbol of the experiences and feelings of life.*

*Amedeo Modigliani created a unique kind of "sculptured" painting. By portraying the human figure as a three-dimensional form with features that evoke a sculptural approach, he revolutionized the art world.*

*Louise Nevelson was another revolutionary. She founded the modern movements of assemblage and environment sculpture.*

*Camille Pissarro earned a unique place for himself in art history for at least two reasons. He was the first major Jewish painter. And through his theories and practices, he founded the Western world's most popular art movement—impressionism.*

# KEEPING POETRY ALIVE IN TWENTIETH-CENTURY ART
## Marc Chagall

ℰℐ

*Marc Chagall was born in Vitebsk, Russia, on July 7, 1887. His surname was originally spelled Chagal; he added the second l and changed the accent from the first to the second syllable, giving the name more of a French sound. He spent most of his adult life in France and became a French citizen in 1937. Chagall became one of the major artists of the twentieth century. He died in Saint-Paul-de-Vence, France, on March 28, 1985.*

CHAGALL
VITRAUX POUR JÉRUSALEM
MUSÉE DES ARTS DÉCORATIFS
PALAIS DU LOUVRE · 107, RUE DE RIVOLI · JUIN - SEPTEMBRE 1961
TOUS LES JOURS · SAUF LE MARDI · DE 10 A 17 HEURES

MARC CHAGALL WORKED IN AN exceptionally wide range of media: paintings; graphic works, such as etchings; book illustrations; set designs for theater and ballet; ceramics and sculpture; mosaics and tapestry designs; and large-scale murals, ceilings, and stained-glass windows. His entire output is marked by a quality that sets him apart from other major twentieth-century artists. In an age that emphasized formal elements in art, he revived the traditional idea that visual arts should symbolize the experiences and feelings of life, just as poetry does.

Chagall wrote poetry throughout his life, and a poetic feeling—especially a lyric of love—permeated his art works. "I want to get close not only to the eyes but also to the hearts of people," he said. His love of people revealed itself early, as in *The Praying Jew* (1914), one of his many paintings of elderly Jews in his native village. Romantic love was a recurring image, especially in the form of entwined lovers, as in *Equestrienne* (1931). He painted his wife many times, as in *Bella in Green* (1934–35). These pictures and others restored the figurative image, which had been supplanted by abstract designs, to a respected place in art between the two world wars.

During the Holocaust, his love turned to anguish, and he symbolized the pain of the era in many works, such as *The Crucified* (1944), a haunting picture of Jews nailed to crosses. In his late years, his love of Old Testament poetry revealed itself in his stained-glass windows, such as the *Jerusalem Windows* (1961), the United Nations *Peace* window (1964), and *The American Windows* (1979).

Through his commitment to symbolizing the emotional life of the people of his time, Chagall became the poet of twentieth-century art.

# CREATION OF SCULPTURAL PAINTING
## Amedeo Modigliani

ॐ

AMEDEO MODIGLIANI HAS ONE OF THE MOST READILY IDENTIFIABLE styles in twentieth-century art. His painting is notable for its unusual sculptural approach.

Modigliani felt like an outsider: he always introduced himself as a Jew; and he drank too much liquor, took drugs, and engaged in sexual promiscuity to distance himself as much as possible from his family's bourgeois background. As an artist, too, he deliberately set himself apart by not joining any group. Other artists affected him only in general terms. For example, from both Cézanne and African art he got the idea of distorting realism to achieve heightened beauty or emotion.

The most important influence on him was the art of sculpture itself. He always wanted to be a sculptor, but he had to concentrate on painting to earn money. Modigliani painted the human figure as a solid, three-dimensional form, often with necks like columns and with twisted noses sharply drawn, as if cut into the planes of the elongated, masklike faces. His portraits all have a family resemblance, but he gave them individuality through the tilt of the head, the slope of the mouth, and so on. He painted a different expression in each of the typically almond-shaped eyes because "with one eye you look out at the world; with the other you look in at yourself."

Modigliani revolutionized the art world with his haunting, graceful sculptural painting.

# FOUNDING ASSEMBLAGE AND ENVIRONMENT SCULPTURE
## Louise Nevelson

ↄ∙

*Louise Nevelson was born in Pereyaslav, near Kiev, Russia, on September 23, 1899. Her original name was Leah Berliawsky, but she was often called by the diminutive Leike. In 1905 she moved with her parents to the United States, where she changed her first name from Leah/Leike to Louise. In 1920 she married a New York shipping broker named Charles Nevelson. After the marriage dissolved in the 1930s, she began her art career in earnest. Her early sculptures were influenced by cubism, and she did not find her individual niche till she returned to impulses nurtured by her roots. She died in New York City on April 17, 1988.*

LOUISE NEVELSON WAS PROBABLY THE MOST ORIGINAL AMERICAN sculptor of the twentieth century. Drawing on her experiences as a child, she found the inspiration to initiate the modern movements in assemblage and environment sculpture.

When she was a child, her father was a junk dealer, and she imitated his collections by gathering sticks, pebbles, marbles, and other objects and displaying them in little boxes. In the 1940s her scavenging instincts resurfaced; she began to build artistic constructions from old pieces of wood, such as furniture fragments. She thus initiated a kind of art called assemblage, art made from bits and pieces of natural or preformed materials.

In the 1950s she expanded her work into "sculptured walls," large wooden reliefs made of boxes and compartments into which she placed abstract shapes and found objects, such as slats and chair legs. She painted each work a single color, at first black, later white or gold. These works made her a leader in environment sculpture, art consisting of an interplay of forms in three-dimensional space and aiming to enclose spectators and to involve them in multiple stimulations. In the 1960s she began to use aluminum and Plexiglas. Late in her career, she took these ideas one step further to large-scale outdoor works built from steel and other materials.

▶

*Homage to the 6 Million, 1958–64, painted wood.*

Israeli Museum/Jerusalem

Nevelson's childhood playing led to her finding a unique place for herself in art history as the primary force behind two important modern art forms.

# FOUNDING IMPRESSIONISM
## Camille Pissarro

❧

CAMILLE PISSARRO, THE FIRST MAJOR JEWISH PAINTER, was the founding father of the impressionist school of painting. His ideas guided younger members of the school, such as Claude Monet and Pierre-Auguste Renoir. Paul Cézanne called Pissarro "the first impressionist."

Pissarro was a political anarchist, a point of view he adopted largely because of the insecurity he felt as a Jew in a gentile society. He applied his anarchist theories to art by rejecting traditional biblical, historical, and allegorical themes and advocating, in their place, the study of nature.

Freed from traditional themes, he felt, artists would also be freed from their traditional role. Instead of recording what they saw, they could record their impression of what they saw, that is, the sensations they experienced under the influence of a specific place, light, time, movement, and atmosphere.

These new goals, in turn, would require new techniques. Colors, for example, no longer having to imitate reality, could be richer, more brilliant, and more expressive of subjective feelings. Forms could be created not by lines but by patches of evanescent colors and tones. Traditional rules of perspective could be broken to achieve special effects.

> *Jacob Camille Pissarro was born in St. Thomas, Danish West Indies, on July 10, 1830. In 1855 he moved to Paris, where he took part in all of the impressionists' exhibitions (1874–86). After a period of experimentation with pointillism, he returned in his late years to a freer, brighter kind of impressionism, which won him much success. He died in Paris on November 13, 1903.*

The Israel Museum, Jerusalem, Israel

◄
*Mirabeau's Garden, the Terrace, Les Damps (Evre),* c. 1892

These became some of the principal characteristics of impressionism. Pissarro, through his leadership of the movement, earned a unique place for himself in art history.

▲ **ARBUS, DIANE** (originally Diane Nemerov; born March 14, 1923, in New York City; died July 26, 1971, in New York City). Photographer who expanded the range of acceptable subject matter in documentary photography by shooting disconcerting studies of ordinary people as well as midgets, nudists, fetuses, transvestites, and other offbeat subjects. Her name change resulted from her marriage (1941–69) to the actor and fashion photographer Allan Arbus.

▲ **BAKST, LÉON NIKOLAEVICH** (originally Lev Samoylovich Rosenberg; born February 8, 1866, in Grodno, Russia; died December 1924 in Paris, France). Artist whose oriental sets and costumes for the Ballets Russes launched a craze for exotic colors and patterns in fashion and interior decoration.

▲ **BRENNER, VICTOR DAVID** (born June 12, 1871, in Shavli, Russia; died April 5, 1924, in New York City). Designer of the first American portrait coin, the Lincoln penny, issued in August 1909.

▲ **CAPA, ROBERT** (originally Endre Ernö Friedmann; born October 22, 1913, in Budapest, Hungary; died May 25, 1954, in Thai-Binh, Indochina). Celebrated war photographer during the Spanish Civil War, World War II, the Israeli struggle to maintain independence, and Indochina, where he became the first American correspondent to be killed in the Vietnam conflict. Cornell Capa (originally Kornel Friedmann; born April 10, 1918, in Budapest), his brother, is a photojournalist known for his portrait photographs.

▲ **CAPP, AL** (originally Alfred Gerald Caplin; born September 28, 1909, in New Haven, Connecticut; died November 5, 1979, in Cambridge, Massachusetts). Cartoonist famed for his *Li'l Abner* comic strip (1934–77).

▲ **EISENSTAEDT, ALFRED** (born December 6, 1898, in Dirschau, West Prussia, Germany; died August 23, 1995, on Martha's Vineyard, Massachusetts). Photographer who pioneered modern photojournalism by developing the techniques of the picture story and of candid-camera news reporting. He symbolized the end of World War II with his famous picture of a sailor kissing a nurse in Times Square, New York City, on V-J Day.

▲ **EPSTEIN, JACOB** (born November 10, 1880, in New York City; died August 19, 1959, in London, England). Sculptor who created monumental neoprimitive stone carvings, such as *Ecce Homo* (1935), that influenced other artists.

▲ **EZEKIEL, MOSES JACOB** (born October 28, 1844, in Richmond, Virginia; died March 27, 1917, in Rome, Italy). The first American sculptor of international reputation.

▲ **FEIFFER, JULES** (born January 26, 1929, in New York City). Cartoonist whose social and political commentary in *Feiffer* (beginning in 1956) popularized the satirical comic strip.

▲ **FRANKENTHALER, HELEN** (born December 12, 1928, in New York City). Creator of a new type of abstract art called color stain painting, a form of color field painting in which paint is soaked or stained into an unprimed canvas so that the paint is integral with it rather than superimposed.

HELEN FRANKENTHALER

Marabeth Cohen-Tyler

▲ GOLDBERG, RUBE (originally Reuben Lucius Goldberg; born July 4, 1883, in San Francisco, California; died December 7, 1970, in New York City). Cartoonist best known for his "Crazy Inventions" feature, which led to a new term in the English language: a *Rube Goldberg* device or scheme is one that attempts to accomplish by complex means what seemingly could be done simply.

▲ GOTTLIEB, ADOLPH (born March 14, 1903, in New York City; died March 4, 1974, in Easthampton, Long Island, New York). Painter who was a leader of the New York School of abstract expressionism; became famous for the "pictograph" (a picture divided into compartments, each filled with shapes representing Freudian symbols or abstract concepts); painted "imaginary [abstract] landscapes"; and, late in his career, created "cosmic landscapes" called "bursts."

▲ HERSHFIELD, HARRY (born October 13, 1885, in Cedar Rapids, Iowa; died December 17, 1974, in New York City). Cartoonist whose strip *Abie the Agent* (1914–40) was the first sympathetic treatment of a Jewish character in American cartooning.

▲ LIPCHITZ, JACQUES (originally Chaim Jacob Lipchitz; born August 22, 1891, in Druskininkai, Lithuania; died May 26, 1973, in Capri, Italy). Arguably the greatest cubist sculptor; the creator of bronze "transparents," which were among the earliest works to combine mass with open space; and, in his later years, sculptor of monumental, expressive figures.

▲ ROSENTHAL, JOE (born October 9, 1911, in Washington, D.C.) Photographer who took the famous picture of the American flag being raised atop Mount Suribachi on Iwo Jima (February 23, 1945).

▲ Segal, George (born November 26, 1924, in New York City). Sculptor who pioneered the artistic use of plaster figures cast from living models.

▲ SENDAK, MAURICE BERNARD (born June 10, 1928, in New York City). Widely regarded as the first illustrator of children's books to convey the most intense feelings of childhood, as in *Where the Wild Things Are* (1963), which he also wrote.

▲ SHUSTER, JOE (originally Joseph Shuster; born July 10, 1914, in Toronto, Canada; died July 30, 1992, in Los Angeles). Artist who, with writer Jerry Siegel, created the comic-strip character Superman in the 1930s.

▲ STIEGLITZ, ALFRED (born January 1, 1864, in Hoboken, New Jersey; died July 13, 1946, in New York City). Photographer who pioneered the recognition of photography as an art.

▲ VISHNIAC, ROMAN (born August 19, 1897, in Pavlovsk, Russia; died January 22, 1990, in New York City). Photographer and microbiologist who, from 1936 to 1940, photographically recorded the faces of eastern European Jews soon to be killed in the Holocaust, and later applied original techniques to photograph live microscopic animals in their free-swimming state.

▲ WEBER, MAX (born April 18, 1881, in Białystok, Russia; died October 4, 1961, in Great Neck, New York). Eclectic painter who pioneered the introduction of modern art to the United States.

# 14

# FILM AND THEATER PRODUCTION, DIRECTION, AND MANAGEMENT

∽

JEWS HAVE ACCUMULATED A LONG LIST OF UNIQUE ACHIEVEMENTS *as leaders in the business of stage and screen entertainment. Samuel Goldwyn led the establishment of Hollywood as the film capital of the world. Founders and/or first heads of studios included Harry Cohn at Columbia Pictures, Louis B. Mayer at MGM, the Warner brothers at Warner Bros., and Adolph Zukor at Paramount Pictures. Carl Laemmle launched Universal Pictures, the star system, and feature-length films. David O. Selznick was the prototype of the independent film producer. Sherry Lansing was the first woman production chief at a major studio. Michael Eisner raised the Disney Company to the world's most prestigious entertainment entity, primarily through film production. Two major directors were Erich von Stroheim, who was the first to bring realism to the screen, and Steven Spielberg, the most successful director of all time.*

*Television, too, has benefited from the achievements of Jews. David Sarnoff initiated the development of commercial radio and television. William S. Paley built CBS into a giant. And, in the 1970s, Norman Lear pioneered modern television programming by flouting old taboos and presenting frank-spoken situation comedies that explored adult themes; his greatest achievement was* All in the Family.

# FOUNDING COLUMBIA PICTURES
## Harry Cohn

಄

*Harry Cohn was born in New York City on July 23, 1891. He quit school early and worked at a variety of jobs, including songplugging for a music publisher. In 1913 he entered the motion-picture industry by producing short films for music publishers. Later he headed Columbia Pictures. He died in Phoenix, Arizona, on February 27, 1958.*

HARSH IN MANNER, LOWBROW IN TASTE, and dictatorial in style, Harry Cohn typified the popular image of the movie mogul of his time. "I don't have ulcers," he boasted, "—I give them." As cofounder and head of production at Columbia Pictures, he was one of the most powerful men in Hollywood.

In 1920 he, Joe Brandt, and Jack Cohn (his brother) founded C.B.C. Film Sales Company in Hollywood. They tired of hearing their company referred to as Corned Beef and Cabbage, so in 1924 they renamed it Columbia Pictures Corporation. Harry Cohn had artistic control over the films and held the titles of vice president (1924–32) and president (1932–58).

Under his leadership, Columbia became one of the most respected film companies in Hollywood. He insisted on a strong story in every film, and he cultivated first-rate directors and performers. One of his most successful directors was Frank Capra, who made *It Happened One Night* (1934), *Mr. Deeds Goes to Town* (1936), *Lost Horizon* (1937), and *Mr. Smith Goes to Washington* (1939). Other directors included John Ford, Leo McCarey, and George Cukor. Cohn promoted the careers of Rita Hayworth, William Holden, and other major stars. During the Cohn era, Columbia made such classics as *Born Yesterday* (1950), *From Here to Eternity* (1953), *On the Waterfront* (1954), and *The Bridge on the River Kwai* (1957).

Because of Cohn's skillful management, Columbia avoided many of the problems faced by other film companies in the late 1940s and early 1950s. Unlike the larger studios, Columbia never invested in a string of theaters, so when the antitrust laws of the late 1940s forced other companies to divested themselves of their theaters, Columbia was unaffected. And while other studios were suffering from competition with television, Columbia became the first major studio to cash in on the new medium by opening a subsidiary, Screen Gems, specifically designed to sell old Columbia films to the small screen.

Harry Cohn proved over and over again that he was a unique giant in the history of the film industry.

# LEADING THE DISNEY RESURGENCE
## Michael Eisner

❧

MICHAEL EISNER HEADS THE WORLD'S MOST PRESTIGIOUS ENTERTAIN-MENT EMPIRE—the Walt Disney Company. When he took over in 1984, the company had been in a decline since the death of the firm's founder, Walt Disney, in 1966. Eisner turned the company around, and in his first decade he increased the Disney profits elevenfold.

When Eisner became the chief executive officer at Walt Disney Productions, the business, which was renamed the Walt Disney Company in 1986, was in poor financial condition. It had had few movie hits in recent years, and even the theme parks, Disneyland and Walt Disney World, were doing only moderately well.

Eisner attacked the problem on many fronts, but his principal solution was to produce hit movies, which not only generated capital by themselves but also opened the door to related new attractions at the theme parks, to related consumer products, and to related television and video marketing. He approved Disney's first R-rated movie, *Down and Out in Beverly Hills* (1986), approved Disney's production of the television series *The Golden Girls* (1985–92) and *Home Improvement* (1991– ), and oversaw the rejuvenation of Disney's trademark work—animated feature films, including *The Little Mermaid* (1989), *Aladdin* (1992), *The Lion King* (1994), and *Pocahontas* (1995).

On July 31, 1995, he announced Disney's purchase of Capital Cities/ABC, making the merged companies one of the most powerful communications enterprises in the world. Eisner's success has been so great that he has become nearly as well identified with Disney products as Walt Disney himself was.

*Michael Dammann Eisner was born in Mount Kisco, New York, on March 7, 1942. His wealthy parents taught him the value of money, but as a teenager he turned away from a possible career in law or business because, he later explained, he read "a Maxwell Anderson essay about how what remains behind in societies is not the wars or the politics but the art." So he majored in English literature and theater at Denison University in Ohio. Soon after graduating in 1964, he began to work at NBC as a clerk and quickly rose through the ranks at CBS and ABC to become a top television programming executive. From 1976 to 1984, he was president of Paramount Pictures.*

---

### ALSO NOTEWORTHY

▲ BELASCO, DAVID (born July 25, 1853, in San Francisco, California; died May 14, 1931, in New York City). Theatrical producer and playwright known for his important innovations in the techniques and standards of staging and design.

▲ KIRSTEIN, LINCOLN EDWARD (born May 4, 1907, in Rochester, New York; died January 5, 1996, in New York City). Cofounder of the School of American Ballet (the premier dance academy in the United States) and the New York City Ballet.

# ESTABLISHING HOLLYWOOD AS THE WORLD FILM CAPITAL
## Samuel Goldwyn

❧

*Samuel Goldwyn was born in Warsaw, Poland, probably in July 1879 (not 1882, as usually listed). His original name was Schmuel Gelbfisz, anglicized as Samuel Goldfish when he came to the United States as a youth. He worked in a glove factory and then as a glove salesman till business slowed down. Entering the motion-picture business, he became one of the most powerful men in Hollywood. He died in Los Angeles on January 31, 1974.*

PARAMOUNT, MGM, GOLDWYN—three of the most prestigious names in Hollywood history, and all are linked by the same man, Samuel Goldwyn. Because of his role in creating so many movie powerhouses, Goldwyn can arguably be called the most important man in establishing Hollywood as the film capital of the world. In contrast with the usual Hollywood practice of his time, Goldwyn, as both executive and producer, made movies slowly and carefully. His goal was high quality and solid production values with each film.

In 1913 Goldwyn, then known as Goldfish, pressured the vaudeville performer and producer Jesse L. Lasky, his brother-in-law, to set up the Jesse L. Lasky Feature Play Company, a three-way partnership with Lasky, Goldfish, and the film director Cecil B. DeMille. They soon made *The Squaw Man* (1914), the first feature-length film produced in Hollywood. In 1916 the company merged with Adolph Zukor's Famous Players to form the Famous Players–Lasky Corporation. Years later, this company would become Paramount Pictures, Inc.

Goldwyn himself, however, left after just a few months in the new partnership. Later in 1916 he formed Goldwyn Pictures Corporation, the name being a blend of *Goldfish* and *Selwyn*, the surname of his new partners, two brothers. Soon Goldfish legally changed his own name to Goldwyn. In 1922 he left this company, which in 1924 merged with two others to become Metro-Goldwyn-Mayer (MGM), the most successful film studio in Hollywood.

Goldwyn then went on to great success as an independent producer. His films included the classics *Arrowsmith* (1931), *Dead End* (1937), *Wuthering Heights* (1939), *The Little Foxes* (1941), *The Best Years of Our Lives* (1946), *Hans Christian Andersen* (1952), and *Guys and Dolls* (1955).

As both a founder of movie studios and a producer, Goldwyn had a golden touch that, more than any other source, put the glitter into Hollywood's image as the world film capital.

# FOUNDING UNIVERSAL PICTURES, THE STAR SYSTEM, AND FEATURE FILMS
## Carl Laemmle

❧

CARL LAEMMLE HOLDS A UNIQUE PLACE in film history for at least three reasons. First, he founded the main precursor of Universal Pictures, an important movie studio. Second, he launched the star system. Third, he proved that there was money to be made in feature-length films.

Laemmle opened a nickelodeon in 1906. Unsatisfied with the product and service available to him, he founded his own production company, the Independent Motion Picture Company of America (IMP) in 1909.

The following year, he hired Biograph's most popular player, Florence Lawrence, known at the time only as "the Biograph Girl" because studios had not yet begun to bill their players. Laemmle, however, changed that policy. He secretly planted a story that Lawrence had been killed, and then he publicly denounced the report and announced that she had signed with his studio. This episode was the beginning of the Hollywood star system, based on glamorizing performers with extravagant publicity.

In 1912 his company merged with several others to form the Universal Film Manufacturing Company, later known as Universal Pictures. In 1913 his company produced the feature-length *Traffic in Souls*, the first film to prove that a longer movie could make a profit.

Laemmle put his son, Carl (originally Julius), in charge of the company's film production in 1929, when the young man was only twenty-one. The son produced some prestigious films, including *All Quiet on the Western Front* (1930), and started the studio's famous series of horror films, such as *Dracula* (1931) and *Frankenstein* (1931).

As founder of Universal, initiator of the star system, and experimenter in feature films, Carl Laemmle put his indelible stamp on film history.

> *Carl Laemmle was born in Laupheim, Württemberg, Germany, on January 17, 1867. In 1884 he came to the United States, where he worked his way up from odd jobs to become a major success in the motion-picture business. He died in Beverly Hills, California, on September 24, 1939.*

# BECOMING THE FIRST WOMAN FILM-PRODUCTION CHIEF
## Sherry Lansing

ଏ৯

*Sherry Lee Lansing was born in Chicago, Illinois, on July 31, 1944. Her natural father died when she was very young, and her mother, Margo Heimann, married a manufacturer named Norton Lansing, whose surname Sherry took. After graduating from Northwestern University (1966), she taught math in the Los Angeles public schools (1966–69), modeled (1969–70), and tried acting, as in the movie Rio Lobo (1970). Later she became an important motion-picture producer and executive.*

SHERRY LANSING WAS THE FIRST WOMAN TO BE PUT IN CHARGE of production at a major film studio. Not merely a figurehead, she has personally produced or overseen the production of many of the best movies of her time.

Courtesy of *The Jewish Chronicle*

Early in her career, Lansing was uncomfortable as an actress but fascinated by the production process. She took some film classes at the University of Southern California and the University of California, Los Angeles, and began to climb the studio ladders: script reader to executive story editor at Wagner International (1970–73); vice president of productions at Heyday Productions (1973–75); executive story editor to vice president of creative affairs at MGM (1975–77); and vice president to senior vice president of productions at Columbia Pictures (1977–80), where she guided the making of *The China Syndrome* (1979) and *Kramer vs. Kramer* (1979).

Her goal, she explained, was "to make movies that stir up your emotions; movies where you root for the people." Hollywood executives saw that she had a knack for making such pictures, and in January 1980 she was named president of Twentieth Century-Fox, the first woman to head production at a major film studio. Compared with most male production chiefs, she was strong but not harsh. "I don't understand why human decency, kindness, respect for people have to be  mutually exclusive from strength," she said. Lansing oversaw the production of *Taps* (1981), *The Verdict* (1982), and other successful pictures at Twentieth Century-Fox.

In 1983 she resigned to form her own company, Jaffe-Lansing Productions, in partnership with Stanley R. Jaffe. One of the company's most popular productions was *Fatal Attraction* (1987).

In November 1992 she was again appointed chief of production at an important studio, this time Paramount Pictures. At Paramount, she personally produced the hit *Indecent Proposal* (1993).

Through her success as the head of major studios, Lansing  opened doors for other women executives in the film industry.

# PIONEERING BOLD TELEVISION SITCOMS
## Norman Lear

ও

NORMAN LEAR, MORE THAN ANY OTHER INDIVIDUAL, pioneered the acceptance of bold, frank-spoken situation comedies on television. He flouted old broadcasting taboos by presenting adult themes, strong language, and realistic characters. In the process, he became the most successful television producer of the 1970s. At least one of his shows was rated in the prime-time top ten for eleven consecutive seasons (1971–82); and during the 1974–75 season, he had five of the top ten shows.

As a television producer, Lear had a definite goal in mind. "I want to entertain," Lear explained, "but I gravitate to subjects that matter, and people worth caring about." While creating a new series, he recalled that his own father was an intolerant man who asserted his position as head of the household by telling his wife to "stifle" herself and by belittling his son (Norman) as "the laziest white kid I ever saw." Those two expressions became favorites of the leading character, Archie Bunker, in Lear's *All in the Family* (1971–79), a landmark sitcom that revolutionized television by introducing such topics as bigotry, impotence, menopause, and homosexuality. After some of the cast members left the show, it was retitled *Archie Bunker's Place* (1979–83).

*All in the Family* yielded the spinoffs *Maude* (1972–78) and *The Jeffersons* (1975–85). The former focused on an aggressive women's libber and tackled such controversial topics as abortion, race relations, and pornography. *The Jeffersons* centered on a black version of Archie Bunker. Black casts also headed *Good Times* (1974–79), a spinoff of *Maude,* and the independent *Sanford and Son* (1972–77). Other Lear productions included the sitcom *One Day at a Time* (1975–84) and the satirical soap opera *Mary Hartman, Mary Hartman,* (1976–77) the first television serial to deal with such previously taboo subjects as adultery, anti-Semitism, and venereal disease.

Lear's programs were acceptable to the public because he made sure that the scripts handled the topics realistically and responsibly. He has continued to develop television series since the 1970s, but his greatest achievements in recent years have been as a social activist, especially in combating the censorship tendencies of the religious New Right in politics. As the chief liberator of television's sitcoms, Lear knows how to battle taboos.

> *Norman Milton Lear was born in New Haven, Connecticut, on July 27, 1922. After serving in World War II, he worked at a variety of jobs. To earn extra money, he wrote comedy skits, which landed him a job as a television writer. During the 1950s he wrote and directed television programs. Later he became one of the most influential producers in the history of the medium.*

# WIELDING THE GREATEST POWER IN HOLLYWOOD
## Louis B. Mayer

᠙

Louis Burt Mayer was born in Minsk, Russia; the date is uncertain, but he set it at July 4, 1885. His original name was Eliezer, or Lazar, Mayer, though the surname may have been assumed by his family only after arriving in the New World. They settled in Canada when he was a child, and in 1904 he set up a junk business in the United States. Later he became a major success in the film industry. He died in Los Angeles on October 29, 1957.

FOR THREE DECADES, LOUIS B. MAYER was the most powerful motion-picture executive in Hollywood. As head of Metro-Goldwyn-Mayer (MGM), the largest and most prestigious film studio, he imposed his personal values on countless movies and developed the star system to its apex.

In 1907 Mayer bought a nickolodeon, and by 1918 he owned a theater chain. To increase his supply of films, he opened in Hollywood the Louis B. Mayer Pictures company and the Metro Pictures Corporation. In 1924 Loew, Inc., bought and merged those two companies and the Goldwyn Pictures Corporation to form Metro-Goldwyn-Mayer.

American Jewish Archives, Cincinnati Campus, Hebrew Union College, Jewish Institute of Religion

Mayer, as the hands-on chief executive, ruled the studio with a ruthless, tyrannical style. He insisted on producing films that reflected his own mass-oriented tastes: escapist fare emphasizing virtue, patriotism, family life, pretty girls, and elaborate sets and costumes. Instead of engaging audiences with thoughtful or controversial topics, he stimulated their interest in stars, including Rudolph Valentino, Greta Garbo, Joan Crawford, and Clark Gable. However, Mayer also insisted on high-quality production values, and under his leadership MGM developed a reputation for turning out some of the best-made films in cinematic history. They included *Ben-Hur* (1926), *Mutiny on the Bounty* (1935), *The Good Earth* (1937), *The Wizard of Oz* (1939), and *Mrs. Miniver* (1942). On a lighter note was the popular Andy Hardy series of the late 1930s and early 1940s.

Because of MGM's great success under Mayer, his film formula was widely copied by other studios. To a great extent, he personally created the typical film style of the 1930s and 1940s.

# BUILDING CBS INTO AMERICA'S TOP TELEVISION NETWORK
## William S. Paley

ری

FOR OVER SIXTY YEARS, WILLIAM S. PALEY PERSONIFIED THE POWER and influence of the Columbia Broadcasting System (CBS). He served as president (1928–46), chairman of the board (1946–83), founder chairman (1983–86), acting chairman (1986–87), and chairman (1987–90). Under his personal, hands-on leadership, Paley built CBS from a tiny new company into a radio and television giant.

In 1927 Paley invested some money in a relative's small radio network, Columbia Phonographic Broadcasting System (the word *Phonographic* was dropped in 1929), and in 1928 he took over as president of the company. Paley quickly built CBS through his ability to deal with stars, his instinct for mass entertainment, and his eye for competent executives. During radio's heyday, he acquired the services of Bing Crosby, Will Rogers, Eddie Cantor, Bob Hope, Jack Benny, George Burns and Gracie Allen, and many other stars. He also set up the radio news-gathering team that would lead to the legendary early-television staff, including Edward R. Murrow.

Paley personally controlled major television programming at CBS. In the 1950s the network series included the sitcom *I Love Lucy,* the western *Gunsmoke,* and Ed Sullivan's variety show. Later came a long list of hits, including the great Norman Lear sitcoms of the 1970s, such as *All in the Family.* CBS led the American television ratings for twenty consecutive years.

The originator of, and driving force behind, this tremendous success at CBS was William S. Paley.

*William S. Paley was born in Chicago, Illinois, on September 28, 1901. Originally he had no middle name. At the age of twelve, he added a middle initial S.; he claimed that it stood for nothing in particular, though, in fact, his father's name was Samuel. After graduating from the Wharton School of Finance at the University of Pennsylvania in 1922, he went to work for the Congress Cigar Company, owned by his father and uncle. When Paley advertised his cigar products on radio, the company's sales skyrocketed. He quickly saw the potential power of radio. "My imagination went wild in contemplating the possibilities of it," he later said. Paley became an important executive in both radio and television. He died in New York City on October 26, 1990.*

### ALSO NOTEWORTHY

▲ LASKY, JESSE LOUIS (born September 13, 1880, in San Francisco, California; died January 13, 1958, in Beverly Hills, California). Motion-picture executive who, with Samuel Goldfish (later Goldwyn) and Cecil B. DeMille, founded the Jesse L. Lasky Feature Play Company (1913), which made the first Hollywood feature-length film, *The Squaw Man* (1914); years later, after mergers and corporate realignments, the company became Paramount Pictures. Also an independent producer of films, such as *Sergeant York* (1941).

# PIONEERING COMMERCIAL RADIO AND TELEVISION

## David Sarnoff

൧

DAVID SARNOFF BROUGHT RADIO AND TELEVISION into millions of homes in the United States. He set up the first American radio broadcasting network, and the Television Broadcasters Association itself called him "the father of American Television."

*David Sarnoff was born in Uzlian, near Minsk, Russia, on February 27, 1891. In 1901 he came to the United States. In 1906 his father died and young Sarnoff quit school to work for a cable company. Without a formal education, he studied technical books to raise himself in the world, and soon he obtained a job as a wireless operator for American Marconi Company. In April 1912 he gained renown as the operator who picked up the first message that the S.S. Titanic was sinking. In 1915 he proposed to his Marconi superiors the idea of the first radio set, which he called a "radio music box," but the proposal was ignored. Later he became a pioneering executive in the radio and television industries. He died in New York City on December 12, 1971.*

American Jewish Archives, Cincinnati Campus, Hebrew Union College, Jewish Institute of Religion

After Radio Corporation of America (RCA) absorbed American Marconi, Sarnoff became general manager in 1921 and vice president in 1922. Later he served as president (1930–47) and chief executive officer (1947–66). In 1926 he founded a history-making subsidiary of RCA: the National Broadcasting Company (NBC), the first radio network in the United States. He foresaw television as early as 1923, when technical advancements were taking place that others did not see in practical terms the way Sarnoff did. In 1928 he set up a special NBC station to experiment with the new medium, and in 1939 RCA, under his guidance, developed an all-electronic television, a tremendous advancement over the earlier mechanical scanner. In the 1950s he pioneered the use of color television.

David Sarnoff, more than any other individual, opened up the commercial possibilities of radio and television for the general public.

# BECOMING THE PROTOTYPE INDEPENDENT HOLLYWOOD PRODUCER
## David O. Selznick

❧

DAVID O. SELZNICK WAS THE PROTOTYPE of the creative, independent Hollywood producer whose input went far beyond the mere financing and administration of film production. He developed a reputation for producing movies that were both commercially and artistically successful.

He produced melodramas, such as *A Star Is Born* (1937), and literary classics, including *The Adventures of Tom Sawyer* (1938). His most popular success was *Gone with the Wind* (1939), for which he not only used multiple writers and directors but also wrote and directed some sections himself. Among the many other outstanding Selznick productions were Alfred Hitchcock's *Spellbound* (1945) and Carol Reed's *The Third Man* (1949). Selznick personally made a star of Jennifer Jones, whose films included *Duel in the Sun* (1946), and he married her in 1949.

Films made through Selznick International were thoughtful and insightful, like the man himself.

> *David Oliver Selznick was born in Pittsburgh, Pennsylvania, on May 10, 1902. His father, Lewis J. Selznick, produced silent films. In 1926 David moved to Hollywood and quickly rose from a script reader to a producer at MGM, Paramount, RKO, and MGM again. In 1936 he established his own company, Selznick International. He died in Los Angeles on June 22, 1965.*

---

### ALSO NOTEWORTHY

▲ **LOEW, MARCUS** (born May 7, 1870, in New York City; died September 5, 1927, in New York City). Motion-picture executive who, in the early 1920s, purchased and combined Metro Pictures Corporation, Goldwyn Pictures Corporation, and Louis B. Mayer Pictures to form Metro-Goldwyn-Mayer (MGM), which, with Loew's famous theater chain as a ready-made market, became the biggest and richest Hollywood studio.

▲ **LUBITSCH, ERNST** (born January 1892 in Berlin, Germany; died November 30, 1947, in Bel Air, California). Film director who created the "Lubitsch touch," a sophisticated comedy style characterized by understatement, visual wit, and a compression of ideas and situations into single shots or brief scenes that encapsulate the essence of a character or the meaning of the entire film. His movies included *Trouble in Paradise* (1932), *Ninotchka* (1939), and *To Be or Not to Be* (1942).

▲ **LUMET, SIDNEY** (born June 25, 1924, in Philadelphia, Pennsylvania). Famed television director of the 1950s and later a motion-picture director noted for presenting moral conflicts in complex individuals. His films included *Twelve Angry Men* (1957), *Long Day's Journey into Night* (1962), *The Pawnbroker* (1965), *Dog Day Afternoon* (1975), and *The Verdict* (1982).

▲ **MANKIEWICZ, JOSEPH L**(EO) (born February 11, 1909, in Wilkes-Barre, Pennsylvania; died February 5, 1993, in Mount Kisco, New York). The first person to win Academy Awards for both writing and directing two films: *A Letter to Three Wives* (1949) and *All about Eve* (1950).

# DIRECTING AN UNRIVALED STRING OF BLOCKBUSTER MOVIES

## Steven Spielberg

❦

*Steven Spielberg was born in Cincinnati, Ohio, on December 18, 1947. As a child, he used his father's 8–millimeter movie camera to film his family. He graduated from California State College (later University) in Long Beach with a major in English (B.A., 1970). His short film* Amblin' *caught the attention of Universal Pictures, where he was hired to direct episodes of television series, such as* Columbo, *and made-for-television movies, including the highly regarded* Duel *(1971), in which a man driving in a car is pursued by the unseen homicidal driver of a huge truck. He then turned to theater films, where he has been phenomenally successful.*

STEVEN SPIELBERG, MOTION-PICTURE DIRECTOR, has risen to unprecedented levels of popularity by knowing his audiences. He has incredible technical virtuosity in combining cinematography, editing, music, and special effects; and he utilizes that skill to manipulate audience response more powerfully than any other filmmaker of his time. Spielberg has put together an unrivaled string of blockbuster hits.

"Making movies is an illusion," he has said, "a technical illusion that people fall for. My job is to take that technique and hide it so well that never once are you taken out of your chair and reminded of where you are." He applied that philosophy to his first major success, *Jaws* (1975), a thriller about the pursuit of a man-eating shark. *Close Encounters of the Third Kind* (1977) and *E.T.: The Extraterrestrial* (1982), science-fiction films, provided Spielberg with many opportunities to display his technical illusions, as did the adventure yarns *Raiders of the Lost Ark* (1981), *Indiana Jones and the Temple of Doom* (1984), and *Indiana Jones and the Last Crusade* (1989). *Hook* (1991) was a fantasy-adventure based on the Peter Pan story, and *Jurassic Park* (1993) showed dinosaurs in the modern world.

Universal Pictures

Even when Spielberg departs from his usual genres, he still succeeds, as in *The Color Purple* (1985), concerning feminism and black oppression, and *Schindler's List* (1993), a powerful story about the Holocaust. In the mid-1990s, he directed the production of *Survivors of the Shoah,* a set of computer-stored video recollections by Holocaust survivors. This master of "technical illusion" seems to have no limits to his range.

# BRINGING REALISM TO SILENT FILMS
## Erich von Stroheim

✌

ERICH VON STROHEIM WAS ONE OF THE MOST CRITICALLY RESPECTED motion-picture directors of the silent era. His special contribution to the art of filmmaking was his uncompromising realism and attention to detail.

He wrote or cowrote his own scripts and often acted in his films as well. His big break came when he directed *Blind Husbands* (1919), followed by *The Devil's Passkey* (1920) and *Foolish Wives* (1922). All three focused on the sexual awakening of married women. *Blind Husbands* was the most sophisticated sex drama to date, and *Foolish Wives* was banned in some American cities. But the films' great achievement was in their unprecedented realistic details in decor, costumes, acting gestures, and characterizations.

*Greed* (1924), his masterpiece and a landmark in grim, brutal, honest realism on film, was based on Frank Norris's novel *McTeague*, a story about the power of money to corrupt. Von Stroheim constructed the film in a unique way, with each scene deriving its meaning from its own carefully planned details, not from its juxtaposition with other scenes. Because of this structure, the film suffered only minimally when von Stroheim's original forty-two reels were cut down by his superiors to ten reels.

He scored major successes with *The Merry Widow* (1925), *The Wedding March* (1928), and *Queen Kelly* (1928). But his extravagant spending on his films, his fanatic insistence on artistic freedom regardless of the cost, and his sophisticated treatment of controversial subjects ended his directing career. Studio executives gave up on him. All of his films from *Foolish Wives* on were heavily edited and shortened by others at the request of his producers. Returning to acting, he appeared in *The Great Gabbo* (1929), *Sunset Boulevard* (1950), and many other movies.

More than any other silent-film director, he anticipated the realism of the sound era. Sergei Eisenstein called him "The Director."

*Erich von Stroheim was born in Vienna, Austria, on September 22, 1885. As an adult he asserted that his original name was Erich Oswald Hans Carl Maria Stroheim von Nordenwald and that his parents were members of the Catholic aristocracy in Austria, but research after his death shows that his parents were Jewish and that his real name was Erich Oswald Stroheim. He arrived in the United States in 1909 and took a series of jobs before settling in Los Angeles. There he entered motion pictures as an extra and rose to bit player, assistant director, and full-fledged actor, usually typecast as a brutal Prussian soldier and billed as "the man you love to hate." His most important work was his direction of several silent-film classics. Later he returned to acting. He died in Maurepas, Seine-et-Oise, France, on May 12, 1957.*

# FOUNDING WARNER BROS.
## Warner Brothers

❦

*The four Warner brothers were Harry Morris (originally Hirsch), born in Krasnashiltz (in Polish, Krasnosielce), Poland, on December 12, 1881; Albert, nicknamed Abe, born in Baltimore, Maryland, on July 23, 1884; Samuel Lewis, born in Baltimore in 1888; and Jack Leonard (originally Jacob), born in London, Ontario, Canada, on August 2, 1892. In 1904 the boys bought a movie projector, with great difficulty and with help from their father, specifically because they thought it would provide a business in which they could all participate. They began showing films on a traveling basis in the Midwest. Soon they were doing so well that they bought theaters, entered the distribution business, started producing pictures themselves, and settled in Hollywood. Harry died in Los Angeles on July 25, 1958. Abe died in Miami Beach, Florida, on November 26, 1967. Sam died in Los Angeles on October 5, 1927. Jack died in Los Angeles on September 19, 1978.*

WARNER BROS.—THE STUDIO THAT PRODUCED THE FIRST GENUINE TALKIES and some of the most colorful, highly respected film classics of all time—began with four young brothers and a single movie projector. They built the business into one of Hollywood's storied empires.

In 1923 they formed Warner Brothers Pictures, Inc. Harry, the president, ran the New York City business headquarters. Abe, the treasurer, headed sales and distribution. Sam and Jack managed the studio in Hollywood. (After Sam's death in 1927, Jack had sole responsibility in Hollywood, and in 1956 he became president of the company.)

By the mid-1920s they were experiencing financial difficulties. Sam persuaded his brothers to develop a patent on Vitaphone, a process for making movies with sound. They did so and subsequently came out with a series of history-making motion pictures that made their company one of Hollywood's major studios. *Don Juan* (1926) had a completely synchronized music track. *The Jazz Singer* (1927) had both synchronized music and some dialogue. *Lights of New York* (1928) was the first full-length all-talking film. *On with the Show* (1929) was the first all-talking color film (it had two colors distributed to make it appear that there were more colors).

From the 1930s on, the Warners developed a reputation for turning out tightly budgeted, technically competent entertainment films. They began the gangster-film craze with their *Little Caesar* (1930); they produced many Busby Berkeley musicals; and they had great success with adventure films, such as *The Adventures of Robin Hood* (1938). Their later classics included *The Maltese Falcon* (1941), *Casablanca* (1943), *The Treasure of the Sierra Madre* (1948), *A Streetcar Named Desire* (1951), and *My Fair Lady* (1964).   In 1969 the studio became Warner Bros., Inc., a subsidiary of Warner Communications. In 1989 the latter merged with Time, Inc., to form Time Warner, Inc., one of the largest media and entertainment corporations in the world.

# FOUNDING PARAMOUNT PICTURES
## Adolph Zukor

&

ADOLPH ZUKOR HELPED FOUND, and for many years was chairman of the board at, Paramount Pictures, one of the film industry's most important production companies. He was also among the developers of the star system, bringing to the screen many of its most glittering names.

In 1912 he left his early partnership with Marcus Loew and earned a fortune on his own as the sole American distributor of *Queen Elizabeth,* starring the French actress Sarah Bernhardt. That success gave him the idea of forming a film-production company featuring Broadway stars in their current stage successes. His Famous Players Film Company started business later that year.

In 1916 it merged with the Jesse L. Lasky Feature Play Company to form Famous Players–Lasky Corporation. After further mergers and reorganizations, it became, in 1935, Paramount Pictures, Inc., with Zukor as chairman of the board.

His special interest, going back to his days with Famous Players, was in cultivating stars. In silent films, his performers included Mary Pickford, John Barrymore, Gloria Swanson, and Rudolph Valentino. In the sound era, he developed Mae West, W.C. Fields, Bing Crosby, Bob Hope, Gary Cooper, Burt Lancaster, and Kirk Douglas. The list of hit movies at Paramount would be nearly endless, but they included *The Ten Commandments* (1923 and 1956), *Going My Way* (1944), and *Psycho* (1960).

As the principal force in creating Paramount and its stars, Zukor left a permanent, personal imprint on film history.

> *Adolph Zukor was born in Ricse, Hungary, on January 7, 1873. As a teenager, he immigrated to the United States. In 1903 he invested in a penny arcade, and from 1904 to 1912 he and Marcus Loew owned a chain of theaters. Later he became a powerful executive in Hollywood film production. He died in Los Angeles on June 10, 1976, at the age of 103.*

---

### ALSO NOTEWORTHY

▲ PREMINGER, OTTO LUDWIG (born December 5, 1906, in Vienna, Austria; died April 23, 1986, in New York City). Motion-picture director who made the classic *Laura* (1944); pioneered the fight for liberalization of screen portrayals of sex, in *The Moon Is Blue* (1953) and *Anatomy of a Murder* (1959), and drugs, in *The Man with the Golden Arm* (1955); and helped end blacklisting by hiring the writer Dalton Trumbo for *Exodus* (1960).

▲ REINHARDT, MAX (originally Max Goldmann; born September 9, 1873, in Baden, near Vienna, Austria; died October 31, 1943, in New York City). Stage director who pioneered the idea of the director as a creative artist, his own spectacular productions being marked by unusual staging methods and elaborate special effects. He assumed the stage name Reinhardt.

▲ ROSE, BILLY (originally Samuel Wolf Rosenberg, later William Samuel Rosenberg; born September 6, 1899, in New York City; died February 10, 1966, in Montego Bay, Jamaica). Stage producer who became the most colorful showman of his time, known as the Bantam Barnum. His famous productions included the lavish *Jumbo* (1935) and the all-black *Carmen Jones* (1943).

▲ SCHULBERG, B(ENJAMIN) P(ERCIVAL) (born January 19, 1892, in Bridgeport, Connecticut; died February 18, 1957, in Miami, Florida). Motion-picture producer who discovered Clara Bow and made her famous as the "It" Girl. Father of the writer Budd Schulberg.

▲ STERNBERG, JOSEF VON (originally Jonas, or Josef, Stern, or Sternberg; born May 29, 1894, in Vienna, Austria; died December 22, 1969, in Hollywood, California). Director of the silent *Underworld* (1927), regarded as the first feature-length gangster film; *Thunderbolt* (1929), the first such sound film; and the classic Marlene Dietrich vehicle *Der blaue Engel* ("The Blue Angel," 1930). Sternberg brought Dietrich to the United States and directed her in several English-language pictures.

▲ THALBERG, IRVING GRANT (born May 30, 1899, in Brooklyn, New York; died September 14, 1936, in Santa Monica, California). Motion-picture production manager who was called the "boy wonder of Hollywood" and established MGM's reputation for consistently high-quality films, such as *The Barretts of Wimpole Street* (1934), *Mutiny on the Bounty* (1935), and *The Good Earth* (1937).

▲ TODD, MIKE (or Michael Todd; originally Avrom Hirsch Goldbogen; born June 22, 1909, in Minneapolis, Minnesota; died March 22, 1958, in an airplane crash near Grants, New Mexico). Broadway and film producer who helped pioneer the wide screens of the 1950s with his Todd-AO process and who produced the movies *Oklahoma!* (1955) and *Around the World in Eighty Days* (1956).

▲ WILDER, BILLY (originally Samuel Wilder; born June 22, 1906, in Sucha, Galicia). Director of motion pictures that broke new ground in the film industry by tackling subjects that other directors would not touch, such as human evil in *Double Indemnity* (1944), alcoholism in *The Lost Weekend* (1945), sexual ambiguities in *Some Like It Hot* (1959), and modern American hypocrisy in *The Apartment* (1960).

▲ WYLER, WILLIAM (born July 1, 1902, in Mulhouse, France; died July 27, 1981, in Beverly Hills, California). Motion-picture director widely regarded as having the greatest technical polish of his time, as in the films *Wuthering Heights* (1939), *Mrs. Miniver* (1942), *The Best Years of Our Lives* (1946), and *Ben-Hur* (1959).

# 15

# FILM AND THEATER PERFORMANCE

ა

JEWISH ACTORS, COMEDIANS, AND DANCERS *have significantly enriched the worlds of film and theater by creating unique performance styles, genres, and characters.*

*Woody Allen evolved his urban Everyman into the most complete comic expression of the age of anxiety. Rabbi Robert A. Alper is the world's only practicing clergyman doing stand-up comedy—intentionally. Lauren Bacall created The Look. Jack Benny revolutionized stage humor by creating a consistent, rounded character. Milton Berle was television's first superstar. Mel Brooks developed film parody into an art form. Lenny Bruce was the prototype "sick" comedian. George Burns stood alone as the Methuselah of show business.*

*Richard Dreyfuss translated his nondescript features into a new star image. John Garfield, in his portrayal of flawed characters, created a new-style film hero. Harry Houdini virtually invented the art of escape. Leslie Howard developed the modern "natural" approach to acting. Al Jolson starred in the first important sound film. Danny Kaye's special niche in entertainment history was as the United Nations official ambassador-at-large to the world's children.*

*The Marx Brothers recorded the screen's purest form of comic anarchy. The dancer-choreographer Jerome Robbins was unique in his dual success in ballet and on Broadway. Edward G. Robinson created the prototype for gangster characters in films. And Ed Wynn's Perfect Fool character was unique in entertainment annals because he blended the qualities of stage comedian and circus clown.*

# CREATION OF THE URBAN EVERYMAN
## Woody Allen

❧

*Woody Allen was born in New York City on December 1, 1935. His original name was Allan Stewart Konigsberg. As a teenager, he earned a job as a comedy writer for television performers, including Sid Caesar. In the early 1960s, Allen himself became a stand-up comedian because he felt that his jokes needed a special kind of delivery. He was invited to write the script for the movie* What's New, Pussycat? *(1965), but he was so disappointed with the way his material was treated that he vowed to make his own films in the future. The result has been an outstanding series of motion pictures written and directed by Allen and centering on his unique comic character.*

W.H. AUDEN, IN HIS POEM *THE AGE OF ANXIETY*, gave a serious voice to mankind's feelings about the tensions and complexities of modern life. The richest comic expression of those feelings lies in the work of Woody Allen. As a stand-up comedian and as a filmmaker, he portrays the ultimate comic neurotic, an intelligent contemporary urban man struggling feebly against the alienation and anxieties in the modern mechanized world.

The character is a carefully crafted artistic creation, not the real Woody Allen. "The things I did on nightclub stages were fantasies or exaggerations from my own life," he has said. "All I was doing was what was funny."

Allen modeled his fictional persona by blending elements from his two favorite comedians, Bob Hope (representing traditional humor) and Mort Sahl (the counterculture). Into that mix, Allen, who suffers from anhedonia (the inability to experience happiness), poured the classic characteristics of the traditional Jewish schlemiel (loser), with his insecurities, self-deprecation, and fear of everyday objects ("My toaster hates me"). The character is deepened through his pondering of the modern existential crisis, constantly debating with himself about spiritual-material conflicts (often expressed as paradoxes, as when he describes his parents' values as "God and carpeting"). "I have an intense desire," he says, "to return to the womb—anybody's." In his films—including *Play It Again, Sam* (1972), *Annie Hall* (1977), *Crimes and Misdemeanors* (1989), and *Husbands and Wives* (1992)—

► Woody Allen **(second from right) directs Jack Warden, Elaine Stritch,** and Mia Farrow in a scene from his film *September.*

Allen has created an urban Everyman who is the most important "little guy" on screen since Charlie Chaplin and the most perfect comic embodiment of Auden's *Age of Anxiety*.

# Becoming the World's Only Rabbi-Comic
## Robert A. Alper

❧

RABBI ROBERT A. ALPER BILLS HIMSELF as "the world's only practicing clergyman doing stand-up comedy...intentionally." Since 1986 he has simultaneously served as a rabbi and performed as a professional comic.

Since childhood, he had always had a gift for making people laugh. As a rabbi, he used humor effectively in his preaching, teaching, and counseling, and he looked forward to making announcements at services so that he could improvise funny lines. Finally, in 1986, he entered a contest for the

Courtesy of Rabbi Alper

Jewish Comic of the Year in Philadelphia and took third place out of a hundred entrants. Hooked on humor, he switched to a part-time rabbi position and began his career as a stand-up comedian. The early going was rough. Some nights he bombed. "Some colleagues," he says, "I'm sure, were judgmental (what? a rabbi judgmental?) until they saw the act." And, of course, he had to win an audience while at the same time distancing himself from the sleaze that characterizes much of the comedy industry.

By the early 1990s he was a solid success—without sacrificing his ethics. He says "that while there was always lots of humor in my rabbinate, I've discovered that there's a lot of rabbi in my humor." Sick people, for example, have told him that after listening to his comedy tapes, their conditions have improved. He refuses to use profanity or suggestive material or to tell jokes about circumcision, Jewish mothers, Jewish American Princesses, or other topics that do not present a positive Jewish image. He does, however, glory in the Jewish milieu. For example: "We follow Jewish tradition in our family. When our son was born, we named him after my grandfather. We call him 'Grandpa.'" And: "We have a Jewish cable news network. Every hour a guy meanders across the screen and says, 'You don't want to know about it.'"

Alper has carved out a unique place for himself as the world's only rabbi-comic.

*Robert Abelson Alper was born in Providence, Rhode Island, on January 29, 1945. Coming from a strong Reform Jewish home, wanting a people-oriented career, and having a rabbi uncle as a model, he chose to enter the field of rabbinics. He graduated from Lehigh University (1966), was ordained at the Hebrew Union College (1972), and became the first Jew to earn a Doctor of Ministry degree at the Princeton Theological Seminary (1984). Alper was a full-time assistant and associate rabbi at Temple Beth Zion in Buffalo, New York (1972–78), a full-time rabbi at Congregation Beth Or in Spring House, Pennsylvania (1978–86), and a part-time rabbi (on High Holy Days and other occasions) at Temple Micah in Glenside, Pennsylvania (1986 to present).*

# CREATION OF THE LOOK
## Lauren Bacall

ɔ

*Lauren Bacall was born in New York City on September 16, 1924. Her original name was Betty Perske. When she was a child, her parents divorced and her mother took the name Bacal, from her maiden name of Weinstein-Bacal. Betty added the extra l when she began to get some stage roles. She also modeled, and when the film director Howard Hawks saw her picture on the March 1943 cover of Harper's Bazaar, he signed her to a movie contract. She married her first costar, Humphrey Bogart, and appeared in several more pictures with him, including Key Largo (1948). In these early movies, she played a femme fatale, but later in her career, she widened her range to include comedies, musicals, and melodramas. Since the 1970s she has been a versatile character actress.*

FEW ACTRESSES HAVE ENJOYED AS POWERFUL A FILM DEBUT as Lauren Bacall did in *To Have and Have Not* (1944). In that movie, she brought to the screen a facial expression so uniquely her own that it was dubbed simply The Look.

Bacall's early film persona was created by her first director, Howard Hawks. For *To Have and Have Not*, he molded her character, Slim, into an insolent, provocative sexpot by drawing from Bacall a sultry voice and a seductive, sophisticated manner. The truth, however, was that she was barely more than a child. And she was so nervous that her head kept shaking. Hawks told her to control her head by bracing her chin in a lowered position and looking up insinuatingly at Bogart when she said, "You know how to whistle, don't you Steve? You just put your lips together and blow." That pose became The Look, which, for many years, men adored and women imitated.

# REVOLUTIONIZING STAGE HUMOR
## Jack Benny

ᴇ∕ᴏ

Cleveland Press

MOST AMERICAN STAGE comedians in the early twentieth century created humor through slapstick, pomposity, exaggerated dialects, or a series of basically unrelated jokes. The first performer to rise to a higher level of comedy was Jack Benny, whose more sophisticated techniques, especially his use of a consistent, rounded characterization, proved to be much more enduring.

Benny understood the need for a new kind of humor. In the 1940s he wrote, "The public today demands more of its humor than a laugh at any price....We try to follow one simple rule: if it hurts, it isn't funny."

He made his comic persona gentle, low-key, and self-effacing. But the character was also realistically flawed, especially by being "the world's worst violin player" and "the stingiest man in show business" (in reality, Benny was a fine violinist and a generous man). Benny did not tell jokes—he built comic scenes. The pace was deliciously slow, with highlights punctuated by his incredible timing, particularly by his use of silence, a skill he probably evolved from his music studies. After being insulted, he would pause before exclaiming, "Well!" When a thief bellowed out, "Your money or your life!" the miserly character paused before replying, "I'm thinking it over!" The character became so well known that Benny could, and did, walk out onto a Las Vegas stage, fold his arms, and look silently at the audience for almost a full minute while the house roared with laughter. His first line was "What are you laughing at?"

Benny paved the way for other comics to build careers on a single, well-crafted character.

*Jack Benny was born in Chicago, Illinois, on February 14, 1894, and raised in Waukegan. His original name was Benjamin Kubelsky. He studied violin at the Chicago School of Music and played the instrument in vaudeville. During navy service (1917–18), he entertained sailors at stage shows; but one night the audience was cool to his violin playing, so he began to ad-lib jokes. Returning to vaudeville, he created acts based on jokes and comic bits on his violin, began to form his unique stage persona, and, in 1921, took the name Jack Benny. He soon became a star in vaudeville and later appeared in many films, notably To Be or Not to Be (1942). But his greatest impact came in The Jack Benny Program on radio (1932–55) and television (1950–65). He died in Beverly Hills, California, on December 26, 1974.*

# BECOMING TELEVISION'S FIRST SUPERSTAR
## Milton Berle

෴

*Milton Berle was born in New York City on July 12, 1908. His original name was Milton Berlinger. When he was only five, his ambitious mother led him into show business. He went on to appear in films, Broadway shows, and nightclubs. In 1932 he hosted a vaudeville show at the prestigious Palace Theater in New York City. That experience led to similar jobs, capped by his stint as host of the Texaco Star Theater on radio (1948–49) and television (1948–53). He has continued to work well into his eighties, not only as a comedian but also as a straight dramatic actor.*

MANY EARLY COMMERCIAL TELEVISION PROGRAMS were variety shows, much in the tradition of vaudeville. The most popular variety series in television history and the medium's first major success was the *Texaco Star Theater*, hosted by the acknowledged master of the variety form, Milton Berle.

Berle was eager to do the *Texaco Star Theater* on both radio, because the program's format was so much like his familiar vaudeville shows, and on television, because he was convinced that his visual brand of humor would do well on the screen. He opened each show with his own routine and then introduced the other acts, in which he often participated. The program was telecast live, and he had no cue cards. When he muffed a line, he actually became funnier by ad-libbing, drawing on his years of experience on vaudeville and nightclub stages. His humor was fast paced, and much of it was physical—pure slapstick and buffoonery, such as wearing outlandish women's clothing. Because of Berle's reputation for stealing other comedians' jokes, the columnist Walter Winchell called him the "thief of badgags." His verbal style was aggressive, flippant, and sometimes insulting ("What is this, an audience or an oil painting?"). In later years, he admitted that his onstage abrasiveness reflected much of his offstage personality, which had been formed by his missing out on a normal childhood and spending years of struggling in the rough world of show business.

On the *Texaco Star Theater*, Berle was phenomenally successful.

▶ The many faces of Milton Berle.

Many American families bought their first television sets specifically to see him. Known affectionately as Uncle Miltie and respectfully as Mr. Television, Berle was the small screen's first superstar.

# RAISING THE FILM PARODY TO AN ART FORM
## Mel Brooks

ɛↄ

A PARODY IS AN ARTISTIC WORK that imitates the style of another work. The effect of the parody is often comic, and the purpose may be either to ridicule or to pay tribute to the original. The man who raised film parody to an art form is Mel Brooks.

Showtime

His parodies of film classics are done with such knowledge of, and obvious affection for, the originals that Brooks's works can rightly be called homages. He patterned *The Producers* (1967), in which he did not appear, after the putting-on-the-show musical films popular in the 1930s; in this case, the show is *Springtime for Hitler,* which, in the picture, becomes a camp hit. *Blazing Saddles* (1974) spoofs Hollywood westerns and includes a black sheriff, a wacky governor, and a Yiddish-speaking Indian chief, the last two parts played by Brooks himself. *Young Frankenstein* (1974), in which he did not appear, borrows from 1930s horror movies. Brooks starred in *High Anxiety* (1977), which is based on the thrillers made by his favorite director, Alfred Hitchcock; *Spaceballs* (1987), which parodies space epics; and *Robin Hood: Men in Tights* (1993), a comic version of the famous 1938 movie *The Adventures of Robin Hood.*

Through these films and others, Brooks has secured a firm place for himself in movie history as the unrivaled king of parody.

Mel Brooks was born in New York City on June 28, 1926. His original name was Melvyn Kaminsky. His mother was responsible for the growth of his imagination. "She really had this exuberant joy of living," he has said, "and she infected me with that." However, when Mel was only two, his father died, leaving him with a permanent sense of loss, outrage, and fear of death. "I'm sure that a lot of my comedy is based on anger and hostility." Another factor was his belief that "as a Jew and as a person," he didn't "fit into the mainstream of American society." As a youth, he learned to clothe his anger in comedy "to spare myself problems— like a punch in the face." He changed his name to Brooks (after his mother's maiden name, Brookman), worked as a comic in the Catskills, wrote for Sid Caesar's famous television variety shows in the 1950s, and in 1960 began a series of comedy recordings as a two-thousand-year-old Jew. His career hit full stride when he turned to films, often functioning as writer, director, and star.

# PIONERING SICK COMEDY
## Lenny Bruce

ༀ

*Lenny Bruce was born in Mineola, New York, on October 13, 1926. His original name was Leonard Alfred Schneider. He early turned to comedy purely as a profession. Later he used the stage to propound a social philosophy. He died in Los Angeles on August 3, 1966.*

LENNY BRUCE REVOLUTIONIZED AMERICAN HUMOR. He was the first major comedian to employ raw, controversial language and imagery in an attempt to expose and destroy the prejudices and repressions of middle-class America.

He began his career as a traditional comic. Then, in the late 1940s, he met a group of new-style comedians in New York City. Chief among them was Joe Ancis, a nonprofessional whose sleazy, improvised material Bruce closely imitated and artistically refined to make it suitable for a public stage. After ten years of perfecting his act, Bruce finally began to attract serious attention in San Francisco in 1958. But as he traveled the nightclub circuit, he began to face repeated arrests on narcotics and obscenity charges. Near the end of his life, he abandoned his stage career to become a free-speech crusader.

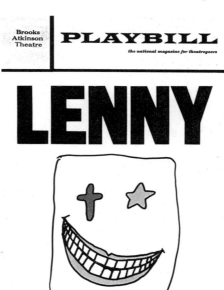

▶ A dramatization of the life of Lenny Bruce opened on Broadway in 1971.

"All my humor is based on destruction and despair," Bruce said. Believing that everyone had occasional dark or selfish thoughts and feelings, he used obscenity as a kind of psychological dynamite to blow away his own and his audience's inhibitions and to lay bare the secret human layers. He attacked organized religion, dwelt on unconventional sex, and joked about such topics as rape, toilets, and amputees.

After he died of a drug overdose, he became a martyr to the counterculture, and he is still the most famous exponent of sick comedy.

# BECOMING THE METHUSELAH
## OF SHOW BUSINESS
## George Burns

Ɛɔ

GEORGE BURNS HELD A UNIQUE PLACE IN SHOW-BUSINESS HISTORY not only because of his longevity but also because of the way he used his age as a comedy asset. Well into his nineties, he was still making public appearances as a comedian.

"For forty years my act consisted of one joke," he wrote of his wife, Gracie Allen. "And then she died." After that, he "really went into show business." He performed a nightclub act with songs, jokes, and reminiscences.

But the big breakthrough in his solo career did not come till he was nearly eighty, when he played an ex-vaudevillian in the film comedy *The Sunshine Boys* (1975). He then rose to superstar status through his performances as the Deity in the movies *Oh, God!* (1977), *Oh, God! Book II* (1980), and *Oh, God! You Devil* (1984). He became incredibly active doing live appearances, making recordings, writing books, appearing on television, and continuing his films, such as *Wisecracks* (1992).

Age was the core of his humor. "Thanks for the standing ovation," he said. "I'm at the point now where I get a standing ovation just for standing." "They're talking about making a movie of my life. I hope they do it quick—I'd like to see it."

In September 1994, after suffering a fall, he had successful surgery to remove fluid from his brain. On January 20, 1996, Burns turned one hundred years old. He died forty-nine days later, the acknowledged Methuselah of show business.

> *George Burns was born in New York City on January 20, 1896. His original name was Nathan Birnbaum. As a child, he sang as he sold crackers on the streets. Soon he entered vaudeville, took a cigar as a prop at the age of fourteen, and adopted the name George (a nickname for an admired older brother, Isadore) Burns (after the Burns Brothers coal company, from whom he stole coal). He went through a series of acts and partners, including a trained seal. In 1923 he teamed up with, and in 1926 married, Gracie Allen, an Irish-American Catholic. He served as a straight man to her zany character, and they became huge hits on vaudeville and, through The George Burns and Gracie Allen Show, on radio (1932–50) and television (1950–58). She retired in 1958 and died in 1964. Burns then performed on his own. He died in his Beverly Hills, California, home on March 9, 1996.*

# FOUNDING A NEW STAR IMAGE
## Richard Dreyfuss

ço

*Richard Dreyfuss was born in New York City on October 29, 1947. In 1956 he moved with his family to Los Angeles, where he immediately decided that he wanted to become an actor. He performed on local stages, appeared on television, and gathered experience in some films, notably as a student in* American Graffiti *(1973). Within a few years, he was a genuine star.*

FILM STARS, AT LEAST THE "HEROES," are traditionally tall, handsome, and macho. Richard Dreyfuss is, truth to tell, none of the above, yet he is one of the great stars of his era. When he hit the big time, he believed that he was setting a trend for future stars. But the trend never came. He remains one of a kind.

With his title role as a poor young Jew pursuing success in *The Apprenticeship of Duddy Kravitz* (1974), Dreyfuss established his basic screen image: an aggressive but ordinary guy. He knew he was difficult to cast, and he said he looked forward to the day when audiences would tire of perfect biceps and admire "short, slightly over-

PM Magazine

weight Jewish neurotics." Good parts did come. In *Jaws* (1975) he played a wise-cracking scientist, in *Close Encounters of the Third Kind* (1977) a utility-company employee pursuing UFOs, and in *The Goodbye Girl* (1977) an egocen-

tric actor. Since *Down and Out in Beverly Hills* (1986) and *Tin Men* (1987), he has concentrated on comedies.

In these and many other films, Dreyfuss has used his self-assertive style to translate his nondescript features into a new image of what a star can be.

### ALSO NOTEWORTHY

▲ ADAMS, JOEY (originally Joseph Abramowitz; born January 6, 1911, in New York City). Comedian who long reigned as the most sought-after entertainer in the borscht belt.

# CREATION OF A NEW-STYLE HERO
## John Garfield

જી

IN THE MID-TWENTIETH CENTURY, A NEW KIND OF LEADING MAN emerged in films. He was not always good at heart, strong in spirit, and victorious in the end. Instead, he was flawed, vulnerable, and sometimes defeated. Such a character was often played by Marlon Brando, Montgomery Clift, James Dean, Dustin Hoffman, Paul Newman, Steve McQueen, and Al Pacino. But the prototype was John Garfield.

John Garfield with Lana Turner in
*The Postman Always Rings Twice.*

His very first picture, *Four Daughters* (1938), established his basic screen image for the rest of his career. He played a young loner and loser who is cynical but appealing. His typical character was a street kid who yearned for society to accept him and his aspirations, but he was doomed to failure. In *They Made Me a Criminal* (1939) he is a boxer in hiding after being framed for a killing. In *The Postman Always Rings Twice* (1946) he is lured by love into adultery and murder. *Body and Soul* (1947) was a landmark in his career, allowing him to show his acting depth and range as his character evolves from an arrogant youthful boxer into a disillusioned middle-aged champ. In *Force of Evil* (1948) he is a lawyer drawn into corruption. In his final screen image, he is an outlaw dying in the gutter in *He Ran All the Way* (1951).

In these and similar roles, he proved to be the forerunner of a new style of hero, one who lacks many traditional heroic qualities but realistically reflects many truths about modern urban life.

*John Garfield was born in New York City on March 4, 1913. His original name was Jacob Garfinkle, but his parents informally called him Julius or Julie. His early experiences with the street life of the urban poor influenced his later social consciousness and rough mannerisms as an actor. He was saved from a life of crime by his junior-high-school principal, Angelo Patri, who encouraged him to take up amateur boxing and to study dramatics at the American Laboratory Theater. The youth began to appear onstage as Julian Garfield and then as Jules Garfield, and in 1934 he joined the famed Group Theater. In 1938 he began his film career with Warner Bros. Under pressure from the studio, he changed his name to John Garfield. He died in New York City on May 21, 1952.*

# Inventing the Art of Escape
## Harry Houdini

ℰℐ

HARRY HOUDINI WAS THE MASTER SHOWMAN of the early twentieth century. Through his unprecedented use of self-publicity, he became the most famous magician of his time, attaining renown even among people who did not care about magic. And he virtually invented the art form of escape.

Early in his career, he struggled unsuccessfully to develop a following. The turning point came during a five-year visit to Europe, where he learned the value of promoting himself. In England he made sure that newspapers covered his escapes from jails, and in Germany he jumped off a public bridge into water while he was fully manacled. In 1905 he returned to America as a celebrity and began performing in urban vaudeville.

*Harry Houdini was born in Budapest, Hungary, on March 24, 1874. His original name was Erik Weisz. As a small child, he moved with his parents to the United States, where his name was Americanized to Erich Weiss. To escape poverty, he created a magic act, learning by watching sideshows and circuses and by reading books. He called himself Harry (derived from his nickname, Ehrie) Houdini (after his idol, the magician Robert-Houdin). With a partner—first a friend, then a brother, then his wife—he played at dime museums, beer halls, and small-time rural vaudeville theaters.*

*Later he added escape tricks to his act and eventually hit the big time. He died in Detroit, Michigan, on October 31, 1926.*

His specialty was "The Challenge Handcuff Act," in which he became the first escape artist to invite people from the audience to shackle him with real handcuffs, not the usual fake variety. In "The Chinese Water Torture Cell Escape," his ankles were padlocked and he was lowered head first into a glass container of water. In "The Straitjacket Escape," he squirmed out of the binding in full view of the audience.

Through his showmanship, self-publicity, and superior skills, he became the first superstar escape artist.

# CREATION OF "NATURAL" ACTING
## Leslie Howard

cᴗ

LESLIE HOWARD CREATED A NEW STYLE OF ACTING. In the 1920s on Broadway and then in the 1930s on film, he eschewed the excessive gestures and overwrought declamations traditional among actors. Instead, he used a "natural" approach, underplaying his parts with a conversational, relaxing manner that reflected his own personality.

Howard never really enjoyed acting. He performed merely to earn enough money to have the freedom to write, produce, and direct his own plays and films. Having no pretensions as an actor, he simply played himself: a dreamy, cultured, intelligent, honorable man often pitted against the brute forces in the world. In *The Scarlet Pimpernel* (1935) he fights the oppressive

*Leslie Howard was born in London, England, on April 3, 1893. His full name was Leslie Howard Steiner. He worked in a bank and served in World War I before making his professional acting debut in 1917. In the 1920s he worked on English and American stages, and in 1930 he began to appear in major motion pictures. He died on June 1, 1943, when his airplane was shot down by German aircraft over the Bay of Biscay.*

French with trickery and daring disguises, not with fists and swords. In *The Petrified Forest* (1936) he is a writer who sacrifices his life for a waitress. In *The First of the Few* (1942, known in America as *Spitfire)* he is an aeronautical engineer who battles the Nazis by designing a fighter plane. He played a linguist in *Pygmalion* (1938), a violinist in *Intermezzo* (1939), a self-debating reluctant soldier in *Gone with the Wind* (1939), and a professor in *Pimpernel Smith* (1941).

Through these and other roles, Howard became the screen's foremost idealistic intellectual and the forerunner of modern realistic actors.

# STARRING IN THE FIRST SOUND FILM
## Al Jolson

❧

*Al Jolson was born in Srednike, Lithuania, sometime during the period 1880–86. Jolson himself did not know the exact date, but he later chose May 26, 1886, as the date he preferred. His original name was Asa Yoelson. In the 1890s he moved with his family to the United States. His father, a cantor, taught him to sing, and soon the boy was singing in the streets for money. He changed his name to Al Joelson and then Al Jolson, appeared in vaudeville, performed as one of Lew Dockstader's Minstrels, returned to vaudeville, and then graduated to Broadway musical shows. In* The Honeymoon Express *(1913) he created his hallmark gestures: falling to one knee and extending his arms in a pathetic appeal while singing. His other Broadway shows included* Sinbad *(1918) and* Big Boy *(1925). Among his films were* The Singing Fool *(1928) and* Mammy *(1930). In the biopic* The Jolson Story *(1946) he dubbed in the singing for Larry Parks (as Jolson). Jolson died in San Francisco, California, on October 23, 1950.*

THE FIRST SIGNIFICANT FEATURE-LENGTH SOUND MOVIE was the Warner Bros. picture *The Jazz Singer* (1927). The story was about a Broadway entertainer, so the studio selected as the star of the film Broadway's greatest attraction, Al Jolson.

*The Jazz Singer* was originally a Broadway play (1925) based on the story "The Day of Atonement," by Samson Raphaelson, who had been inspired to write the work by watching Jolson perform. Jolson wanted to play the lead in the Broadway version, but Raphaelson balked because he knew that the story would become secondary to Jolson's powerful musical personality, so the role went to George Jessel. However, when Jessel asked for special financial considerations to make the movie, the studio gladly replaced him with Jolson.

The picture is mostly silent, with songs and bits of dialogue audible. The first spoken words occur when Jolson, after singing "Dirty Hands, Dirty Face," says "Wait a minute! Wait a minute! You ain't heard nothin' yet," and then introduces his next song, "Toot, Toot, Tootsie." Jolson's character is Jakie Rabinowitz, a cantor's son who runs away from home to become the jazz singer Jack Robin. When his father dies, Jack gives up his big chance on Broadway and goes home to take up his father's duties at the synagogue. For the screen version, a final segment was added showing Jack singing in a Broadway musical entitled *The Jazz Singer*.

Before this film, many people thought that sound pictures would be a passing fad. But *The Jazz Singer* was such a tremendous success, largely because of Jolson's performance, that no one could doubt that talkies were here to stay.

# Representing UNICEF to the World's Children

## Danny Kaye

☙

FOR THE LAST THIRTY YEARS OF HIS LIFE, Danny Kaye reigned as the world's prince of clowns. He laid the groundwork for that status through his unprecedented comic versatility in stage performances and in films. But his rise into a class of his own resulted from his work as the official ambassador-at-large to the world's children for the United Nations International Children's Emergency Fund (UNICEF).

In 1954 a UNICEF official asked Kaye to entertain disadvantaged children around the world and help raise funds for the group's work. Kaye devoted most of his energy for the rest of his life to that cause. He traveled to remote areas of Europe, Asia, Africa, and Latin America—anyplace where there were children undernourished, diseased, or orphaned by war. Exuding an obviously genuine affection for the children, he entertained them while teams of UNICEF workers administered medical and other aid. Language was no barrier; he had learned as long ago as 1934, during a working trip to the Orient, how to communicate comedy to non-English-speaking audiences by using pantomime, mugging, and nonsense singing.

Because his humor was always kind, humble, and universal in appeal, he was internationally recognized as a human treasure. When he died in 1987, he was universally mourned as the lost clown prince of UNICEF.

*Danny Kaye was born in New York City on January 18, 1913. His original name was David Daniel Kaminski (family members spelled the surname various ways, including Kominsky). He entertained other kids to survive on the tough streets, quit high school to be a toomler on the borscht circuit, and worked in vaudeville and burlesque. His career skyrocketed in 1940 when his wife, the songwriter Sylvia Fine, began to tailor her songs for his talent for dialect (especially Russian and French) singing and patter (humorous, rapid-fire) songs. He became famous in such films as* The Secret Life of Walter Mitty *(1947),* The Inspector General *(1949), and* Hans Christian Andersen *(1952). Later he had a television show (1963–67), comically conducted symphony orchestras, and played dramatic roles, as in* Skokie *(television, 1981). He died in Los Angeles on March 3, 1987.*

# CREATING THE WILDEST COMIC ANARCHY IN FILM HISTORY
## Marx Brothers

ᶜᵇ

*All the Marx Brothers were born in New York City—Chico (pronounced Chicko, not Cheeko, originally Leonard) on August 21, 1887; Harpo (originally Adolph, later Arthur) on November 23, 1888; Groucho (originally Julius) on October 2, 1890; Gummo (originally Milton) on October 23, 1892; and Zeppo (originally Herbert) on February 25, 1901. Show business was in their blood: their maternal grandparents had operated a traveling theatrical troupe in Germany, and one of their uncles was the famous vaudevillian Al Shean in the comedy team of Gallagher and Shean. The boys' mother, Minnie, encouraged her sons to carry on the family tradition. She formed them into a team of varying membership, first as singers and then as a comedy act. The four oldest boys worked together for several years till Gummo was drafted during World War I and he was replaced by Zeppo. By 1919 the team was the biggest attraction in vaudeville. Then they conquered Broadway in the musicals*

THE MARX BROTHERS CREATED A UNIQUE KIND OF COMEDY. No other team or individual has so well combined nonsense, slapstick, satire, pantomime, black humor, and witty dialogue. At the heart of their comedy was their refusal to be molded by the pompous powers of convention. The boys thumbed their noses at the Establishment (often personified on stage and screen by the stately actress Margaret Dumont, their favorite comic foil). A Marx Brothers performance was a wild conglomeration of pure madcap energy.

They began their movie career with filmed versions of *The Cocoanuts* and *Animal Crackers* in 1929 and 1930 respectively, followed by *Monkey Business* (1931), *Horse Feathers* (1932), and *Duck Soup* (1933). In these films, plots barely begin when the Marx Brothers start to destroy them by shifting attention to a series of tangential comedy routines showcasing the boys in various combinations.

The principal figure was Groucho, who wore an ill-fitting frock coat, a parody of the society he mocked. He also had a painted-on mustache, constantly smoked and flicked a cigar, insinuatingly twitched his eyebrows, uttered savage wisecracks at everyone and everything, and sang comic songs with a unique nasal twang. He expressed the essence of the Marx Brothers spirit when he sang "Whatever It Is, I'm against It" in *Horse Feathers*.

Chico's humor was largely based on his use of a mock Italian accent and his misuse of the English language. In *The Cocoanuts*, for example, he confused *viaduct* and *why a duck*. He also applied comedy to his pianism, as in his technique of "shooting the keys," that is, pointing his index finger like a pistol, using his thumb as a "trigger," and striking a key.

Harpo portrayed a totally uninhibited childlike mute. He chased women (literally) and pulled a face called a Gookie (puffing out his cheeks and crossing his widened eyes). His props included a fright wig, a bicycle horn (which he honked at women to attract their attention), and an overcoat with enormous inside pockets, where he stored such useful items as a blowtorch, an ice-cream cone, a cup of coffee, and a ton of hardware. He created many beautiful interludes in the films with his harp playing.

## COMIC ANARCHY *(continued)*

Zeppo provided romantic relief. He got the girl but not the gags.

After *Duck Soup,* Zeppo left the group and the other three continued to make films, such as *A Night at the Opera* (1935), *A Day at the Races* (1937), *At the Circus* (1939), *A Night in Casablanca* (1946), and, their last picture as a team, *Love Happy* (1950). Chico and Harpo went on to appear in nightclubs and elsewhere. Groucho gained new fame on his radio (1947–51) and television (1950–61) quiz show *You Bet Your Life.*

The Cocoanuts *(1925) and* Animal Crackers *(1928). There followed a legendary career in films. Chico died in Beverly Hills, California, on October 11, 1961. Harpo died in Los Angeles on September 28, 1964. Gummo died in Palm Springs, California, on April 21, 1977. Groucho died in Los Angeles on August 19, 1977. Zeppo died in Palm Springs on November 30, 1979.*

Universal Pictures

◄
**The Marx Brothers (Chico, Groucho, and Harpo,** *left to right)* **with Margaret Dumont** *(right).*

The Marx Brothers never played Jews on-screen, but they exuded the Jewish urban experience through their streetwise Lower East Side language, their ingenious (albeit eccentric) debates reminiscent of the Talmud, and especially their sense of alienation from the mainstream of society. In vaudeville they pulverized their audiences with ad-libbed comical chaos. On Broadway, even with mandatory scripts, they still insisted on ad-libbing frequently. And in films, especially their first five, they recorded the nearest thing to comic anarchy in screen history.

# CHOREOGRAPHING BALLET AND BROADWAY BLOCKBUSTERS
## Jerome Robbins

❧

*Jerome Robbins was born in New York City on October 11, 1918. His original name was Jerome Rabinowitz. When he was a teenager, his older sister turned his attention to dancing. His later versatility already showed itself in his early studies, which included ballet, modern, Spanish, and Oriental dance forms. In the 1930s he worked as a chorus boy in some Broadway shows. In 1940 he joined the Ballet Theatre, rising from minor roles to leading parts to choreographer. In 1949 he became a choreographer with the New York City Ballet. From 1958 to 1961 he ran his own company, Ballets: U.S.A. During the 1960s he worked on Broadway, in films, and on television. In 1969 he returned to the New York City Ballet.*

JEROME ROBBINS—DANCER, CHOREOGRAPHER, AND DIRECTOR—holds a unique place in the world of American dance. No one else has matched his dual success in ballet and on Broadway. On Broadway, in particular, he created a whole new function for dance within the play.

The first ballet he created was *Fancy Free* (1944), with music by Leonard Bernstein. Robbins also choreographed Bernstein music in the ballets *Facsimile* (1946), *Age of Anxiety* (1950), and *Dybbuk Variations* (1974). Other Robbins ballets included *The Goldberg Variations* (1971) and *Glass Pieces* (1983).

His ideal form of theater was an amalgamation of all the forms of theatrical art. He envisioned a company whose members could sing, dance, and act in a variety of styles. His Broadway work reflected those ideals in his pathbreaking use of the dance as an integral component of the play, both delineating character and propelling the plot. His acknowledged masterpiece was *West Side Story* (1957), which he conceived, directed, and choreographed to music by Bernstein. The work was a landmark in extending the expressive range of the Broadway musical, and the organic dances played a key role in the success of the show. His other Broadway hits included *On the Town* (1945), which was an expansion of *Fancy Free*, *Call Me Madam* (1950), *The King and I* (1951), and *Fiddler on the Roof* (1964).

Through his ballet successes and his Broadway innovations, Jerome Robbins created a new fusion in American dance. He danced to his own tune.

# CREATING THE PROTOTYPE OF THE GANGSTER CHARACTER
## Edward G. Robinson

❦

ONE OF THE MOST IMPORTANT FILM GENRES IN THE 1930S was the gangster picture. Prohibition had created many powerful, well-known criminals, and Hollywood capitalized on their fame by making movies based on their exploits. The undisputed master portrayer of such gangster roles was Edward G. Robinson.

For many years he worked as a reliable supporting actor on the New York City stage. Then, in 1927, he scored his first big success, starring as a gangster in the play *The Racket*. That experience led to offers from Hollywood, where he had a long, successful career in a wide rage of roles, such as a sensitive scientist in *Dr. Ehrlich's Magic Bullet* (1940), a hunter of Nazis in *The Stranger* (1946), an overseer of slaves in *The Ten Commandments* (1956), and a serene philosopher in *Soylent Green* (1973).

But it was in his gangster roles that he made his greatest impact on film history. Hollywood soon typecast him in such parts because of his success on Broadway in *The Racket*. He became a major film star through his portrayal of a ruthless mobster in *Little Caesar* (1931). There followed similar roles in such films as *The Little Giant* (1933), *Barbary Coast* (1935), *The Last Gangster* (1937), *Brother Orchid* (1940), and *Key Largo* (1948). In real life, he was a well-read, cultivated man. He eventually said that the gangster part was "a character of whom I was growing wearier and wearier all the time." But with his rugged features, strutting walk, incomparable sneer, and—most important of all—great technical ability as an actor, he turned his gangster persona into the most memorable tough guy in screen history and the prototype for innumerable future film thugs.

*Edward G. Robinson was born in Bucharest, Romania, on December 12, 1893. His original name was Emanuel Goldenberg. In 1902 he moved with his family to the United States, where he turned to acting because he "longed for recognition." While studying in New York City at the American Academy of Dramatic Arts, he was urged to change his name, and he selected Edward (after the current king of England) Robinson (after a character in an English comedy); as a reminder of his roots, he used the middle initial G. for Goldenberg. Robinson began as a stage actor and then had an outstanding career in films. He died in Los Angeles on January 26, 1973.*

# INVENTING THE PERFECT FOOL
## Ed Wynn

∾

*Ed Wynn was born in Philadelphia, Pennsylvania, on November 9, 1886. His original name was Isaiah Edwin Leopold. He began entertaining as a small child by putting on ladies' hats in his father's hat store and clowning around for the customers. As a teenager, he ran away from home, changed his name to Ed Wynn (by splitting the two syllables of his real middle name), and entered vaudeville. Later he reached the zenith of his career in his own Broadway variety shows, often as producer, director, writer, and composer in addition to star. In his radio series* The Fire Chief *(1932–35) he introduced the technique of combining comedy with the sponsor's commercial messages. He also hosted* The Ed Wynn Show *on television (1949–51). Late in his career, he played dramatic roles, notably in the live television play* "Requiem for a Heavyweight" *(1956) on the* Playhouse Ninety *anthology series, and comedy parts, as in the Disney movie* Mary Poppins *(1965). Ed Wynn died in Beverly Hills, California, on June 19, 1966.*

MORE THAN ANY OTHER STAGE COMEDIAN, Ed Wynn made himself resemble the traditional image of a circus clown. He whitened his face, grease-painted his eyebrows, put on horn-rimmed glasses, emphasized his prominent nose and red-lipped mouth, covered his pear-shaped frame with zany hats and misfit clothes, and wore over-sized flapping shoes. He called his character the Perfect Fool.

Wynn said he was a "method comedian," that is, one for whom the material was secondary to his method of putting it over. His style was his comedy. By the time he created his show *The Perfect Fool* (1921), his style and stage persona were fully formed. From 1921 on, he billed himself as the Perfect Fool. His trademarks included a lisp, a squeaky voice, a high-pitched giggle, fluttering hands, and a constant look of surprise and wonderment. He loved wordplay; as a showboat impresario he said, "I bred my cast upon the waters," and his favorite exit line was "I'll be back in a flash with more trash." The character was known for his preposterous inventions, including an eleven-foot pole "to use on people you wouldn't touch with a ten-foot pole" and a pianocycle (a piano plus a tricycle).

Ed Wynn (*right*) with son, Keenan Wynn.

In his clownlike characteristics, the Perfect Fool was unique in stage history.

▲ **ADLER FAMILY.** The most famous family in the American Yiddish theater. Jacob P(avlovitch) Adler (born February 12, 1855, in Odessa, Ukraine; died April 1, 1926, in New York City) was the preeminent Yiddish actor of his time. With his second wife, the stage actress Dinah Adler (née Shtettin), he had his daughter Celia (born 1890; died January 31, 1979, in New York City), often referred to as the First Lady of the Yiddish Theater. His third wife, Sarah Adler (née Levitzky; born 1858 in Odessa, Ukraine; died April 28, 1953, in New York City) was the greatest Yiddish actress of her time. Jacob and Sarah had seven children, including Frances (born 1891 in New York City; died December 13, 1964, in New York City), a Yiddish stage actress; Jay (born 1896; died September 24, 1978, in Woodland Hills, California), a character actor on the stage and in films, such as *Lust for Life* (1956); Stella (born February 10, 1902, in New York City; died December 21, 1992, in Los Angeles), a Yiddish- and English-language stage actress who became America's most important teacher of the system of Method acting in which actors create characters through textual analysis and imagination (for a different type of Method acting, see Lee Strasberg); and Luther (born May 4, 1903, in New York City; died December 8, 1984, in Kutztown, Pennsylvania), a distinguished actor in the Yiddish theater, on Broadway, and in movies, such as *Wake of the Red Witch* (1949), *Cast a Giant Shadow* (1966), and *Voyage of the Damned* (1976).

▲ **AMSTERDAM, MOREY** (born December 14, probably 1908, in Chicago, Illinois). Comedian who headlined the first Los Angeles experimental television program (1939); was a panelist on the television game show *Stop Me If You've Heard This One* (1945), the first series telecast with a live studio audience; and played Buddy Sorrell in the sitcom *The Dick Van Dyke Show* (1961–66).

MOREY AMSTERDAM

▲ **ARTHUR, BEATRICE** (originally Bernice Frankel; born May 13, 1926, in New York City). Actress who is the acknowledged queen of comic characters of the commanding, acerbic type, such as Vera Charles in the Broadway musical *Mame* (1966), the title character in the television sitcom *Maude* (1972–78), and Dorothy in the television sitcom *The Golden Girls* (1985–92).

▲ **BARA, THEDA** (originally Theodosia Goodman; born July 20, probably 1885, in Cincinnati, Ohio; died April 7, 1955, in Los Angeles). Actress who became the first star created by Hollywood publicity, the screen's first sex symbol, and the most celebrated vamp of silent films. Through her first movie, *A Fool There Was* (1915), she created the popular catchphrase "Kiss me, my fool!" She always gave 1890 as the year of her birth, but because she graduated from high school in 1903 and because she admitted she would lie about her age, most researchers today place her birth in 1885 (no birth certificate has been found). Hollywood publicists claimed that *Theda Bara* was created as an anagram for *Arab Death,* but in fact *Theda* was merely a contraction of *Theodosia,* and *Bara* was derived from the middle name of her maternal grandfather.

Israel Film Archives

THEDA BARA

▲ **BAYES, NORA** (originally Dora Goldberg; born about 1880, perhaps in Milwaukee, Wisconsin; died March 19, 1928, in New York City). Singing actress who, in 1907, starred in the first edition of Florenz Ziegfeld's *Follies.*

GERTRUDE BERG

▲ BERG, GERTRUDE (originally Gertrude Edelstein; born October 3, 1899, in New York City; died September 14, 1966, in New York City). Actress who created, produced, wrote, directed, and starred in *The Goldbergs* (radio, 1929–34, 1937–45, and 1949–50; television, 1949–55), which paved the way for modern situation comedies and soap operas by its use of recurring characters (notably her own, Molly) in everyday settings.

SHELLEY BERMAN

▲ BERMAN, SHELLEY (originally Sheldon Berman; born February 3, 1926, in Chicago, Illinois). The first big-time comedian to personify the neuroses, frustrations, and absurdities of modern life; the first performer to popularize the "comedy concert," consisting of one-act miniatures and comic lectures; and the first comedian to appear at Carnegie Hall.

SARAH BERNHARDT

▲ BERNHARDT, SARAH (original name and birthdate uncertain, partly because there is no surviving birth certificate from the actual time of her birth and partly because she was an illegitimate offspring of a prostitute; original name probably Henriette-Rosine Bernard; born October 22 or 23, 1844, in Paris, France; died March 26, 1923, in Paris). The dominant stage actress of her time and the first great actress to appear in films.

▲ BLANC, MEL(VIN JEROME) (born May 30, 1908, in San Francisco, California; died July 10, 1989, in Los Angeles). The world's all-time greatest performer of cartoon voices, including those for Bugs Bunny, Daffy Duck, Porky Pig, Road Runner, Sylvester the cat, Tweety Pie the canary, Woody Woodpecker, and Yosemite Sam.

ELAYNE BOOSLER

▲ BOOSLER, ELAYNE (born August 18, 1952 in New York City). The principal forerunner of the new breed of women comics who address topical issues from a women's point of view without being self-demeaning or pandering to men.

▲ BORGE, VICTOR (originally Börg Rosenbaum; January 3, 1909, in Copenhagen, Denmark). Entertainer who is a unique blend of stand-up comic and concert pianist. From 1953 to 1956, he gave 849 performances of *Comedy in Music,* the longest-running one-man show in Broadway history.

▲ BRICE, FANNY (originally Fannie Borach; born October 29, 1891, in New York City; died May 29, 1951, in Los Angeles). Actress-singer-clown who broke ground for later comediennes by performing Broadway, radio, and film comedy without exploiting sexuality or homemaking. *Photo credit:* American Jewish Archives, Cincinnati Campus, Hebrew Union College, Jewish Institute of Religion.

FANNY BRICE

SID CAESAR

▲ CAESAR, SID (full name, Isaac Sidney Caesar; born September 8, 1922, in Yonkers, New York). Comedian and actor who is in a class of his own in his aping of languages, sound effects, and human types. His talents accounted for the only early television variety series, *Your Show of Shows* (1950–54), that deliberately appealed to the audience's intelligence and ability to figure out situations for themselves.

EDDIE CANTOR

▲ **CANTOR, EDDIE** (originally Isidore Itzkowitz; born January 31, 1892, in New York City; died October 10, 1964, in Los Angeles). Comic actor, nicknamed Banjo Eyes, who performed on stage, on radio, and in films with a unique blend of energy, cheerfulness, boyish charm, and sincere human warmth. He headed, and coined the name of, the March of Dimes, the fund-raising drive to fight polio.

▲ **CROSBY, NORM(AN LAWRENCE)** (born September 15, 1927, in Boston, Massachusetts). Comedian who has developed malapropisms into a fine art.

▲ **CRYSTAL, BILLY** (originally William Crystal; born March 14, 1948, in New York City). Comedian, mimic, and actor who played Jodie Dallas, the first openly homosexual character in the history of television, on the sitcom *Soap* (1977–81); created the national catchphrase "You look maaaaaavelous" in his guise as the character Fernando on *NBC's Saturday Night Live* (1984–85); and starred in several hit movies, including *City Slickers* (1991).

BILLY CRYSTAL

TONY CURTIS

▲ **CURTIS, TONY** (originally Bernard Schwartz; born June 3, 1925, in New York City). Actor who carved out a unique place in film history by distinguishing himself in four distinct categories: a handsome, athletic personality, as in *Houdini* (1953); a dramatic lead, as in *Sweet Smell of Success* (1957); a light comedy actor, as in *Some Like It Hot* (1959); and a mature character actor, as in *Mafia Princess* (television, 1986).

▲ **DOUGLAS, KIRK** (originally Issur Danielovitch Demsky; born December 9, 1916, in Amsterdam, New York). Actor who is the all-time master of rage on film, as in *Champion* (1949), *The Bad and the Beautiful* (1952), *Paths of Glory* (1957), *Lonely Are the Brave* (1962), and *Amos* (television, 1985).

▲ **FALK, PETER** (Michael) (born September 16, 1927, in New York City). Actor who played the Los Angeles policeman Lieutenant Columbo, television's most eccentric detective, in the crime-drama series *Columbo* (1971–77 and 1989–90) and in many television movies.

▲ **FLANAGAN, BUD** (originally Chaim Reeven Weintrop, anglicized on his birth certificate as Robert Winthrop; born October 14, 1896, in London, England; died October 20, 1968, in London). British comedian who summed up the great music-hall comic tradition and left a permanent record of that art in his film performances, as in *Underneath the Arches* (1937).

DUSTIN HOFFMAN

Columbia Pictures

▲ **HOFFMAN, DUSTIN** (**LEE**) (born August 8, 1937, in Los Angeles). Hollywood's preeminent antihero in the 1960s, as in *The Graduate* (1967), and 1970s, as in *Lenny* (1974).

▲ **HOLLIDAY, JUDY** (originally Judith Tuvim; born June 21, 1922, in New York City; died June 7, 1965, in New York City). The preeminent performer of dumb-blond roles, notably in *Born Yesterday* (stage, 1946; film, 1950).

JUDY HOLLIDAY

Columbia Pictures

BERT LAHR

▲ **LAHR, BERT** (originally Irving Lahrheim; born August 13, 1895, in New York City; died December 4, 1967, in New York City). The last great American comedian nurtured in classic burlesque before it degenerated into a peep show. Best known as the Cowardly Lion in the film *The Wizard of Oz* (1939).

▲ **LEONARD, JACK E.** (originally Leonard Lebitsky; born April 24, 1911, in Chicago, Illinois; died May 10, 1973, in New York City). The first entertainer to build an entire career as an insult comedian.

▲ **LEWIS, JERRY** (originally Joseph Levitch; born March 16, 1926, in Newark, New Jersey). Comedian and comedy actor who, on stage and in films, created the persona of the "idiot kid" and then raised the character to a universal level by transforming the kid's heartache into Everyman's anguish and releasing the pressure through comic exaggeration. Because of his artistry and because of his volunteer work since 1950 on behalf of the Muscular Dystrophy Association, Lewis has attained a unique status as the "clown with compassion."

JERRY LEWIS

▲ **LORRE, PETER** (originally Ladislav Loewenstein, also spelled Laszlo Löwenstein; born June 26, 1904, in Rózsahegy, Hungary; died March 23, 1964, in Los Angeles). The screen's preeminent psycopath and neurotic villain, notably in the German film *M* (1931).

▲ **MARCEAU, MARCEL** (original surname, Mangel; born March 22, 1923, in Strasbourg, France). The world's greatest mime, especially known for his character Bip, the sad, white-faced clown he created in 1947.

PETER LORRE

JACKIE MASON

▲ **MASON, JACKIE** (originally Yacov Moshe Maza; born June 9, probably 1930, in Sheboygan, Wisconsin). America's most successful overtly Jewish stand-up comedian. He dominated Broadway in the late 1980s with his one-man show *The World According to Me!*

▲ **MENKEN, ADAH ISAACS** (originally Adah Bertha Theodore; born 1835 in Chartrain, near New Orleans, Louisiana; died August 10, 1868, in Paris, France). Leading lady who shocked audiences by being the first American actress to wear flesh-colored tights on the stage, giving the illusion of nudity. She derived her stage name by combining her first name, Adah, with the middle and last names of her first husband, Alexander Isaac (adding an *s* for euphony) Menken.

▲ **MIDLER, BETTE** (born December 1, 1945, in Honolulu, Hawaii). Singer-actress known as the Queen of Camp because of her 1970s–80s bizarre song-and-comedy stage shows. Later a fine comedy actress in films, such as *Ruthless People* (1986).

▲ **MOGULESKO, SIGMUND** (originally Zelig Mogulesko; born December 16, 1858, in Kaloraush, Bessarabia; died February 4, 1914, in New York City). The first great comedian of the modern Yiddish theater.

BETTE MIDLER

▲ **MUNI, PAUL** (originally Mehilem Meyer ben Nachum Favel Weisenfreund; born September 22, 1895, in Lemberg, Austria; died August 25, 1967, in Montecito, California). Actor known as the Man of Many Faces because of his ability to transform himself to fit a multitude of roles, such as a scarred thug in *Scarface* (1932), a French scientist in *The Story of Louis Pasteur* (1936), a Chinese farmer in *The Good Earth* (1937), and a Mexican statesman in *Juarez* (1939).

▲ **MYERSON, BESS** (born July 16, 1924, in New York City). The first and only Jewish Miss America (1945). The title served as a springboard for her later careers on television and in public service.

BESS MYERSON

▲ **NICHOLS AND MAY.** Comedy team consisting of Mike Nichols (originally Michael Igor Peschkowsky; born November 6, 1931, in Berlin, Germany) and Elaine May (originally Elaine Berlin; married and divorced Marvin May; born April 21, 1932, in Philadelphia, Pennsylvania). In the depth of their characterizations, they broke new ground for later satirists. Probably the best improvisational duo ever. After they split up the act (1962), Nichols became a renowned director, with such credits as the Broadway play *The Odd Couple* (1965) and the film *The Graduate* (1967). May scripted the popular movie *Tootsie* (1982).

▲ **PICON, MOLLY** (born June 1, 1898, in New York City; died April 6, 1992, in Lancaster, Pennsylvania). The preeminent performer to emerge from the American Yiddish variety theater.

▲ **RACHEL** (or Mademoiselle Rachel; originally Élisa Félix, also recorded as Elisabeth Felix; born February 28, 1820, also recorded as March 24, 1820, or February 28, 1821, in Mumpf, Switzerland; died January 3, 1858, in Le Cannet, France). Leading lady responsible for the revival of French classical dramatists, especially Racine and Corneille.

▲ **RAINER, LUISE** (born January 12, about 1910, in Vienna, Austria). The first actor or actress to win two Oscars and the first to win two in a row, for *The Great Ziegfeld* (1936) and *The Good Earth* (1937).

▲ **RUBINSTEIN, IDA LVOVNA** (born about 1885 in Saint Petersburg, Russia; died September 20, 1960, in Vence, France). Dancer who starred in the first production of the Ballets Russes in Paris (1909–10) and who commissioned some of the twentieth century's most important ballets, including Ravel's *La Valse* (composed 1919–20, danced 1928) and Stravinsky's *Persephone* (1934).

▲ **SAHL, MORT(ON)** (born May 11, 1927, in Montreal, Canada). Comedian who, in the 1950s, paved the way for a new generation of entertainers by breaking most of the traditional rules of nightclub comedy. Instead of the usual dress suit, he wore casual slacks and a sweater; instead of telling jokes with punchlines, he gave stream-of-consciousness monologues and sardonic social observations; instead of being inoffensive, he feared no taboos and created the famous signature phrase "Is there any group I haven't offended?"

▲ **SALES, SOUPY** (originally Milton Supman; born January 8, 1926, in Franklinton, near Wake Forest, North Carolina). Comedian who is the world's greatest proponent of pure silliness, pies in the face, and corny gags ("Show me a sculptor who works in the basement and I'll show you a low-down chisler"). He acquired his nickname, Soupy, from his childhood playmates who punned it from his family name, Supman.

▲ **SCHACHT, AL(EXANDER)** (born November 12, 1892, in New York City; died July 14, 1984, in Waterbury, Connecticut). The Clown Prince of Baseball, a former baseball player who performed comical pantomime skits during ball games, including many World Series and All Star contests.

▲ **SCHWARTZ, MAURICE** (originally Avrom Moishe Schwartz; born June 15, 1889, in Sudilkov, Ukraine; died May 10, 1960, in Tel Aviv, Israel). Actor who founded the Yiddish Art Theater in New York City and was called the John Barrymore of the Yiddish Theater.

PETER SELLERS

▲ **SELLERS, PETER** (born September 8, 1925, in the Southsea district of Portsmouth, England; died July 24, 1980, in London, England). Arguably the best comedy chameleon in film history, famed for creating brilliant, hilarious screen characterizations of incredible variety, often playing multiple parts within a single movie. His best-known role was that of the bumbling French police detective Inspector Jacques Clouseau in the Pink Panther series of films. Sellers was born of a Jewish mother and non-Jewish father.

▲ **SHORE, SAMMY** (originally Semelah, anglicized as Samuel, Shore; born 1925 in Chicago, Illinois). Long regarded as the best warm-up (opening-act) comedian in show business. He initiated the comedy-club format when he opened his Comedy Store in Los Angeles in 1972.

▲ **SILVERS, PHIL** (originally Philip Silver; born May 11, 1911, in New York City; died November 1, 1985, in Los Angeles). The all-time master of comic fast-talking-swindler roles, as in the television sitcom *You'll Never Get Rich* (by the end of the run, called *The Phil Silvers Show,* 1955–59; later syndicated as *Sergeant Bilko).*

PHIL SILVERS

▲ **STEINBERG, DAVID** (born August 9, 1942, in Winnipeg, Canada). Comedian with a unique stage personality based on an informal manner and intellectual style. In the late 1960s, he broke a long-standing taboo against religious humor on television (in one bit, when God tells Moses, "I am that I am," Steinberg's Moses coughs politely and says, "Thanks for clearing that up").

▲ **STRASBERG, LEE** (born November 17, 1901, in Budanov, Austria-Hungry; died February 17, 1982, in New York City). Artistic director of the famed Actors Studio (1948–82), where he became America's preeminent teacher of the system of Method acting in which actors draw on their personal experiences to create the emotions of characters (for a different type of Method acting, see Stella Adler).

▲ **SUSSKIND, DAVID** (born December 19, 1920, in New York City; found dead February 22, 1987, in New York City). Television producer who hosted *Open End* (1958–67), the first important television program with no set time limit and the first to feature in-depth interviews with such major figures as Soviet Premier Nikita Khrushchev and American Vice President Richard M. Nixon.

▲ **TAMIRIS, HELEN** (originally Helen Becker; born April 23, 1903, in New York City; died August 4, 1966, in New York City). One of the founders of modern dance, and of that group, the one most accomplished in ballet and the one most committed to presenting social themes in her performances.

▲ **THOMASHEFSKY, BORIS** (born May 12, 1868, in Kiev, Ukraine; died July 9, 1939, in New York City). One of the founders of the American Yiddish theater. Grandfather of conductor Michael Tilson Thomas.

▲ **THREE STOOGES.** Comedy team who, through television reruns of their 190 Columbia Pictures short films (1934–59), became the most famous exponents of violent slapstick clowning in the old burlesque-vaudeville tradition. In their vaudeville days, the team worked with Ted Healy under various billings, such as Ted Healy and His Racketeers. The trio consisted of Shemp Howard (originally Samuel Horwitz; born March 17, 1895, in New York City; died November 22, 1955, in Los Angeles), his brother Moe Howard (originally Moses Horwitz; born June 19, 1897, in New York City; died May 4, 1975, in Los Angeles), and Larry Fine (originally Louis Fineberg [sometimes spelled Fineburg/Feinberg]; born October 5, 1902, in Philadelphia, Pennsylvania; died January 24, 1975, in Woodland Hills, California). In 1932 Shemp left the team, and he was replaced by another brother, Curly Howard (originally Jerome Lester Horwitz; born October 22, 1903, in New York City; died January 18, 1952, in San Gabriel, California). When illness forced Curly's retirement in 1946, Shemp returned. After Shemp's death in 1955, he was replaced by Joe Besser, with Joe De Rita taking the third spot in some 1960s films.

▲ **WARFIELD, DAVID** (originally David Wollfeld; born November 28, 1866, in San Francisco, California; died June 27, 1951, in New York City). Widely regarded as the greatest American actor of the early twentieth century.

▲ **WEBER AND FIELDS.** Comedy team consisting of Joe Weber (originally Moisha Weber; born August 11, 1867, in New York City; died May 10, 1942, in Los Angeles) and Lew Fields (originally Moisha Schanfield; born January 1, 1867, in New York City; died July 20, 1941, in Los Angeles). They became the first "modern" comedians by emphasizing jokes and dialect (German-Yiddish) rather than grotesque appearances and behavior, the first to popularize the burlesquing of contemporary plays, and reputedly the originators of the classic joke "Who was that lady I saw you with last night?" "That was no lady. That was my wife!"

▲ **WEINER, MARC** (born 1952 in Far Rockaway, New York). Comedian who was the first to "Weinerize" members of his audience, that is, to "crush" them into half-human and half-puppet characters on his *Weinerville* cable-television show (on Nickelodeon since 1993).

Courtesy of Nickelodeon

MARC WEINER

▲ **WELCH, JOE** (originally Joseph Wolinski; born May 15, 1873, in New York City; died July 15, 1918, in Westport, Connecticut). The prototype Jewish vaudeville comedian, imitated by hundreds of later dialect comics.

▲ **WILDER, GENE** (originally Jerome Silberman; born June 11, 1935, in Milwaukee, Wisconsin). The greatest deadpan comic actor since Buster Keaton. Wilder's films include *The Producers* (1967), *Blazing Saddles* (1974), *Young Frankenstein* (1974), and *The Woman in Red* (1984).

# 16
# SPORTS AND GAMES
‿

UNIQUE ACHIEVEMENTS BY JEWISH ATHLETES *abound in many sports. In track and field, Harold Abrahams was the first European runner to win a sprint championship in the modern Olympic Games. In basketball, Red Auerbach won more professional championships than any other coach, Dolph Schayes revolutionized the forward position, and Abe Saperstein founded the Harlem Globetrotters. In weightlifting, Isaac Berger was the first man to press double his own bodyweight. In football, Benny Friedman changed the game forever with his passing attack, and Sid Luckman became the first T-formation quarterback. In baseball, Hank Greenberg and Sandy Koufax set many major-league records. In swimming, Mark Spitz won a record seven gold medals in a single Olympics. In boxing, there have been many world champions of Jewish background, including Benny Leonard and Barney Ross.*

# A European Finally Wins an Olympic Sprint Championship
## Harold Abrahams

છ

IN THE EARLY MODERN OLYMPIC GAMES, which began in 1896, track sprints (short races) were dominated by Americans. But in 1924 that domination was interrupted by a British Jew—Harold Abrahams.

Abrahams came from an athletic family, but his drive to succeed in track came largely from his desire to fight the anti-Semitism that he found in the British Establishment. At the 1920 Antwerp Games, he failed to make the finals in the 100-meter dash. Six months before

Jewish Sports Hall of Fame

the 1924 Games, in Paris, he hired a personal coach, Sam Mussabini, and underwent rigorous training.

At the Games themselves, he encountered four extremely fast Americans and, at first, thought little of his own chances of winning. On July 6, he won his first 100-meter heat in 11.0 seconds. In the second round, later that day, he tied the Olympic record of 10.6. On July 7, in the semifinals, disaster almost struck: the runner on his right moved early and Abrahams hesitated because he thought a false start would be called, but it was not; however, even with the bad start, he won the race in 10.6. Four hours later came the finals. This time things went smoothly, and he used his famous "drop finish," winning by two yards, again in 10.6. Abrahams was the first European to win an Olympic sprint title.

The story of his Olympic victory was the subject of the film *Chariots of Fire* (1981).

# AN ISRAELI EARNS AN OLYMPIC MEDAL
## Yael Arad

ᗍ

YAEL ARAD, A JUDOIST, was the first representative of Israel to win a medal in the Olympic Games.

In 1991 her career took a big leap forward when she won third place in the world championships. The Israeli press began to build her up, and, Arad admitted, many feared "that this exaggerated praise would ruin me." But she stood the test and captured the gold medal in the prestigious French Open in early 1992. She seemed more than ready for the Olympics later that year.

*Israel Government Press Office*

*Yael Arad was born in Tel Aviv, Israel, on May 1, 1967. At the age of eight, she followed her eleven-year-old brother to his judo lessons and immediately fell in love with the sport. "Judo is a very intelligent sport," she explained. "If you're good at it, you sense it right away." When she was ten, she began to win a long string of Israeli championships in her age and weight class. In the late 1980s and early 1990s, she gained experience in important European matches.*

However, during the French Open, she injured a knee, which required surgery in March 1992. With her dream to win an Olympic medal on the line, she had to work extra hard, not only on physical strength and judo technique but also on repairing her damaged knee. Her efforts paid off on July 30, 1992, when she was awarded the silver medal at the Barcelona Olympics.

Arad thus became the first Israeli to win an Olympic medal. She dedicated her medal to the Israeli athletes who were murdered at the 1972 Munich Olympics.

---

### ALSO NOTEWORTHY

▲ **ALCOTT, AMY** (born February 22, 1956, in Kansas City, Missouri). Golfer who became a winner more quickly than any other woman pro golfer (in February 1975, in only her third tournament).

**ABE ATTELL**

▲ **ALLEN, MEL** (originally Melvin Allen Israel; born February 14, 1913, in Birmingham, Alabama). Sports announcer known as the Voice of the New York Yankees. He coined the baseball expressions "Going, going, gone" (to describe the flight of a home run ball) and "Fall Classic" (to describe the World Series).

**AMY ALCOTT**

▲ **ATTELL, ABE** (nicknamed Little Champ; originally Albert Knoehr; born February 22, 1884, in San Francisco, California; died February 6, 1970, in Liberty, New York). World featherweight boxing champion (1901–1912). His family called him Abe in honor of Abraham Lincoln.

# WINNING NINE NBA TITLES
## Red Auerbach

*Arnold Jacob Auerbach was born in Brooklyn, New York, on September 20, 1917. In high school, he made the All-Scholastic second team in basketball. He also played at George Washington University, where he earned an M.A. in physical education in 1941. After coaching high-school teams and serving in the navy, he coached the Washington Capitals (1946–49) of the Basketball Association of America (the forerunner of the National Basketball Association [NBA]), the Tri-City Blackhawks (1949–50) of the NBA, and the Boston Celtics (1950–66) of the NBA. When he retired from coaching in 1966, he stayed with the Celtics in an executive capacity.*

RED AUERBACH WAS THE MOST SUCCESSFUL PROFESSIONAL BASKETBALL COACH in history. He coached the Boston Celtics to nine NBA championships, including eight in a row. No other pro basketball coach has ever won that many titles. His 1,037 victories stood as a record for nearly thirty years.

The Celtics owner, Walter Brown, gave Auerbach a free hand. The year before Auerbach took over, the team finished last in its division. During his first six seasons, the team finished second four times. The turning point was the acquisiton of center Bill Russell for the 1956–57 season, when the Celtics won the NBA title. After losing in the finals in 1958, Auerbach went on to win eight straight titles, 1959–66. Other key members of the team during those years included Bill Sharman, John Havlecek, and K.C. Jones.

Boston Celtics

The key to Auerbach's success as a coach was his insistence on team play, not individual stars. He imposed strict discipline on everyone equally. He made everyone feel important: "You take a washed-up guy," he explained, "and if you instill in him his pride again and create desire, you can squeeze a good year or two out of him." He motivated his players with the same thing that motivated him—winning. "Show me a good loser," he would say, "and I'll show you a loser."

Auerbach himself was not a good loser. As a nine-time NBA title holder, all he knew was winning.

### ALSO NOTEWORTHY

▲ **BARNA, GYOZO VICTOR** (born August 24, 1911, in Budapest, Hungary; died February 28, 1972, in Lima, Peru). Winner of sixteen world table tennis championships, including five singles titles. He undoubtedly would have won more but for a serious arm injury sustained in an auto accident when he was only twenty-three. Probably the greatest table tennis player ever.

# PRESSING DOUBLE BODYWEIGHT
## Isaac Berger

Isaac Berger, a weightlifter, WON MEDALS IN THREE CONSECUTIVE Olympics, and he set many world records. But perhaps his most extraordinary achievement was to become the first athlete in history to press double his bodyweight.

He won a gold medal in his weight class, featherweight, at the 1956 Olympic Games in Melbourne. In 1960 he took the silver at the Rome Olympics. And in the 1964 Tokyo Games, he won another silver. Among his many world-record-setting achievements was an incredible performance just before the 1960 Olympics, breaking, in one competition, records in all three lifts (press, snatch, and clean and jerk) as well as in total poundage.

Berger's most memorable achievement came at the 1957 Maccabiah Games in Israel. With Prime Minister David Ben-Gurion among the spectators, Berger cleaned 258 pounds (117.1 kilograms) from the floor to his chest. The silent audience heard him groan as he struggled to press the bar overhead. Suddenly they roared with approval as the judges raised their white flags, signifying that the lift was legal. Berger's achievement was not only a new featherweight world record in the press but also the first world record of any kind to be established in Israel. Most impressive of all was the fact that it was the first time any man had ever pressed double his bodyweight. No matter how many times the world record might be broken in the future, Berger's place in sports history as the first to perform this remarkable feat is assured.

*Isaac ("Ike") Berger was born in Jerusalem, Palestine, on November 13, 1936. In 1949 he moved with his family to the United States. In 1952 Berger began weight training, tired of being, at 4'11" and 102 pounds, an easy target for bullies. Just three years later he began winning senior United States weightlifting titles. During the 1950s and 1960s, he was one of the most celebrated weightlifters in the world. After the 1964 Tokyo Olympics he retired, becoming involved in various business ventures with exercise products and officiating as a cantor in synagogues.*

# BECOMING FOOTBALL'S FIRST GREAT PASSER
## Benny Friedman

&

*Benny Friedman was born in Cleveland, Ohio, on March 18, 1905. At the University of Michigan, he was a first-team All-American quarterback in 1925 and 1926. He also played defense and placekicked. From 1927 to 1934, he played professional football with four different teams, including the New York Giants (1929–31). Later he coached college football, notably at Brandeis University (1949–63). He died in New York City on November 23, 1982.*

IN MODERN AMERICAN FOOTBALL, the forward pass is a key element in the excitement of the game. The player who, more than anyone else, brought aerial electricity to football was Benny Friedman.

He pioneered the transition of football from a sport of pure brawn to one of brains. Before Friedman, most quarterbacks would pass only in desperation, when it was third and long or when the team was far behind in points. Friedman introduced the offense of balance and surprise. He called for the pass as often as the run, and he was one of the first who dared to pass from his own end zone. His passing skills were extraordinary. Red Grange, the legendary running back, called Friedman the best quarterback he had ever seen. Because of Friedman, the professional football rules committee slenderized the football to improve its flight.

All modern fans and players who enjoy the aerial attack owe a debt of gratitude to Benny Friedman, football's first great passer.

## ALSO NOTEWORTHY

▲ **BARRON, HERMAN** (born December 23, 1909, in Port Arthur, New York; died June 9, 1976, in Pompano Beach, Florida). The first great Jewish golfer.

▲ **BERENSON, SENDA** (born March 19, 1868, in Biturmansk, Lithuania; died February 16, 1954, in Santa Barbara, California). Sportswoman who introduced women's basketball to the United States.

▲ **BERGMANN, RICHARD** ("the Old Lion") (born 1919 in Vienna, Austria; died April 5, 1970). Table tennis star who, in 1937, became the youngest player to capture the world singles title.

▲ **BUXTON, ANGELA** (born August 16, 1934, in Liverpool, England). Tennis player who was the first Jewish woman to win a Wimbledon title, taking the doubles championship (with Althea Gibson) in 1956.

# PIONEERING PRO FOOTBALL INNOVATIONS
## Sid Gillman

❧

PROFESSIONAL FOOTBALL owes much of its modern appearance and philosophy to Sid Gillman. He was one of the game's true innovators.

With the Rams, Gillman introduced many now-familiar features. He emphasized, much more than other coaches, the pass (developed even further with the Chargers). He was the first to put a player's name on his jersey. He helped introduce the two-platoon system.

*Sidney Gillman was born in Minneapolis, Minnesota, on October 26, 1911. After playing end for Ohio State in the early 1930s, he held many collegiate jobs as an assistant and head coach, but the one he wanted, head coach at Ohio State, was withheld from him because, he suspected, he was a Jew. So he moved up to the pros, coaching the Los Angeles Rams (1955–59) and the Los Angeles, later San Diego, Chargers (1960–71). After some years away from coaching, he returned for brief jobs, as with the Philadelphia Eagles in the 1980s.*

Perhaps Gillman's most important innovation was his use of film. He was the first to film practice sessions and the first to cut game films and organize them according to plays. Sometimes he would watch films eighteen hours a day. His idea to use films came from the fact that his family had been in the film busines in Minneapois in the 1920s and 1930s. When asked the secret to coaching success, he replied, "The movie projector. You've gotta... constantly test your theories, examine your ideas to see where they hold up, to get better ideas."

Gillman's ideas did hold up. Today his innovations are standard practices in pro football.

---

### ALSO NOTEWORTHY

▲ CALLAHAN, MUSHY (originally Vicente Morris Scheer; born November 3, 1905, in New York City). World junior welterweight boxing champion (1926–30). He converted to Catholicism.

▲ COHEN, ROBERT (born November 15, 1930, in Bone, Algeria). World bantamweight boxing champion (1954–56).

# BECOMING THE FIRST JEW ELECTED TO THE BASEBALL HALL OF FAME
## Hank Greenberg

ɔ

*Henry Benjamin Greenberg was born in New York City on January 1, 1911. Soon after graduating from high school (1929), he signed with the Detroit Tigers and spent a few seasons with minor league teams. From 1933 to 1946 he played with Detroit, and in 1947, his last year, he played with the Pittsburg Pirates. The record that he was proudest of was his 183 runs batted in (RBIs) during the 1937 season, the most RBIs ever by an American League right-hander. He finished his career with 331 home runs, 1276 RBIs, and a .313 batting average. Later he was an executive with the Cleveland Indians and the Chicago White Sox, and he made a fortune as a stock investor. He died in Beverly Hills, California, on September 4, 1986.*

HANK GREENBERG WAS THE best Jewish baseball player of the game's first one hundred years. He was also one of the handful of greatest right-handed hitters of all time.

His most memorable year was 1938. By the All Star break, he had hit twenty-two homers and was on pace to break Babe Ruth's record of sixty for the season. The first playing day after the break was a doubleheader, in which he hit four consecutive home runs, two at the end of the first game and two at the start of the second. "From then on," he later admitted, "why, I was shooting for home runs, chasing the record."

During his career, Greenberg often faced anti-Semitism, but the worst of it came in this year, while he was pursuing the beloved Babe's record. He heard racial epithets from fans and players, and he received hate mail. "Sure, there was added pressure being Jewish," he later admitted. But "I was representing a couple of million Jews among a hundred million Gentiles." And "I came to feel that if I, as a Jew, hit a home run, I was hitting one against Hitler."

Greenberg fell two homers short of Ruth's mark. But he set two other major league records: most games (eleven) in which a player hit two home runs, and most homers (fifty-eight) in a season by a first baseman. His home run total that year also tied the major league record (set in 1932 by Jimmy Foxx) for right-handers.

In 1956 Hank Greenberg became the first Jew elected to the Baseball Hall of Fame.

# DOMINATING THE HANDBALL COURTS
## Victor Hershkowitz

VICTOR HERSHKOWITZ WAS THE MOST VERSATILE, dominating handball player ever.

"I've always felt that being a Jew made me play and try harder to defeat my adversaries," he said. He wanted "to show the nation in this sport that I was proud of being a Jew." Hershkowitz won forty-three titles, including nine straight three-wall national championships (1950–58), an unprecedented feat. From 1947 to 1967, he won at least one national title each year (except 1959) in one-wall, three-wall, or four-wall competition. In 1952 he performed the incredible feat of winning all three categories in the same year. From 1950 through 1955, he won six straight international three-wall championships.

*Victor Hershkowitz was born in Brooklyn, New York, on October 5, 1918. After he graduated from high school in 1936, he held various jobs and discovered handball. During periods of unemployment, he practiced longer and harder. Later he worked as a postman (1947–50) and fireman (1950–73), practicing and competing in his spare time.*

Hershkowitz was the only player to attain equal greatness in one-wall, three-wall, and four-wall handball. The United States Handball Association rated him the best all-around handball player in history.

### ALSO NOTEWORTHY

▲ COPELAND, LILLIAN (born November 25, 1904, in New York City; died July 7, 1964, in Los Angeles). Track-and-field star who won nine national titles in the shot put, discus, and javelin; took the gold medal in the discus in the 1932 Olympic Games; and set several world records.

LILLIAN COPELAND

HOWARD COSELL

▲ COSELL, HOWARD WILLIAM (born March 25, 1918, in Winston-Salem, North Carolina; died April 23, 1995, in New York City). Sports broadcaster who revolutionized his profession by publicly proclaiming his opinions on players and issues.

▲ DANILOWITZ, ABRAHAM PHINEAS ("Pinky") (born August 1, 1908, in Krugersdorp, Transvaal, South Africa). Bowls player who, in 1958, broke the world record of twenty-seven straight singles victories by winning eighty-four games in a row.

# WINNING MEDALS IN
# FOUR STRAIGHT OLYMPICS
## Irena Kirszenstein-Szewinska

_Irena Kirszenstein was born in Leningrad, the Soviet Union, on May 24, 1945. Later her parents returned with Irena to their native Poland. Irena's mother encouraged her to join a local sports club, and the girl became a sprinter and long jumper. In 1967 she married her coach, Junusz Szewinska. After her athletic career was over, she worked as an economist in Warsaw._

IRENA KIRSZENSTEIN-SZEWINSKA WON MEDALS in each of the first four Olympic Games she competed in—a feat never before accomplished by any runner, male or female. She also broke many world records.

At the 1964 Tokyo Olympics, Irena took second place in the 200 meters, second in the long jump, and first as a member of the 400-meter relay team. At the 1968 Mexico City Olympics, she won the 200 meters and took third in the 100 meters. At the Munich Olympics in 1972, she captured a bronze medal in the 200 meters. At the Montreal Olympics in 1976, she won the gold medal in the 400 meters. She broke world records many times, including the 200 meters in 22.0 seconds in 1974 and the 400 meters in 49.0 seconds in 1977.

What she enjoyed most about track was the challenge of competition, especially in big meets, such as the Olympics. When asked if her triumphs were victories for the Communist system, she answered, "I run because it gives me great pleasure and satisfaction. I run for me."

Because of her Olympic accomplishments and her world records, Kirszenstein-Szewinska was widely regarded as the greatest female track athlete of her time, and many still believe she was the best of all time.

### ALSO NOTEWORTHY

▲ DAVIS, AL(LEN) (born July 4, 1929, in Brockton, Massachusetts). Football coach and owner who, from 1963 to the mid-1980s, led the Oakland, later Los Angeles, Raiders to the best winning percentage (over 70 percent) of any professional sports franchise in America. In 1995 he took the team back to Oakland.

# SETTING RECORDS IN STRIKEOUTS, SHUTOUTS, AND NO-HITTERS
## Sandy Koufax

ఈ

SANDY KOUFAX WAS A UNIQUE ATHLETE in many ways. He struggled longer and harder than any other great baseball pitcher to reveal his greatness: his first six seasons were mediocre, while his last six were as good as any pitcher has ever had in the history of the game. He suffered more pain than any other consistent winner, and he retired, because of arm trouble, when he was still the best in the league, after having a great season. Yet in spite of all of those delays and physical problems, he was elected to the Baseball Hall of Fame in 1972, the youngest, at thirty-six, ever to receive that honor. Many of his pitching records still stand.

During his first six seasons, 1955–60, Koufax showed strikeout power, but he was wild, giving up too many walks, getting behind batters on the count, and therefore being forced to serve up easy-to-hit pitches right down the middle of the plate. Through those six seasons, he lost more games than he won. He thought seriously of quitting.

But before the 1961 season, Dodger coaches and teammates convinced him to take a smaller windup and to ease up on his throw. Koufax developed a loose, easy pitching motion and surprised himself by improving not only his control but also his speed. The payoff was spectacular. From 1961 through 1966, he won 129 and lost only 47.

However, in 1962 his physical ailments began. In that year, a blood clot caused a loss of circulation in his left index finger. Koufax, a left-hander, faced the prospect of having the finger amputated. Anticoagulants finally brought the condition under control. In 1964 he hurt his left elbow sliding into second base. Soon his left arm was

Sandy Koufax was born in Brooklyn, New York, on December 30, 1935. His original name was Sanford Braun. When he was three, his parents divorced, and several years later his mother married a man named Irving Koufax. Sandy Koufax pitched at the University of Cincinnati and then, in 1955, joined the Brooklyn Dodgers. In 1958 the team moved to Los Angeles. He retired after the 1966 season. Later he worked on television as a baseball commentator, and from 1979 to 1990 he coached the Dodger pitchers.

Jewish Sports Hall of Fame

# RECORD STRIKEOUTS, SHUTOUTS, AND NO-HITTERS *(continued)*

swollen from the wrist to the shoulder. X rays revealed that he had traumatic arthritis. In 1965 he had to put ice on the arm after each game to keep the swelling down. In 1966 the pain worsened, and he could not fully straighten his arm. Pills, shots, and therapy had little effect. At the end of the season, he retired. "I don't want to take a chance of completely disabling myself," he explained, "and losing the use of my left arm."

In his short career, Koufax left a legacy of great records. He set the major league season record for strikeouts, 382 in 1965. He set the major league record for season shutouts by a left-hander, eleven in 1963. He was the first major leaguer to pitch four no-hitters. He set the major league record for most strikeouts in a four-game World Series, 23 in 1963. And he performed a host of other achievements, such as becoming the first National Leaguer to strike out the side on only nine pitches.

Because of his outstanding pitching records in the face of unusually difficult physical circumstances, Koufax earned a special place for himself in baseball history.

## ALSO NOTEWORTHY

▲ **DREYFUSS, BARNEY** (born February 23, 1865, in Freiburg, Germany; died February 5, 1932, in New York City). Baseball executive who created the modern World Series (1903) and built the first major league stadium, Forbes Field (1909).

▲ **FIELDS, JACKIE** (originally Jacob Finkelstein; born February 9, 1908, in Chicago, Illinois; died June 3, 1987, in Las Vegas, Nevada). Welterweight boxing champion of the world (1929–30, 1932–33). The youngest American ever to box for a United States Olympic team, winning the gold medal at the 1924 Paris Olympics when he was only sixteen.

**BARNEY DREYFUSS**

▲ **FISCHER, BOBBY** (originally Robert James Fischer; born March 9, 1943, in Chicago, Illinois). Chess master who was the youngest player in the world ever to attain the rank of grand master (1958, a record that lasted till 1992) and the first American officially to hold the title of world chess champion (1972–75).

▲ **FLATOW, ALFRED** (born 1869 in Germany; died at a death camp during World War II, exact place and date unknown). Gymnast who won the parallel bars competition in the first modern Olympics (Athens, 1896).

**NAT FLEISCHER**

▲ **FLEISCHER, NAT** (known as Mr. Boxing; originally Nathaniel Stanley Fleischer; born in New York City on an unknown date, but Fleischer selected November 3, 1887; died June 25, 1972, in New York City). Boxing promoter and writer who became the most influential figure in modern professional boxing through his efforts to reform the sport (as by insisting on better medical care for boxers, by establishing boxing commissions, and by initiating a rating system) and through his writings, including sixty books and his *Ring* magazine, the first comprehensive coverage of boxing in the world.

# BECOMING THE GREATEST JEWISH BOXER IN HISTORY
## Benny Leonard

༄

BENNY LEONARD WAS WIDELY REGARDED AS THE GREATEST Jewish sports figure of his time, and he has been called the best Jewish boxer in history. From 1917 to 1924, he reigned as the world lightweight champion.

In 1917 Leonard knocked out Freddie Welsh in the ninth round to become the lightweight champion of the world. In 1920 Charlie

White knocked Leonard out of the ring during a match, but Leonard came back to knock out White in the ninth. In January 1925 Leonard retired as the undefeated champ.

One sports writer said that "Leonard moved with the grace of a ballet dancer and wore an air of arrogance that belonged to royalty. His profile might have been chiseled by a master sculptor, and there wasn't a mark of his trade upon it to mar its classic perfection." Another writer offered this tribute to Leonard: "He has done more to conquer anti-Semitism than a thousand textbooks."

> Benny Leonard was born in New York City on April 7, 1896. His original name was Benjamin Leiner. He lived in a tough neighborhood where, he later said, "you had to fight or stay in the house." He began sparring with gloves at the age of eleven. When he was sixteen, he began his professional career. He changed his surname to Leonard so that his parents would not know that he was boxing. During World War II, he was with the United States Maritime Service. In 1943 he began to work as a boxing referee. He died in New York City on April 18, 1947.

### ALSO NOTEWORTHY

▲ **FRANKLIN, SIDNEY** (originally Sidney Frumkin; born June 11, 1903, in New York City; died April 26, 1976, in New York City). The first Jewish bullfighter. He took the name Franklin because he admired Benjamin Franklin.

▲ **GOTTLIEB, EDDIE** (born September 15, 1898, in Kiev, Ukraine; died December 7, 1979, in Philadelphia, Pennsylvania). Basketball coach and administrator who, in 1946, helped to organize the Basketball Association of America, which later became the National Basketball Association (NBA), and was coach and owner of the Philadelphia Warriors when the team won the first league championship (1947).

▲ **GUBNER, GARY JAY** (born December 1, 1942, in New York City). Strength athlete who, in 1962, set an indoor world record in the shot put and four junior world records as a weightlifter in the heavyweight class.

# ESTABLISHING THE T FORMATION AND BECOMING THE FIRST JEW ELECTED TO THE PRO FOOTBALL HALL OF FAME

## Sid Luckman

*Sidney Luckman was born in Brooklyn, New York, on November 21, 1916. At Columbia University, he played tailback, but he was a triple-threat man as a runner, punter, and passer. In 1938 he was named an All-American. From 1939 to 1947, he played professional football with the Chicago Bears. After retiring, he became a business executive.*

SID LUCKMAN WAS FOOTBALL'S FIRST MODERN T-formation quarterback. He was also the greatest long-range passer of his time, and he led his team, the Chicago Bears, to four National Football League (NFL) championships.

When Luckman joined the Bears, the coach, George Halas, was in the process of developing a new kind of offense, based on the T for-

Football Hall of Fame

mation, in which the fullback lines up behind the center and quarterback with one halfback stationed on each side of the fullback. "Sid made himself a great quarterback," Halas later said. "No one else did it for him. He worked hard, stayed up nights studying and really learning the T. Sid wasn't built for quarterback. He was stocky (5'11", 190 pounds), not fast, and not a great passer in the old tradition. But he was smart and he was dedicated."

In 1940 Luckman gave the new T formation credibility when he led the Bears to a 73–0 victory over the Washington Redskins for the NFL title. His team also won titles in 1941, 1943, and 1946. He himself was selected an All-Pro every year from 1941 through 1944, as well as in 1947. In 1943, when he was voted the Most Valuable Player in the league, he set two NFL records: seven touchdown passes in one game, and twenty-eight for the season. In 1965 Luckman became the first Jew elected to the Pro Football Hall of Fame.

# HOLDING THE LIGHTWEIGHT AND WELTERWEIGHT BOXING CHAMPIONSHIPS
## Barney Ross

୯ର

BARNEY ROSS WAS THE FIRST PROFESSIONAL BOXER to hold the world lightweight (1933-35) and welterweight (1934–38) crowns simultaneously.

In June 1933 he won the lightweight title by outpointing Tony Canzoneri. In May 1934 he won the welterweight championship by outpointing Jimmy McLarnin, who had made a reputation by stopping Jewish fighters. From May to September 1934 Ross held both the lightweight and the welterweight championships. In September 1934 McLarnin won a rematch by decision. In April 1935 Ross gave up the lightweight title because he could no longer make the weight.

Ring Magazine

In May 1935 he regained the welterweight title by again outpointing McLarnin. This time Ross held the title till May 1938, when Henry Armstrong outpointed him. "The real secret of his success," Ross's manager said, "is his ability to come back after being hit and press the fighting."

During Ross's boxing days, a Chicago rabbi told him, "You must set an example of decency and goodness so that the world will know what horrible lies Hitler is telling." In his double-championship years and afterward, Ross lived up to the rabbi's wish, both in and out of the ring.

*Barney Ross was born in New York City on December 23, 1909. His original name was Barnet David Rosofsky. When he was two, he moved with his parents to Chicago, Illinois. In 1924 his father was killed while his grocery store was being robbed. "Everything that happened to me afterward," the boxer recalled, "happened because of that senseless, stupid murder." His mother was unable to support her five children, so the family split up, some going to an orphanage. Changing his name to Barney Ross so that his mother would not know what he was doing, he entered boxing and earned enough money to reunite the family. After his career was over, he tried business and acting. In World War II, he was a hero at Guadalcanal but contracted malaria, which led to an addiction to morphine. In 1946 he went to a rehabilitation center and cured himself. For the rest of his life, he fought drug racketeers and helped addicts. His story formed the basis of the movie* Monkey on My Back *(1957). He died in Chicago on January 17, 1967.*

# FOUNDING THE HARLEM GLOBETROTTERS
## Abe Saperstein

cͻ

Abraham Saperstein was born in London, England, on July 4, 1903. He came to America with his parents when he was five, and he grew up in Chicago, Illinois. After playing some semipro baseball, he tried professional basketball, playing, at 5'5", for five dollars a game. Later he entered basketball management. He died in Chicago on March 15, 1966.

ABE SAPERSTEIN FOUNDED THE WORLD-FAMOUS HARLEM GLOBETROTTERS, the clown princes of basketball.

In 1927 he took over an all-black American Legion basketball team called the Savoy Big Five, named for Chicago's Savoy Ballroom. He changed the name to the Harlem Globetrotters. "We chose Harlem," he later explained, "because, well, because Harlem was to the fellows what Jerusalem is to us. And Globetrotters? Well, we hoped to travel." Saperstein was the owner, coach, and trainer.

Originally, the team played straightforward, serious games. But the team was so good, with won-lost records the first two years of 101–6 and 145–13, that Saperstein soon had difficulty finding opponents. He then changed the focus of the team to entertainment, introducing humorous, razzle-dazzle play in which his talented clowns could show off their ball-handling magic. By 1940 the team was finally making money, and by 1950 it was world famous. The movie *Go, Man, Go* (1954) was about Saperstein and his team.

"Wars, depressions, chaos, and one crisis after another are commonplace all around the world," Saperstein once said. "Our fans, and there are millions of them, are looking for an escape from worry and tension when they come out to see us play, and we never want to fail them." The Harlem Globetrotters, the world's most unusual sports-entertainment act, never fail their fans. They are still going strong.

# BECOMING THE FIRST MODERN BASKETBALL FORWARD
## Dolph Schayes

cx

DOLPH SCHAYES HELPED TO ESTABLISH the game of professional basketball in its present form. He was the first to show that a forward could combine the power of a center with the grace of a guard.

When Schayes joined the Syracuse Nationals in the NBA, he was switched from center to forward. He soon showed the league and the fans a new kind of forward: big, fast, mobile. He could hit two-handed set shots, but he could also drive by defenders for lay-ups. And he was an excellent rebounder, assist man, and free-throw shooter. Such versatility had never before been seen in a forward. When he left the league, he held many records, notably those for most career points (over 19,000) and most career free throws made (almost 7,000). The many skills of modern NBA forwards can be traced back directly to Dolph Schayes.

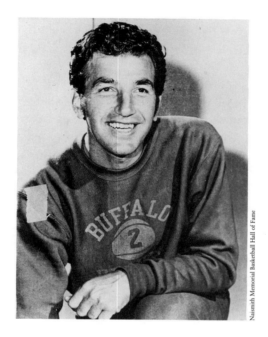

Naismith Memorial Basketball Hall of Fame

His son, Dan Schayes (born May 10, 1959, in Syracuse, New York), was the only Jewish player in the NBA in the late 1980s and early 1990s.

*Adolph Schayes was born in New York City on May 19, 1928. He inherited his love of sports and his height from his father, a 6'4" Romanian Jew who was an avid sports fan. At New York University, Dolph Schayes, at 6'8" and 220 pounds, played center, earning an All-American spot in his senior year (1948). He then played professional basketball with the Syracuse Nationals. In 1964 the team moved to Philadelphia and became the 76ers. In that year, Schayes retired from playing and began a two-season stint (1964–66) as coach of the team. He then served as supervisor of National Basketball Association (NBA) referees (1966–70), and later he entered business.*

### ALSO NOTEWORTHY

▲ HAJOS-GUTTMANN, ALFRED (originally Alfred Guttmann; born February 1, 1878, in Budapest, Hungary; died November 12, 1955). The first Olympic swimming champion, winning the 100-meter and 1200–meter freestyle events at the 1896 Athens Games.

# Winning Seven Gold Medals in One Olympics
## Mark Spitz

෴

*Mark Andrew Spitz was born in Modesto, California, on February 10, 1950. He began swimming as a toddler, and by eight he was already engaged in serious formal training. He was motivated by his father, who impressed on the boy that "swimming isn't everything—winning is." By the age of ten, Mark Spitz held seventeen national age-group records. Later he became a world-record holder and Olympic champion. After he retired, he worked as a real-estate developer in the Los Angeles area.*

ARGUABLY THE BEST SWIMMER OF ALL TIME, Mark Spitz set thirty-five world records during his career. His greatest achievement came in the 1972 Olympic Games. Before those Games, no swimmer had won more than four gold medals in a single Olympics, and the record for any Olympic athlete was five (held by a fencer). In 1972 Spitz won an incredible seven gold medals—all in world-record times.

In 1967 he set his first world record, in the 400-meter freestyle. At the 1968 Mexico City Olympics, he took second in the 100-meter butterfly and third in the 100-meter freestyle, and he won gold medals as a member of two relay teams. While attending Indiana University (1969–72), he won eight national collegiate championships and became the first Jewish recipient of the coveted Sullivan

Trophy as the outstanding amateur athlete of 1971.

At the 1972 Munich Olympics, Spitz won his first gold medal on August 28, swimming the 200-meter butterfly in 2:00.70. That evening he won his second gold when he anchored the 400-meter freestyle relay team to victory. The next day he won his third gold by by swimming the 200-meter freestyle in 1:52.78. On August 31, he won his fourth and fifth gold medals, for the 100-meter butterfly in 54.27 and the 800-meter freestyle relay race. On September 3, he took the 100-meter freestyle in 51.22 for his sixth gold. And he capped his performance as the most successful athlete in Olympic history on September 4, when he swam the butterfly leg on the 400–meter medley relay, winning his seventh gold medal.

"I feel that being a Jewish athlete has helped our cause," he said. "We have shown that we are as good as the next guy." Mark Spitz—winner of seven gold medals in a single Olympics—was perhaps a little better than the next guy.

NAT HOLMAN

▲ HOLMAN, NAT(HANIEL) (known as Mr. Basketball; born October 1896 in New York City; died February 12, 1995, in New York City). Innovative basketball player and coach. As a professional player in the 1920s, he devised the revolutionary pivot play. In 1950 he coached the City College of New York to both the National Invitation Tournament (NIT) and National Collegiate Athletic Association (NCAA) championships, the first time any coach accomplished the "grand slam" of basketball. He created what came to be called "New York basketball," which featured finesse and intelligence.

▲ HOLZMAN, WILLIAM ("RED") (born August 10, 1920, in New York City). Basketball coach who led the New York Knicks to eighteen straight victories during the 1969–70 season, at that time an NBA record; to two NBA titles (1970 and 1973); and, by 1982, to 613 regular-season wins, at that time the most among active coaches and second only to Red Auerbach on the all-time list.

▲ JACOBS, HIRSCH (born April 8, 1904, in New York City; died February 13, 1970, in Miami Beach, Florida). Racehorse trainer who developed more winners (3,569) than anyone else in thoroughbred history.

▲ JACOBS, JIM(MY) (originally James Jacobs; born February 18, 1931, in Saint Louis, Missouri; died March 23, 1988, in New York City). Handball player who won fifteen national titles and revolutionized his sport by utilizing masterful ceiling shots to force an opponent to the rear of the court, where the opponent could not make "kill" shots. Jacobs also became the world's foremost private collector of boxing films and helped manage three world boxing champions, including Mike Tyson.

▲ JAFFEE, IRVING (born September 15, 1906, in New York City; died March 20, 1981, in San Diego, California). Speed skater who broke the five-mile world record in 1927.

▲ KAPLAN, LOUIS ("KID") (born December 4, 1902, in Kiev, Russia; died October 26, 1970, in Norwich, Connecticut). World featherweight boxing champion (1925–27).

▲ KRICKSTEIN, AARON (born August 2, 1967, in Ann Arbor, Michigan). Tennis player who, at the age of sixteen years and two months, became the youngest ever to win a Grand Prix tournament (Tel Aviv Grand Prix, October 1983).

▲ LASKAU, HENRY HELMUT (born September 12, 1916, in Berlin, Germany). Walking champion who won forty-two American national titles and set a world indoor record for the mile (1950).

▲ LEVINSKY, BATTLING (originally Barney Lebrowitz; born June 10, 1891, in Philadelphia, Pennsylvania; died February 12, 1949, in Philadelphia). World light heavyweight boxing champion (1916–20). He set a record by fighting three main events in one day (January 1, 1915), all no-decisions totaling thirty-two rounds.

Mike Groll/Buffalo Bills

**MARV LEVY**

▲ **LEVY, MARV** (full name, Marvin Daniel Levy; born August 3, 1928 [or 1929], in Chicago, Illinois). Football coach who led the Buffalo Bills to an unprecedented four straight Super Bowls (1991–94), all of which they lost.

▲ **LEWIS, TED** (**"KID"**) (originally Gershon Mendeloff; born October 24, 1894, in London, England; died October 20, 1970, in London). World welterweight boxing champion (1915, 1917–19).

▲ **McCOY, AL** (originally Al Rudolph; born October 23, 1894, in Rosenhayn, New Jersey; died August 22, 1966, in Los Angeles). World middleweight boxing champion (1914–17).

▲ **MARTIN, SYLVIA WENE** (originally Sylvia Wene; born 1928 in Philadelphia, Pennsylvania). Bowler who set many world records, including being the first woman to bowl more than one perfect (300) game.

▲ **MELNIK, FAINA** (born June 9, 1945, in Bakota, Ukraine, the Soviet Union). Discus thrower who broke the world record many times during 1971–76.

▲ **MENDOZA, DANIEL** (born July 5, 1764, in London, England; died September 3, 1836, in London). Bareknuckle boxer known as the father of modern scientific boxing because of his emphasis on defense and his use of rapid, rather than hard, punching. Though only 5'7'' and 160 pounds, he held the heavyweight championship of England (and thus, in effect, the world) during 1791–95, the first Jew to hold the title.

**DANIEL MENDOZA**

▲ **MIX, RON(ALD)** (born March 10, 1938, in Los Angeles). An offensive lineman who was unanimously chosen to the all-time American Football League (AFL) team by the Pro Football Hall of Fame (1970), and later to the AFL-NFL (National Football League) 1960–84 All-Star Team.

▲ **MYERS, LAURENCE EUGENE** (**"Lon"**) (born February 16, 1858, in Richmond, Virginia; died February 15, 1899, in New York City). The greatest short-distance runner of the nineteenth century, holding, at one time or another, world records in the 100, 440, and 880 yards, and American records at every distance from 50 yards to one mile.

▲ **PIKE, LIPMAN EMANUEL** (born May 25, 1845, in New York City; died October 10, 1893, in New York City). Baseball player who, in 1866, became the game's first professional when the Philadelphia Athletics paid him to play third base (the first all-professional team was formed in Cincinnati in 1869).

▲ **PINCUS, JACOB** (**"JAKE"**) (born September 13, 1838, in Baltimore, Maryland; died January 23, 1918, in New York City). The foremost American jockey of his day and the trainer of the first American-bred horse to win the English Derby (1881).

▲ **PODOLOFF, MAURICE** (born August 18, 1890, in Elizabethgrad, Russia; died November 24, 1985, in New Haven, Connecticut). The first and only head of the short-lived Basketball Association of America (1946–49), the precursor of the National Basketball Association (NBA), which he led till 1963.

▲ **PRINSTEIN, MYER** (born 1880 in Russia; died March 10, 1925). Track-and-field star who won four Olympic gold medals (1900–1908) and twice held the world record in the long jump.

▲ **REULBACH, EDWARD MARVIN** ("BIG ED") (born December 1, 1882, in Detroit, Michigan; died July 17, 1961, in Glens Falls, New York). The only baseball player ever to pitch two shutouts in a doubleheader (1908, against Brooklyn).

▲ **ROSEN, AL** ("FLIP") (full name, Albert Leonard Rosen; born February 29, 1924, in Spartanburg, South Carolina). Baseball player who was the first unanimous choice as Most Valuable Player in the American League (1953).

AL ("FLIP") ROSEN

▲ **ROSENBLOOM, MAXIE** ("Slapsie [or Slapsy] Maxie") (born September 6, 1904, in New York City; died March 6, 1976, in South Pasadena, California). Light heavyweight boxing champion of the world (1930–34).

▲ **ROTH, MARK** (born April 10, 1951, in Brooklyn, New York). Bowler who had a record high average of 221.662 in 1979, and from 1976 to 1990 had over a 215 average, the best long-term average in professional bowling history.

▲ **RUBENSTEIN, LOUIS** (born September 23, 1861, in Montreal, Canada; died January 3, 1931, in Montreal). The first famous figure skater in North America, winning the unofficial world championship in 1890.

▲ **SAVITT, RICHARD** ("DICK") (born March 4, 1927, in Bayonne, New Jersey). Tennis player who is the only Jew to date to win the Wimbledon singles title (1951).

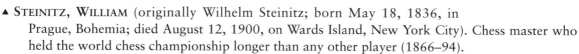

MARK ROTH

▲ **STEINITZ, WILLIAM** (originally Wilhelm Steinitz; born May 18, 1836, in Prague, Bohemia; died August 12, 1900, on Wards Island, New York City). Chess master who held the world chess championship longer than any other player (1866–94).

▲ **SZEKELY, EVA** (born April 3, 1927, in Hungary). Swimmer who set ten world records and established over a hundred Hungarian records. Her daughter, Andrea Gyarmati, broke the world record in the 100-meter butterfly in 1972.

# INDEX

❧

Austria, chancellor of, 19
Authors. *See* Writers.
*Auto-da-Fé (Act of Faith)* (Canetti), 155
*Awake and Sing!* (Odets), 167
Axelrod, Julius, 50, 66

Baal Shem Tov, 39, 40
Bacall, Lauren, 20, 239, 242
Bacharach, Burt, 182
Baeck, Leo, 39, 41
Baeyer, Adolf von, 87, 88
Bakst, Léon Nikolaevich, 220
*The Bald Soprano* (Ionesco), 166
Balfour Declaration, 23
Ballet
    choreographers of, 239, 256
    dancers, 263, 265
    schools for, 225
Ballets: U.S.A., 256
Baltimore, David, 51, 82
*Bambi* (Salten), 168
Bankers, 149. *See also* Financiers.
Bara, Theda, 259
Bárány, Robert, 49, 52
*Barefoot in the Park* (Simon), 164
Barna, Gyozo Victor, 270
Barron, Herman, 272
Barrymore, John, 237
Baruch, Bernard Mannes, 13, 50
Baruch, Simon, 13, 50
Baseball. *See* Sports.
Basketball. *See* Sports.
Bayes, Nora, 259
Beadle, George W., 70
Beame, Abraham David, 13
Beaux Arts Trio, 181
Beer, Wilhelm, 88, 209
*Beggar on Horseback* (Kaufman), 167
Begin, Menachem, 11, 13, 176, 177
Belasco, David, 225
Bell, Alexander Graham, 137, 138
Bellow, Saul, 151, 153
Benacerraf, Baruj, 49, 53
Ben-Gurion, David, 11, 14, 271
Benjamin, Judah Philip, 15
Benny, Jack, 231, 239, 243
Ben-Porat, Miriam, 34
Berenson, Senda, 272
Berg, Gertrude, 260
Berg, Paul, 54, 63
Berger, Isaac, 267, 271
Bergmann, Richard, 272
Bergson, Henri, 119, 121
Berle, Milton, 239, 244
Berlin, Irving, 179, 183
Berliner, Emile, 137, 138
Berman, Shelley, 260
Bernays, Edward L., 144

Bernhardt, Sarah, 237, 260
Bernstein, Carl, 172
Bernstein, Elmer, 181
Bernstein, Leonard, 176, 179, 184–85, 210, 256
Berson, Solomon, 85
Besser, Joe, 265
Bethe, Hans A., 87, 89
Beth Jacob network of schools, 32
*Betrayal* (Pinter), 168
*Bet Yoseph (House of Joseph)* (Caro), 42
*Biloxi Blues* (Simon), 164
Blanc, Mel, 260
Blaustein, Louis, 144
Blinder, Naoum, 206
Blitzstein, Marc, 181
Bloch, Ernest, 179, 186
Bloch, Felix, 89
Bloch, Konrad, 49, 54
Block, James W., 61
Bloomingdale, Lyman Gustave, 144
Blowitz, Henri, 172
Blum, Léon, 15
Blumberg, Baruch S., 55
Blume, Judy, 154
Blumenfeld, Felix, 193
Boas, Franz, 123
Bock, Jerry, 181
Bogart, Humphrey, 242
Bohr, Aage, 107
Bohr, Neils, 87, 90
Boosler, Elayne, 260
Borge, Victor, 260
Born, Max, 87, 91
Botanists, 50
Bothe, Walther, 91
Bouffes-Parisiens theater, 200
Boulanger, Nadia, 187
Bow, Clara, 238
Bowling. *See* Sports.
Boxer, Barbara, 11, 15, 17
Boxer, Stewart, 15
Boxers. *See* Sports.
Brandeis, Louis D., 33, 35
Brando, Marlon, 249
Brandt, Joe, 224
Brenner, Victor David, 220
Breuer, Josef, 31, 123
Brewster, Mary, 135
Brice, Fanny, 260
*The Bridal Canopy* (Agnon), 152
Briscoe, Robert, 15
Brodsky, Adolph, 184
Brodsky, Joseph, 154
*Broken Glass* (Miller), 160
Brooks, Mel, 239, 245
Brown, Herbert C., 92
Brown, Michael S., 56, 64
Bruce, Lenny, 239, 246